FURTHER PRAISE FOR KERNEL TO CANON

In *Jacob's Journey*, Dr. Tzemah Yoreh offers a comprehensive demonstration of his version of the "Supplementary Hypothesis". While the "Documentary Hypothesis" claims that the Hebrew Bible is comprised of separate texts by separate authors - glued together to form a composite urn, Yoreh proposes how the biblical text is built from a coherent source that can be unearthed through careful scholarly analysis… *Jacob's Journey* enables scholars, clergy, students, and lay readers to engage with valuable scholarship in an accessible and congenial form. Yoreh's personal commitment to the text and its making refreshes stale academic methods and inspires profound inquiry into the Hebrew Bible.

Bonna Devora Haberman, PhD
Author of: *ReReading Israel: The Spirit of the Matter, and Israeli Feminism Liberating Judaism: Blood and Ink*.

How far can one go in reading the Bible? While Derrida once remarked "il n'y a or que texte" (that there is nothing but text), Yoreh goes a step further in reading the Bible as a palimpsest— interwoven through the warp of disquieting nuance and the woof of glorious complexity. Yoreh is a master teacher and student of the supplementary paradigm of textual accretion in reading Bible and his passion for it is contagious. This new work opens the fascinating world of textual quirks to the non-specialists and specialist alike, by challenging us to read with an eye for crossing canonical borders, one that opens the reader to a primordial poem of repetitions, contradictions, radical stylistic shifts, ultimately asking every reader to be a part of this new way of seeing ancient text. Nothing could be more important for all Abrahamic communities in evolving their sacred scriptures.

Rabbi Aubrey L. Glazer, Ph.D. (JCCH of Harrison, New York)
Author of: *A New Physiognomy of Jewish Thinking: Critical Theory After Adorno as Applied to Jewish Thought (Continuum Studies in Jewish Thought)*.

In the Beginning © 2013 by Tzemah Yoreh

Cover illustration © 2013 by Chava Megan Evans

Cover layout and design by Lenore Cohen

Interior layout and design by Tzemah Yoreh

First Printing

ISBN 978-0-9857108-8-0

Modern Scriptures

http://www.modernscriptures.com

Tzemah Yoreh

In the beginning

Kernel to Canon

For my friend Hagay, though he'll probably not read it

ACKNOWLEDGMENTS

Many people were instrumental in getting this all important second book off the ground. First and foremost I'd like to thank my first editor Abigail Phelps who, despite being very busy, persevered and helped me write a book of which I am proud.

I am very grateful to my baby son Boaz, who allowed me to work, when I had no right to expect it. My spouse Aviva continues to push me to greater heights; her support is critical to me in every way.

Although many of my teachers at Hebrew University would disagree with the arguments throughout this series, I owe them a great debt for the scholarship I learnt at their feet. I would especially like to thank my erstwhile PhD advisor Israel Knohl, for teaching me so much and for being an inspiration to me of how to balance scholarship and popularization.

The CLAL Institute for Jewish Leadership has provided me with a place to work, and has helped me disseminate the series. In particular I'd like to thank Rabbi Irwin Kula for believing in my projects, and helping me reimagine myself and my work.

Ebible.org, generously provides a free open source English translation of the Bible which I tweaked for my purposes. The author of tanach.us worked even harder and provided a usable and accurate copy of the Leningrad Codex. My own website biblecriticism.com seeks to emulate their generosity of spirit.

TABLE OF CONTENTS

SERIES INTRODUCTION — i

IN THE BEGINNING: OVERVIEW — 1

GENESIS 1-2 — 4
    1-2 – J — 4
    1-2 – J + P — 8
    1-2 – J + P + B — 14

GENESIS 3 — 22
    3 – J — 22

GENESIS 4-5 — 28
    4-5 – J — 28
    4-5 – J + P — 34
    4-5 – J + P + B — 40

GENESIS 6 — 46
    6 – J — 46
    6 – J + P — 48
    6 – J + P + B — 50

GENESIS 7 — 56
    7 – J — 56
    7 – J + P — 58

GENESIS 8	64
8 – J	64
8 – J + P	66
GENESIS 9	70
9 – J	70
9 – J + P	72
GENESIS 10	76
10 – P	76
10 – P + B	78
GENESIS 11	82
11 – J	82
11 – J + P	84
APPENDIX: DOCUMENTARY HYPOTHESIS	89
Introduction	89
The Yahwistic Source	92
The Priestly Source	106
The Redactors	120

INTRODUCTION

This section is a general introduction to the Supplementary Hypothesis. If you have read previous volumes, or are familiar with the methodology and sources I posit, please feel free to skip this section.

Allow me to tell you a sordid tale: the tale of Dinah and the massacre of the Shechemites. The story begins in Genesis 34:1, when Dinah, Jacob's daughter, is raped by Shechem, the Hivite governor of a city bearing his name. Dinah's brothers are predictably outraged, and when Shechem comes to them with a marriage proposal, which, to add insult to injury, essentially calls for the absorption of all of their family and property, they begin to plot their revenge. They agree to Shechem's proposal, but only on the condition that he and all of the male inhabitants of his city circumcise themselves. While the men are recuperating and incapacitated, two of Dinah's brothers rampage through Shechem, killing every male of the city and making off with their belongings. This is the canonical text, the story that we encounter when we open up a Bible and read the book of Genesis. It is short, brutal, and deeply unsettling.

As grim as this story is, there is another version that is even shorter and more brutal. According to this alternate version, Dinah still catches Shechem's eye, but, rather than rape her, he respectfully requests her hand in marriage. Dinah's brothers, seeing an opportunity, agree, again on the condition that he and all the male inhabitants of his city be circumcised. While the men recuperate, all of Dinah's brothers descend upon the city to kill the men and plunder their households. The moral dilemma raised by the canonical tale as to whether or not Dinah's brothers are justified in their retaliation is not an issue here. Morality is entirely absent; all that is left is horror.

Where did this second story come from? From the same place as the first story: Genesis 34. Upon close examination, the first story proves to be disjointed enough that Bible aficionados such as myself have concluded that it could not have been the work of just one author. Rather, there seem to be two authors at work, one supplementing the other, so that the second story is actually contained within the first. Indeed, it seems that upon reading the horrifying account of how Dinah's opportunistic brothers massacred the innocent inhabitants of one of Canaan's major cities, a later author felt the need to add a layer of damage control. He thus inserted his contention that Shechem had raped Dinah (not just chastely pined after her), that Shechem was a Hivite (one of the nations that the Israelites are commanded to exterminate), that the marriage proposal was essentially a ruse to acquire property, and that in any case, only two of the brothers were actually responsible for the massacre. In this way, the later supplementer brought Genesis 34 as we know it into this world.

This earlier story is revealed by the conceptual toolkit of the Supplementary Hypothesis, which theorizes that the Bible was written in stages by several authors, each adding to the narrative of the one who preceded him. Using the Supplementary Hypothesis, we can discover these older narratives. We can peel back the textual layers like an onion, revealing new stories and hidden details. Only by patiently chipping away at the later narrative layers of the book of Genesis do we discover that Abraham may actually have sacrificed Isaac, or that Jacob may have had only seven sons instead of twelve. Without these tools, there would be no way for us to know that the Israelites' sojourn in Egypt lasted only a few generations, not 430 years, and that when they escaped from Egypt, they numbered just 3,000, not 3,000,000. We would not know that according to the original story, the ancient Israelites escaped from Egypt immediately after the plague of darkness, or that only seven commandments were given at Mount Sinai, not ten.

The supplementary paradigm of textual accretion in the Bible explains all sorts of confusing textual quirks (repetitions, contradictions, radical stylistic shifts, etc.), and complements our general understanding of how early Jewish and Christian texts and traditions developed—each generation receiving and respecting their predecessors' myths and traditions, while at the same time adapting them to their own time and place. This process is ongoing today, as Christians, Jews, and other religious groups continue to reread and reinterpret their religious texts. By showing us how we can dig down to the bedrock of the Pentateuchal text, the Supplementary Hypothesis affords us new insights into the origins and evolution of arguably the most important and influential book ever written, and the intentions, concerns, and agendas that pervade it. This is invaluable information, whether we as individuals look to the Bible as a source of spiritual authority and guidance, or merely wish to better understand the modern world that it has been so instrumental in creating.

BIBLICAL SOURCES

The Supplementary Hypothesis raises some obvious questions: if, as the theory goes, the Pentateuch began with a core narrative that was supplemented by successive writers, then who wrote that original narrative, and who added the material that transformed it into the book we know today?

The Elohistic Source (Higlighted in Gray)

E, the Elohistic source, is the first source, the author of the foundational narrative of the Pentateuch. (Note that here, and throughout this volume, I refer to each of the Biblical sources as an individual. This is based on the coherence I find within each of the sources. It is not entirely clear, however, whether each source represents a single person or a group working together.) It is likely that the Elohistic text was composed in the mid- to late eigth century BCE, toward the end of the heyday of the northern Ephraimite Kingdom, one of the two kingdoms that occupied Biblical Israel. The Kingdom of Ephraim was the larger and more urban of the two, and had its capital at Samaria, the city after which the Samaratins are named. To its south lay the smaller, but better-known Kingdom of Judah, whose capital city was Jerusalem. It seems likely that E lived and wrote during this period because it marked the first literary flowering in ancient Israel. We know this based on the books of Amos and Hosea, composed at about that time, and from a wealth of inscriptions that we can confidently date to that period.

The book of E, so called because it uses Elohim as its exclusive name for the deity of the Pentateuch, is composed of five story cycles focusing on five early Israelite heroes: Abraham, Jacob, Joseph, Moses, and Balaam. The stories of Abraham and Balaam are placed at the beginning and end of the Elohistic document, respectively, so that the two men can serve as models for how one should fear the remote and awesome God of the Elohistic source. The Jacob, Joseph, and Moses cycles, which comprise the bulk of the E narrative, chronicle Israel's metamorphisis from a family into a people.

The Yahwistic Source (Highlighted in Yellow)

J, the Yahwistic source, wrote in the late eighth or early seventh century BCE in the southern Kingdom of Judah. J was responsible for the first major metamorphosis of the Biblical narrative. By combining the book of E, the Book of the Covenant (a law code found in Exodus 21–24), and the northern book of Judges (predecessor to the canonical book of Judges), and supplementing them with his own text, he composed a cohesive historical work which chronicles the events from the creation of the world to the crowning of King David in nine story cycles, focusing on the Israelite line.

J's independent narrative is characterized by well-rounded characters and double entendres. Eve's Hebrew name, for example, which is introduced by J, may derive either from the Hebrew word for "life"—a fitting name for the mother of all humankind—or it may mean "female snake," which is also fitting, considering her role in the expulsion from Eden. J's deity is a God orphaned from his brothers and sisters of Canaanite and Mesopotamian mythologies. Like those deities, J's God is almost all immanence and no transcendence. Indeed, J's God is the most human of all of God's depictions in the Pentateuch—he is no longer remote, as he was in E, but rather reveals himself in human form, has human insecurities (his intense worry about the threat of Babel is one example), and is intimately involved in human affairs. J's God also goes by the name Yahweh, or "the Lord," rather than Elohim, or "God." Despite all this, J makes it clear right from the beginning that his Yahweh is the same as E's Elohim—both names refer to the one God who created the world.

J's editorial style is highly invasive. In adding his own voice to that of his predecessor, E, he often overwhelms the reader with his point of view to the extent that E's original narrative threads are no longer apparent. It is extremely difficult, for example, to discern that Moses, not God, was originally the hero of the Exodus—that he performed all of the plagues himself, led the Israelites out of Egypt, split the sea, and caused the Egyptian army to drown—because J undercuts and diminishes Moses by portraying him as an unwilling leader and a stutterer, dependent on Aaron, and merely an instrument of God's power.

The Priestly Source (*Not Highlighted*)

P, the Priestly Source, is the Pentateuchal (and, to a lesser extent, the Prophetical) source most concerned with the priests, the temple, the regulation of sacrifices (e.g. what to bring on which day), and organization in general, including censuses, the division of labor among the various clans of Levites, and the hierarchy among the tribes. The bulk of the Priestly texts are found at the end of Exodus (specifically Exodus 25–40), throughout Leviticus, in Numbers 1–10, and in Joshua 13–21.

The goal of P's narratival texts is largely to provide a basis for his laws. Thus, his innovation of the creation of the world in seven days is the basis for his oft-repeated Sabbath law. P's flood narrative is needed as background for God's covenant with humanity, and to accentuate the sanctity of life and the absolute prohibition against shedding the blood of another. The story of Abraham's journey to Canaan and God's promise to give him progeny is a necessary prelude to the covenant of circumcision. God's salvation of Israel from the Egyptians is seen as an enactment of the Abrahamic covenant, and is itself a prelude to the more global covenant with Israel. The plague of the firstborn and the Israelites' subsequent expulsion from Egypt is the basis for the extensive Passover laws. The journey to Mount Sinai and the succinct ten commandments serve as a starting point for a much broader body of laws, encompassing the whole of Leviticus and much of Numbers.

Another important feature of the P source is his copious addition of lists to the text. Many of these lists are genealogies (e.g. Gen. 5, 11, 36), but they can also be lists of stations on Israel's journey throughout the desert (e.g. Num. 33), cities (e.g. Josh. 14–21), and censuses (e.g. Num. 1–3). The primary reason for these additions is that they impart an authenticity and authority which cannot be conveyed as readily through narrative. The human mind is trained to accept exact, quantitative information of the sort provided by the Priestly lists at face value—we are more inclined to accept as authoratative a figure like 54.3%, for example, than the verbal description "more than half," even when both are equally true. By inundating the reader with lists, P attempts to enhance the authority of the Bible, and to ensure that his version of events is accepted over possible alternatives.

In contrast to J, P was a hands-off redactor, preferring to make his additions at the beginnings and ends of narratives. He thereby usually preserved his predecessors' accounts, very likely because he wished to preserve the internal order of those accounts. Note that his creation list and his genealogical lists appear entirely before and after J's account of creation and expulsion from Eden, respectively. Both additions alter our understanding of the surrounded material in important ways without being invasive. For example, P changes Jacob's name to

Israel in Genesis 35, after it has already been changed by the angel with whom Jacob struggled in Genesis 32. It is likely that P does this in order to dull the impact of the theologically challenging narrative in Genesis 32, wherein a mere human wrestles with and defeats a celestial being, and replace it with a more staid version of events. Only when the matter at hand is of grave importance to P, as in the case of the pillaging of the innocent inhabitants of Shechem, does he delve fully into the text and whitewash the whole episode. P's sense of morality and order, based on dichotomy and hierarchy, thus governed his narrative supplementation just as much as it governed his legal composition.

The Holiness Code

H, or the Holiness Code, was first recognized as a short body of Priestly legal texts beginning in Leviticus 19. My teacher Israel Knohl, however, argues in his book, *The Sanctuary of Silence*, for a much more extensive source placed chronologically after P, a view which I accept. The H source popularized Priestly law for the masses after the Temple was gone, and functioned as an intermediary between Priestly lists and laws and the surrounding narrative. H mainly features in Exodus-Numbers, and is confined in the Book of Genesis to just a few verses.

The Bridger

B, the Bridger, was the final redactor of J's historiographical project, adding popular myths, genealogies, and narrative bridges between distant story cycles (referring to this author as B is my own innovation, but the role he plays in the composition of Biblical narrative is widely acknowledged.) He connects, for example, the books of Genesis, Exodus and Joshua, using Joseph's bones as a bridge—Joseph's deathbed request in Genesis 50 that his bones be buried with the other patriarchs is taken on by Moses in Exodus 13, and then by Joshua, until, finally, Joseph's bones are actually buried in Joshua 24. A distinctive marker of the Bridger's genealogies is his use of a particular form of the passive Hebrew verb "yulad," or "born to." This vocabulary marker coincides with non-Israelite and sometimes not entirely monotheistic tales and lists, such as the mysterious tale of the sons of God marrying the daughters of man in Genesis 6; the account of Nimrod, the great king of yore, in Genesis 10; and the list of Edomite kings in Genesis 36. In this way, B, a post-exilic writer living at a time when the Israelites were a small, non-sovereign ethnic group, adds a cosmopolitan flavor to Biblical narrative, perhaps making a case that the Bible is relevant for a wider audience than just the Jews. Other episodes that were likely composed by this author include Abraham defeating four powerful kings with a mere 318 soldiers in Genesis 14, and Balaam conversing with his donkey in Numbers 22. These texts share a fantastic element rarely found in Biblical narrative, and are most likely later additions to their respective Pentateuchal frameworks.

EVIDENCE OF MULTIPLE AUTHORSHIP

As is apparent from the above discussion, the Supplementary Hypothesis asserts that the Pentateuch was composed by several different writers. This reflects an overwhelming academic consensus on Biblical authorship, even among scholars who do not subscribe to the Supplementary Hypothesis in particular.

So, how do we know that more than one author is at work in the Bible? There are a number of tried and true methods that scholars have developed for uncovering the plurality of voices within a given text.

Repetitions

Close readers of the Biblical text will notice that elements of some Biblical stories repeat themselves. This happens for a variety of reasons. Sometimes repetition is simply stylistic—many songs have choruses that are repeated many times, for emphasis or for aesthetic reasons. So, too, with stories—some details are juicier or more important than others and bear repeating. The commandment to observe the Sabbath, for example, a crucial one as evidenced by its inclusion in the Ten Commandments, is repeated in the Pentateuch more than ten times.

Another reason that details are repeated so often is that originally, many of the Biblical tales were recounted orally, and storytellers didn't want their audiences to forget the most pertinent details. Thus, for example, Pharaoh's dreams, which herald critical future events, are told and retold a number of times in Genesis 41.

Finally, there are those repetitions that indicate multiple authorship. Originally, it was thought that repeated details indicated two or three separate storylines that included a similar series of events. These separate storylines were supposedly combined by a later author who retained parts of each. For example, in the Biblical text, human beings were created twice, Noah was commanded about the Ark twice, Abraham presented his wife as his sister twice, and Jacob's name was changed twice.

What some earlier critics neglected to account for were the important differences between each of these so-called parallel accounts. Human beings may have been created twice, but the first time, the two sexes were created at the same time and in the image of God; the second time, they were created separately, the man out of dust from the earth, and the woman from the ribs or the side of the man. Similarly, Noah was commanded in one account to bring animals into the Ark two by two, but in the other account, he was commanded to make a distinction between pure and impure animals—the pure animals were to be brought into the ark seven by seven, and the impure animals two by two. In one account, it is strongly implied that Sarah had sex with the monarch to whom Abraham presented her; in the other account, she explicitly did not. In one account, Jacob physically fought God to a standstill, and thus earned a blessing; in the other account, Jacob respectfully offered a libation, and God rewarded him for his faithfulness by changing his name.

In these and many other cases, it can be shown that repetitions do not merely offer a slightly divergent account, but that they are responding to and transforming our understanding of the earlier account. According to what we have now identified as the later storyline, human beings are not mere dust from the earth—they are beings created in God's own image, a detail which is repeated a number of times for emphasis. According to the later storyline, the distinction between pure and impure animals does not need to be made because it does not apply until God reveals the law to Moses at Mount Sinai. Thus, every animal is paired up two by two without exception, a correction which is repeated many times throughout Genesis 7–9. According to the later storyline, the monarch does not cohabit with Sarah—a detail which is repeated at least three times—and we are invited to understand the earlier storyline in the same way. According to the later storyline, Jacob's name is changed in a sober ceremony, not through a highly unorthodox struggle with an angel. These revisionist retellings raise an intriguing question: are we meant to hold them together with the earlier stories, or to erase the earlier stories from our minds?

According to the Supplementary Hypothesis, Biblical narrative is layered. No editor took a blowtorch to the parts of the Bible he disagreed with and destroyed them; if he had, we would not find these repetitions and contradictions. Instead, Biblical narrative began with a coherent, foundational bedrock, which over time accreted more and more storylines. Unlike geological processes, though, this process of addition was deliberate. What happened if one author disagreed with his predecessor's storyline or worldview? He did not simply take an axe to the narrative; instead, he attempted to bury his predecessor's point of view by repeating his own over and over again, thus skewing our understanding of the story in new ways. Every generation of readers sees the world differently, and thus every generation of writers seeks to adapt their predecessors' cultural heritage to their own situation. We are not meant simply to dismiss earlier stories; rather, the intention of later writers is to transform our understanding of those stories via their additions.

Contradictions

Contradictions are closely related to repetitions. What is a contradiction, after all, if not the repetition of a detail in a divergent way? Some contradictions are more blatant than others, such as the implication that Sarah is still alive at the end of Genesis 24, despite having been buried in Genesis 23, or E's implication that Abraham actually did sacrifice Isaac in Genesis 22:19, when Isaac appears alive and well in later chapters. This type of textual inconsistency was the most difficult for early exegetes to account for—it is one thing to reconcile somewhat dissimilar storylines, but it is far more difficult to reconcile A and not-A. In such cases, the only reasonable inference can be that different authors are at work.

Style and genre

Biblical literature is a pastiche of many different styles of writing, including narrative prose, genealogical lists, poetry, and prophecy, to name but a few. One does not necessarily need to posit a change in authorship when the genre switches from narrative prose to genealogies, but it is definitely a possibility. Take, for example, the book of Chronicles, which begins with nine chapters of genealogies. It is generally accepted to have been written by a different author than the book of Judges, which is almost exclusively narratival, and it is also clearly distinct from the book of Psalms, which is exclusively poetic. Similarly, within the book of Genesis, one may reasonably posit different authors for Genesis 36, which is predominantly genealogical, and Genesis 18, which is exclusively narrival. This being said, one must be very careful with this criterion—just as you and I can write in more than one style, so, too, could Biblical authors. It is commonly supposed by Biblical critics, for example, that Genesis 1, which is narrival, and Leviticus 1, which is legal, were both written by P. As in any scientific endeavor, one should try to rely upon more than one criterion for determining plurality of authorship.

Vocabulary

Every author uses different words to convey their ideas. I, for example, used the word "narrival" several times in the preceding paragraph, a term which might be too neologistic for another writer. This is also true of Biblical authors; perhaps even more so, since proper English writing style discourages repetitions in word choice, whereas Biblical Hebrew does not. For example, one Biblical author, E, shows a consistent preference for the Hebrew term "amah" for handmaiden, while J prefers the analogous term "shifchah." The most famous example of this is the Biblical authors' aforementioned distinct preferences in terminology for the deity of the Old Testament—both E and P prefer the term "Elohim" throughout the book of Genesis, whereas J almost exclusively uses the term "Yahweh."

Some modern scholars of Biblical narrative have largely abandoned divergent lexica and styles as valid criteria for distinguishing between authors, relying instead upon contradiction and narrative coherence. I believe that this is a result of the repeated (and justified) attacks against an earlier generation of Bible scholars—in particular, those who accepted the Documentary Hypothesis—regarding the abuse of these criteria. However, the field of Biblical criticism was founded upon these criteria, and abandoning them entirely to suit a particular permutation of a particular hypothesis is, I believe, an extremely doctrinaire move that risks undermining the validity of this scholarly endeavor.

◆

Even with the aid of all of the tools described above, determining by whom a particular passage was written is often quite difficult. No writer, unless he or she is an excruciatingly exact scientist, completely escapes inconsistencies or repetitions, and it can be challenging to determine which of these inconsistencies are indicative of multiple authorship, and which are merely fluctuations within a given writer's style or storytelling. In light of this difficulty, one of the best measures of effective philology is not how much evidence it can marshal of differences in style, narrative detail, or word choice, but rather the extent to which it provides new insights into the text.

Breaking the Biblical urn into innumerable tiny pieces, and then failing to put it back together in new and interesting patterns, is a futile exercise that merely results in the destruction of a perfectly good urn. I sincerely hope that despite whatever disagreements any reader may have with the tools I employ or the conclusions I reach, at the very least I have provided a new and illuminating way of looking at the Biblical text.

THE BEGINNING: OVERVIEW

Like beautifully layered rock formations lining the walls of a desert canyon, so is the Biblical text. Story is piled upon story until the foundations are invisible. Those foundations tell a different story—one that only a trained geologist can tease from the rock; one that only a Biblical philologist, trained in the dissection of literature, can find in the text. This way of examining Biblical literature was pioneered in early nineteenth century German scholarship, and is referred to as the Supplementary Hypothesis. The Supplementary Hypothesis seeks to chart the accretive process of the composition of Biblical narrative. It pulls apart the canonical text and isolates the earliest storyline. It then attempts to draw out each of the stages of additions to this early storyline, culminating with the canonical text that we have today.

If there is one biblical story people are familiar with it is the story of how it all began, how God created the world in seven days, how Adam and Eve ate from the forbidden fruit and were banished from the garden, how God destroyed the world in a flood and Noah and his three sons rebuilt it. The well-known story as told in the Book of Genesis was, however, not the first version of the tale. In the first version, the kernel if you will, the world wasn't created in seven days, it was already there, God was not an aloof deity creating everything with a mere word, but insecure and very corporeal. The story of creation as we know it developed through the accretive additions of two authors to this kernel who had very different ideas than this first author.

To find out more about this story and how I got to it, read on!

As outlined in the introductory booklet which you received with your book, the Supplementary Hypothesis posits five distinct voices contributing to the narrative of the first four books of the Pentateuch. The Deuteronomistic authors (D), as their name implies, appear only in Deuteronomy (the fifth book), and are primarily concerned with the time the Israelites spend in the desert.

Let us peel away the layers one by one:

We begin with the canonical text. This is the version you will find in bookstores and on Bible websites; it's the story that the rabbi will tell you about in synagogue, and the pastor will tell you about in church. God created the universe and all that was in it in six days, except for darkness, the waters, and the mysterious deep. On the first day he created light, on the second day land, on the third day plants, on the fourth day the sun, the moon, and the stars, on the fifth day animals, and on the six day human beings. On the seventh day he rested. The story then focuses on the Garden of Eden and Adam. Adam was placed in the Garden of Eden to tend to it, lacking a companion God took one of Adam's ribs and fashioned it into a woman, Eve. The snake then tempted Eve to eat from the tree of life, and when she does she and Adam are banished from the garden. Eve gives birth to two children Cain and Abel. Cain offers some fruit to God, Abel offers some sheep. God prefers Abel's sacrifice. Cain gets jealous and kills Abel. As a punishment he is made to wander the earth to the end of days. Adam and Eve then give birth to a third son Seth, who is the ancestor of Noah.

At this time the sons of God come and copulate with human beings who have spread across the earth, the product of these unions are heroic demigods (the disjointedness of this part of the story and its lack of relationship to what comes before is also apparent in the canonical text). God becomes sick of human conduct and decides to wipe the slate clean with a flood, but chooses Noah and his family to save. Noah builds an ark, where he stows two pairs of every animal species and then waits out the flood in his ark, after a little less than a year he sends out birds to check if the land has dried, when the dove comes back with an olive branch he knows that the earth is once more inhabitable. Noah offers a sacrifice to God and God promises never again to bring a flood.

The first crop Noah decides to plant is grapes from which he makes wine and promptly gets drunk. His youngest son, Ham, sees his father naked and depending on your reading of the text may have had sex with him. Noah's other children cover their father. Upon waking Noah curses his youngest son and blesses his older children. Noah's sons repopulate the earth and give birth to seventy nations, among these nations' scions is Nimrod the first emperor. The seventy nations gather together and build a giant tower, God perceiving this as a threat sows confusion among the builders causing them to speak mutually unintelligible languages and thus they scatter over the earth.

After ten generations through Noah's eldest son Shem, Abraham is born and they begin their trek to Canaan.

That is the story of Creation as we know it today, but if we peel away one layer, the Bridging Redactor, or the Bridger, there are no more gods copulating with human women giving birth to herculean figures. Nimrod is no longer a mighty emperor, and there are a lot less nations. The focus narrows (though not exclusively) to Shem and his children since they are the forefathers of Abraham and the Israelites.

Peel off the next layer – the Priestly layer – and you will hardly recognize the story. The world didn't need to be created in seven days, it was always there. Instead of God being aloof he is jealous and afraid and quite corporeal, first he banishes Adam and Eve from the garden scared they may eat from the tree and challenge him, then he destroys the tower of Babel lest they reach heaven. In this kernel Adam and Eve don't give birth to a third son, it is Cain their eldest son's children who inherit the earth. Instead of three sons Noah has four sons and instead of a yearlong flood forty days are enough to destroy humanity. After the flood, the covenant between God and human beings is unfortunately never delineated, all God cares about is the Israelite line, who will appear on the world stage in Genesis 12.

These kinds of radical differences between the kernel (in this case J, though often it's E) and the canonical text are pervasive throughout the Pentateuch. When I lecture about J, my students are often surprised to learn that in J's version of events, we are all descended from a murderer. God actually forgave Cain and he turns out to be the ancestor of Noah in J's version of events. In this and many other respects, J's story of the creation is very different from what those familiar with the canonical text may recall. In the chapters that follow, I invite you to sit back and enjoy this uniquely divergent account and its development into the canonical text we have today.

THE CREATION STORY: GENESIS 1–2

In the beginning, there is only water, wind and darkness. Then God (Elohim) differentiates the light from the darkness, and creates the world and all that is in it in six days. He begins by distinguishing between water and land. He then plants trees, and places the sun, moon and stars in their correct constellations. On the fifth day he creates animals, and on the sixth day, pairs of human beings after his own image. On the seventh day he rests.

Chapter 2 zeroes in on the creation of man, who is fashioned by the Lord (Yahweh) from dust. The Lord plants a garden in Eden, which he commands man to tend. In the garden, there are two special trees: the Tree of Knowledge, and the Tree of Life. Man is lonely, so the Lord creates animals to serve as companions. The animals, however, do not alleviate his loneliness, so the Lord takes a rib from Man's chest and fashions Woman.

GENESIS 1–2: THE J KERNEL

2:4 In the day that Yahweh God made the earth and the heavens, 2:5 no plant of the field was yet on the earth, and no herbs of the field had sprouted yet; for Yahweh God had not caused it to rain upon the earth. There was no one to till the ground, 2:6 but a mist arose from the earth, and watered the entire ground. 2:7 Yahweh God fashioned a man from the earth upon the ground, and breathed the breath of life into his nostrils; and man became a living thing. 2:8 Yahweh God planted a garden eastward, in Eden, and there he placed the man whom he had formed. 2:9 Yahweh God caused every tree that is pleasant to the sight and good for food to grow out of the ground; and the Tree of Life was in the midst of the garden, and the Tree of the Knowledge of Good and Evil. 2:15 Yahweh God took the man, and put him into the garden of Eden to tend to it and to preserve it. 2:16 Yahweh God commanded the man, thusly, "you may freely eat of every tree of the garden; 2:17 but of the Tree of the Knowledge of Good and Evil, you shall not eat of it; for on the day that you eat of it you will surely die."

GENESIS 1–2: THE J KERNEL (HEBREW)

2:4 בְּיוֹם עֲשׂוֹת יְהוָה אֱלֹהִים אֶרֶץ וְשָׁמָיִם: 2:5 וְכֹל ׀ שִׂיחַ הַשָּׂדֶה טֶרֶם יִהְיֶה בָאָרֶץ וְכָל־עֵשֶׂב הַשָּׂדֶה טֶרֶם יִצְמָח כִּי לֹא הִמְטִיר יְהוָה אֱלֹהִים עַל־הָאָרֶץ וְאָדָם אַיִן לַעֲבֹד אֶת־הָאֲדָמָה: 2:6 וְאֵד יַעֲלֶה מִן־הָאָרֶץ וְהִשְׁקָה אֶת־כָּל־פְּנֵי־הָאֲדָמָה: 2:7 וַיִּיצֶר יְהוָה אֱלֹהִים אֶת־הָאָדָם עָפָר מִן־הָאֲדָמָה וַיִּפַּח בְּאַפָּיו נִשְׁמַת חַיִּים וַיְהִי הָאָדָם לְנֶפֶשׁ חַיָּה: 2:8 וַיִּטַּע יְהוָה אֱלֹהִים גַּן־בְעֵדֶן מִקֶּדֶם וַיָּשֶׂם שָׁם אֶת־הָאָדָם אֲשֶׁר יָצָר: 2:9 וַיַּצְמַח יְהוָה אֱלֹהִים מִן־הָאֲדָמָה כָּל־עֵץ נֶחְמָד לְמַרְאֶה וְטוֹב לְמַאֲכָל וְעֵץ הַחַיִּים בְּתוֹךְ הַגָּן וְעֵץ הַדַּעַת טוֹב וָרָע:

2:15 וַיִּקַּח יְהוָה אֱלֹהִים אֶת־הָאָדָם וַיַּנִּחֵהוּ בְגַן־עֵדֶן לְעָבְדָהּ וּלְשָׁמְרָהּ: 2:16 וַיְצַו יְהוָה אֱלֹהִים עַל־הָאָדָם לֵאמֹר מִכֹּל עֵץ־הַגָּן אָכֹל תֹּאכֵל: 2:17 וּמֵעֵץ הַדַּעַת טוֹב וָרָע לֹא תֹאכַל מִמֶּנּוּ כִּי בְּיוֹם אֲכָלְךָ מִמֶּנּוּ מוֹת תָּמוּת:

GENESIS 1–2: THE J KERNEL – CONTINUED

2:18 Yahweh God said, "It is not good that the man is alone; I will make a suitable helper for him." 2:19 Yahweh God formed all animals of the field, and every bird of the sky, out of the ground, and brought them to the man to see what he would call them. Whatever the man called every living creature, that was its name. 2:20 The man gave names to all livestock, and to the birds of the sky, and to every animal of the field; but for the man no suitable helper was found.

2:21 Yahweh God caused a deep sleep to fall upon the man, and he slept; and he took one of his ribs, and closed up the flesh in its place. 2:22 He fashioned the rib, which He (Yahweh God) had taken from the man, into a woman, and brought her to the man. 2:23 The man said, "This is now a bone of my bones, and flesh of my flesh. She will be called 'woman,' because she was taken from man." 2:24 It is for this reason that man leaves his father and his mother, and cleaves to his wife, and they become one flesh. 2:25 They were both naked, the man and his wife, and were not ashamed.

J's creation story is easy to distinguish from Chapter 1's ordered account. Instead of Elohim creating the world and all that is in it more or less from scratch, it is a deity with the compound name Yahweh Elohim (The Lord God) who creates all life forms in an already existing world. This compound name represents J's equation of Israel's private deity, Yahweh (The Lord), with the general deity, Elohim (a generic name for deities), thereby asserting that Israel's God created the world. Following the creation story (i.e. Genesis 2-3), J will use the name "Yahweh" exclusively when he refers to the deity of the Bible.

Instead of enumerating a list, J tells us a story. It is the story of a deity who is much more human than the remote, non-corporeal deity of Genesis 1 and modern monotheism. Instead of using the abstract verb "to create," J employs more hands-on terminology, like "to make," "to fashion," "to blow," and "to plant." Thus, The Lord God fashions the first human man (without the female counterpart found in P) out of "dust" and blows life into him. This first human being ("man" or "Adam") is placed in the newly planted Garden of Eden and is commanded by the Lord God to tend to it.

Mysteriously, two trees exist in the Garden of Eden that The Lord God didn't plant—the Tree of Knowledge, and the Tree of Life—suggesting that powers beyond The Lord God's are at work. J, unfortunately, does not elaborate.

GENESIS 1–2: THE J KERNEL (HEBREW) – CONTINUED

2:18 וַיֹּאמֶר֙ יְהוָ֣ה אֱלֹהִ֔ים לֹא־ט֛וֹב הֱי֥וֹת הָֽאָדָ֖ם לְבַדּ֑וֹ אֶֽעֱשֶׂהּ־לּ֥וֹ עֵ֖זֶר כְּנֶגְדּֽוֹ: 2:19 וַיִּצֶר֩ יְהוָ֨ה אֱלֹהִ֜ים מִן־הָֽאֲדָמָ֗ה כָּל־חַיַּ֤ת הַשָּׂדֶה֙ וְאֵת֙ כָּל־ע֣וֹף הַשָּׁמַ֔יִם וַיָּבֵא֙ אֶל־הָ֣אָדָ֔ם לִרְא֖וֹת מַה־יִּקְרָא־ל֑וֹ וְכֹל֩ אֲשֶׁ֨ר יִקְרָא־ל֧וֹ הָֽאָדָ֛ם נֶ֥פֶשׁ חַיָּ֖ה ה֥וּא שְׁמֽוֹ: 2:20 וַיִּקְרָ֨א הָֽאָדָ֜ם שֵׁמ֗וֹת לְכָל־הַבְּהֵמָה֙ וּלְע֣וֹף הַשָּׁמַ֔יִם וּלְכֹ֖ל חַיַּ֣ת הַשָּׂדֶ֑ה וּלְאָדָ֕ם לֹֽא־מָצָ֥א עֵ֖זֶר כְּנֶגְדּֽוֹ: 2:21 וַיַּפֵּל֩ יְהוָ֨ה אֱלֹהִ֧ים ׀ תַּרְדֵּמָ֛ה עַל־הָאָדָ֖ם וַיִּישָׁ֑ן וַיִּקַּ֗ח אַחַת֙ מִצַּלְעֹתָ֔יו וַיִּסְגֹּ֥ר בָּשָׂ֖ר תַּחְתֶּֽנָּה: 2:22 וַיִּבֶן֩ יְהוָ֨ה אֱלֹהִ֧ים ׀ אֶֽת־הַצֵּלָ֛ע אֲשֶׁר־לָקַ֥ח מִן־הָֽאָדָ֖ם לְאִשָּׁ֑ה וַיְבִאֶ֖הָ אֶל־הָֽאָדָֽם: 2:23 וַיֹּאמֶר֮ הָֽאָדָם֒ זֹ֣את הַפַּ֗עַם עֶ֚צֶם מֵֽעֲצָמַ֔י וּבָשָׂ֖ר מִבְּשָׂרִ֑י לְזֹאת֙ יִקָּרֵ֣א אִשָּׁ֔ה כִּ֥י מֵאִ֖ישׁ לֻֽקֳחָה־זֹּֽאת: 2:24 עַל־כֵּן֙ יַֽעֲזָב־אִ֔ישׁ אֶת־אָבִ֖יו וְאֶת־אִמּ֑וֹ וְדָבַ֣ק בְּאִשְׁתּ֔וֹ וְהָי֖וּ לְבָשָׂ֥ר אֶחָֽד: 2:25 וַיִּֽהְי֤וּ שְׁנֵיהֶם֙ עֲרוּמִּ֔ים הָֽאָדָ֖ם וְאִשְׁתּ֑וֹ וְלֹ֖א יִתְבֹּשָֽׁשׁוּ:

GENESIS 1–2: J + P

1:1 In the beginning when God created the heavens and the earth, 1:2 the earth was a formless void, and darkness covered the face of the deep, while a wind from God swept over the face of the waters. 1:3 Then God said, "Let there be light;" and there was light. 1:4 And God saw that the light was good; and God separated the light from the darkness. 1:5 God called the light Day, and the darkness he called Night. And there was evening and there was morning, the first day.

1:6 And God said, "Let there be a plane in the midst of the waters, and let it distinguish between water and water." 1:7 So God made the plane and separated the waters that were under the plane from the waters that were above the plane. And it was so. 1:8 God called the plane Sky. And there was evening and there was morning, the second day.

1:9 And God said, "Let the waters under the sky be gathered together into one place, and let the dry land appear." And it was so. 1:10 God called the dry land Earth, and the waters that were gathered together he called Seas. And God saw that it was good.

1:11 Then God said, "Let the earth sprout vegetation: plants with seed, and fruit trees of every kind on earth that bear fruit with the seed in it." And it was so. 1:12 The earth brought forth vegetation: plants yielding seed of every kind, and trees of every kind bearing fruit with the seed in it. And God saw that it was good. 1:13 And there was evening and there was morning, the third day.

1:14 And God said, "Let there be lights upon the surface of the sky to separate the day from the night; and let them be signs for seasons and for days and years, 1:15 and let them be luminaries upon the surface of the sky to light up the earth." And it was so. 1:16 God made the two great luminaries—the greater luminary to rule the day and the lesser luminary to rule the night—and the stars. 1:17 God placed them upon the surface of the sky to give light upon the earth, 1:18 to rule over the day and over the night, and to separate light from darkness. And God saw that it was good. 1:19 And there was evening and there was morning, the fourth day.

1:20 And God said, "Let the waters bring forth swarms of living creatures, and let birds fly above the earth across the sky's surface." 1:21 So God created the great sea monsters and every living creature that moves, of all types, that swarm in the waters and every winged bird of every kind. And God saw that it was good. 1:22 God blessed them, saying, "Be fruitful and multiply and fill the waters in the seas, and let birds multiply upon the earth." 1:23 And there was evening and there was morning, the fifth day.

GENESIS 1–2: J + P (HEBREW)

1:1 בְּרֵאשִׁ֖ית בָּרָ֣א אֱלֹהִ֑ים אֵ֥ת הַשָּׁמַ֖יִם וְאֵ֥ת הָאָֽרֶץ: 1:2 וְהָאָ֗רֶץ הָיְתָ֥ה תֹ֙הוּ֙ וָבֹ֔הוּ וְחֹ֖שֶׁךְ עַל־פְּנֵ֣י תְה֑וֹם וְר֣וּחַ אֱלֹהִ֔ים מְרַחֶ֖פֶת עַל־פְּנֵ֥י הַמָּֽיִם: 1:3 וַיֹּ֥אמֶר אֱלֹהִ֖ים יְהִ֣י א֑וֹר וַֽיְהִי־אֽוֹר: 1:4 וַיַּ֧רְא אֱלֹהִ֛ים אֶת־הָא֖וֹר כִּי־ט֑וֹב וַיַּבְדֵּ֣ל אֱלֹהִ֔ים בֵּ֥ין הָא֖וֹר וּבֵ֥ין הַחֹֽשֶׁךְ: 1:5 וַיִּקְרָ֨א אֱלֹהִ֤ים ׀ לָאוֹר֙ י֔וֹם וְלַחֹ֖שֶׁךְ קָ֣רָא לָ֑יְלָה וַֽיְהִי־עֶ֥רֶב וַֽיְהִי־בֹ֖קֶר י֥וֹם אֶחָֽד: פ

1:6 וַיֹּ֣אמֶר אֱלֹהִ֔ים יְהִ֥י רָקִ֖יעַ בְּת֣וֹךְ הַמָּ֑יִם וִיהִ֣י מַבְדִּ֔יל בֵּ֥ין מַ֖יִם לָמָֽיִם: 1:7 וַיַּ֣עַשׂ אֱלֹהִים֘ אֶת־הָרָקִיעַ֒ וַיַּבְדֵּ֗ל בֵּ֤ין הַמַּ֙יִם֙ אֲשֶׁר֙ מִתַּ֣חַת לָרָקִ֔יעַ וּבֵ֣ין הַמַּ֔יִם אֲשֶׁ֖ר מֵעַ֣ל לָרָקִ֑יעַ וַֽיְהִי־כֵֽן: 1:8 וַיִּקְרָ֧א אֱלֹהִ֛ים לָֽרָקִ֖יעַ שָׁמָ֑יִם וַֽיְהִי־עֶ֥רֶב וַֽיְהִי־בֹ֖קֶר י֥וֹם שֵׁנִֽי: פ

1:9 וַיֹּ֣אמֶר אֱלֹהִ֗ים יִקָּו֨וּ הַמַּ֜יִם מִתַּ֤חַת הַשָּׁמַ֙יִם֙ אֶל־מָק֣וֹם אֶחָ֔ד וְתֵרָאֶ֖ה הַיַּבָּשָׁ֑ה וַֽיְהִי־כֵֽן: 1:10 וַיִּקְרָ֨א אֱלֹהִ֤ים ׀ לַיַּבָּשָׁה֙ אֶ֔רֶץ וּלְמִקְוֵ֥ה הַמַּ֖יִם קָרָ֣א יַמִּ֑ים וַיַּ֥רְא אֱלֹהִ֖ים כִּי־טֽוֹב: 1:11 וַיֹּ֣אמֶר אֱלֹהִ֗ים תַּֽדְשֵׁ֤א הָאָ֙רֶץ֙ דֶּ֗שֶׁא עֵ֚שֶׂב מַזְרִ֣יעַ זֶ֔רַע עֵ֣ץ פְּרִ֞י עֹ֤שֶׂה פְּרִי֙ לְמִינ֔וֹ אֲשֶׁ֥ר זַרְעוֹ־ב֖וֹ עַל־הָאָ֑רֶץ וַֽיְהִי־כֵֽן: 1:12 וַתּוֹצֵ֨א הָאָ֜רֶץ דֶּ֠שֶׁא עֵ֣שֶׂב מַזְרִ֤יעַ זֶ֙רַע֙ לְמִינֵ֔הוּ וְעֵ֧ץ עֹֽשֶׂה־פְּרִ֛י אֲשֶׁ֥ר זַרְעוֹ־ב֖וֹ לְמִינֵ֑הוּ וַיַּ֥רְא אֱלֹהִ֖ים כִּי־טֽוֹב: 1:13 וַֽיְהִי־עֶ֥רֶב וַֽיְהִי־בֹ֖קֶר י֥וֹם שְׁלִישִֽׁי: פ

1:14 וַיֹּ֣אמֶר אֱלֹהִ֗ים יְהִ֤י מְאֹרֹת֙ בִּרְקִ֣יעַ הַשָּׁמַ֔יִם לְהַבְדִּ֕יל בֵּ֥ין הַיּ֖וֹם וּבֵ֣ין הַלָּ֑יְלָה וְהָי֤וּ לְאֹתֹת֙ וּלְמ֣וֹעֲדִ֔ים וּלְיָמִ֖ים וְשָׁנִֽים: 1:15 וְהָי֤וּ לִמְאוֹרֹת֙ בִּרְקִ֣יעַ הַשָּׁמַ֔יִם לְהָאִ֖יר עַל־הָאָ֑רֶץ וַֽיְהִי־כֵֽן: 1:16 וַיַּ֣עַשׂ אֱלֹהִ֔ים אֶת־שְׁנֵ֥י הַמְּאֹרֹ֖ת הַגְּדֹלִ֑ים אֶת־הַמָּא֤וֹר הַגָּדֹל֙ לְמֶמְשֶׁ֣לֶת הַיּ֔וֹם וְאֶת־הַמָּא֤וֹר הַקָּטֹן֙ לְמֶמְשֶׁ֣לֶת הַלַּ֔יְלָה וְאֵ֖ת הַכּוֹכָבִֽים: 1:17 וַיִּתֵּ֥ן אֹתָ֛ם אֱלֹהִ֖ים בִּרְקִ֣יעַ הַשָּׁמָ֑יִם לְהָאִ֖יר עַל־הָאָֽרֶץ: 1:18 וְלִמְשֹׁל֙ בַּיּ֣וֹם וּבַלַּ֔יְלָה וּֽלֲהַבְדִּ֔יל בֵּ֥ין הָא֖וֹר וּבֵ֣ין הַחֹ֑שֶׁךְ וַיַּ֥רְא אֱלֹהִ֖ים כִּי־טֽוֹב: 1:19 וַֽיְהִי־עֶ֥רֶב וַֽיְהִי־בֹ֖קֶר י֥וֹם רְבִיעִֽי: פ

1:20 וַיֹּ֣אמֶר אֱלֹהִ֔ים יִשְׁרְצ֣וּ הַמַּ֔יִם שֶׁ֖רֶץ נֶ֣פֶשׁ חַיָּ֑ה וְעוֹף֙ יְעוֹפֵ֣ף עַל־הָאָ֔רֶץ עַל־פְּנֵ֖י רְקִ֥יעַ הַשָּׁמָֽיִם: 1:21 וַיִּבְרָ֣א אֱלֹהִ֔ים אֶת־הַתַּנִּינִ֖ם הַגְּדֹלִ֑ים וְאֵ֣ת כָּל־נֶ֣פֶשׁ הַֽחַיָּ֣ה ׀ הָֽרֹמֶ֡שֶׂת אֲשֶׁר֩ שָׁרְצ֨וּ הַמַּ֜יִם לְמִֽינֵהֶ֗ם וְאֵ֨ת כָּל־ע֤וֹף כָּנָף֙ לְמִינֵ֔הוּ וַיַּ֥רְא אֱלֹהִ֖ים כִּי־טֽוֹב: 1:22 וַיְבָ֧רֶךְ אֹתָ֛ם אֱלֹהִ֖ים לֵאמֹ֑ר פְּר֣וּ וּרְב֗וּ וּמִלְא֤וּ אֶת־הַמַּ֙יִם֙ בַּיַּמִּ֔ים וְהָע֖וֹף יִ֥רֶב בָּאָֽרֶץ: 1:23 וַֽיְהִי־עֶ֥רֶב וַֽיְהִי־בֹ֖קֶר י֥וֹם חֲמִישִֽׁי: פ

GENESIS 1–2: J + P – CONTINUED

1:24 And God said, "Let the earth bring forth living creatures of all types: cattle and creeping things and wild animals of the earth of all types." And it was so. 1:25 God made wild animals of the earth of all types, and the cattle of all types, and everything that creeps upon the ground of all types. And God saw that it was good.

1:26 Then God said, "Let us make humankind in our image, according to our likeness; and let them have dominion over the fish of the sea, and over the birds of the air, and over the cattle, and over all the wild animals of the earth, and over every creeping thing that creeps upon the earth." 1:27 So God created humankind in his image; he created them in the image of God; he created them male and female. 1:28 God blessed them, and God said to them, "Be fruitful and multiply, and fill the earth and subdue it; and have dominion over the fish of the sea and over the birds of the air and over every living thing that moves upon the earth." 1:29 God said, "See, I have given you every plant with seeds that is upon the face of all the earth, and every tree with seed in its fruit, as food for you. 1:30 And to every beast of the earth, and to every bird of the air, and to everything that creeps on the earth, everything that has the breath of life, I have given every sprouting plant as food." And it was so. 1:31 God saw everything that he had made, and indeed, it was very good. And there was evening and there was morning, the sixth day.

2:1 The heavens and the earth were finished, and all their vast array. 2:2 On the seventh day God finished his work which he had made; and he rested on the seventh day from all his work which he had made. 2:3 God blessed the seventh day, and made it holy, because he rested in it from all his work which he had created and made.

2:4 This is the history of the heavens and of the earth when they were created: in the day that Yahweh God made the earth and the heavens, 2:5 no plant of the field was yet on the earth, and no herbs of the field had sprouted yet; for Yahweh God had not caused it to rain upon the earth. There was no one to till the ground, 2:6 but a mist arose from the earth, and watered the entire ground. 2:7 Yahweh God fashioned a man from the earth upon the ground, and breathed the breath of life into his nostrils; and man became a living thing. 2:8 Yahweh God planted a garden eastward, in Eden, and there he placed the man whom he had formed. 2:9 Yahweh God caused every tree that is pleasant to the sight and good for food to grow out of the ground; and the Tree of Life was in the midst of the garden, and the Tree of the Knowledge of Good and Evil. 2:15 Yahweh God took the man, and put him into the garden of Eden to tend to it and to preserve it. 2:16 Yahweh God commanded the man, thusly, "you may freely eat of every tree of the garden;

GENESIS 1–2: J + P (HEBREW) – CONTINUED

1:24 וַיֹּאמֶר אֱלֹהִים תּוֹצֵא הָאָרֶץ נֶפֶשׁ חַיָּה לְמִינָהּ בְּהֵמָה וָרֶמֶשׂ וְחַיְתוֹ־אֶרֶץ לְמִינָהּ וַיְהִי־כֵן: 1:25 וַיַּעַשׂ אֱלֹהִים אֶת־חַיַּת הָאָרֶץ לְמִינָהּ וְאֶת־הַבְּהֵמָה לְמִינָהּ וְאֵת כָּל־רֶמֶשׂ הָאֲדָמָה לְמִינֵהוּ וַיַּרְא אֱלֹהִים כִּי־טוֹב: 1:26 וַיֹּאמֶר אֱלֹהִים נַעֲשֶׂה אָדָם בְּצַלְמֵנוּ כִּדְמוּתֵנוּ וְיִרְדּוּ בִדְגַת הַיָּם וּבְעוֹף הַשָּׁמַיִם וּבַבְּהֵמָה וּבְכָל־הָאָרֶץ וּבְכָל־הָרֶמֶשׂ הָרֹמֵשׂ עַל־הָאָרֶץ: 1:27 וַיִּבְרָא אֱלֹהִים ׀ אֶת־הָאָדָם בְּצַלְמוֹ בְּצֶלֶם אֱלֹהִים בָּרָא אֹתוֹ זָכָר וּנְקֵבָה בָּרָא אֹתָם: 1:28 וַיְבָרֶךְ אֹתָם אֱלֹהִים וַיֹּאמֶר לָהֶם אֱלֹהִים פְּרוּ וּרְבוּ וּמִלְאוּ אֶת־הָאָרֶץ וְכִבְשֻׁהָ וּרְדוּ בִּדְגַת הַיָּם וּבְעוֹף הַשָּׁמַיִם וּבְכָל־חַיָּה הָרֹמֶשֶׂת עַל־הָאָרֶץ: 1:29 וַיֹּאמֶר אֱלֹהִים הִנֵּה נָתַתִּי לָכֶם אֶת־כָּל־עֵשֶׂב ׀ זֹרֵעַ זֶרַע אֲשֶׁר עַל־פְּנֵי כָל־הָאָרֶץ וְאֶת־כָּל־הָעֵץ אֲשֶׁר־בּוֹ פְרִי־עֵץ זֹרֵעַ זָרַע לָכֶם יִהְיֶה לְאָכְלָה: 1:30 וּלְכָל־חַיַּת הָאָרֶץ וּלְכָל־עוֹף הַשָּׁמַיִם וּלְכֹל ׀ רוֹמֵשׂ עַל־הָאָרֶץ אֲשֶׁר־בּוֹ נֶפֶשׁ חַיָּה אֶת־כָּל־יֶרֶק עֵשֶׂב לְאָכְלָה וַיְהִי־כֵן: 1:31 וַיַּרְא אֱלֹהִים אֶת־כָּל־אֲשֶׁר עָשָׂה וְהִנֵּה־טוֹב מְאֹד וַיְהִי־עֶרֶב וַיְהִי־בֹקֶר יוֹם הַשִּׁשִּׁי: פ

2:1 וַיְכֻלּוּ הַשָּׁמַיִם וְהָאָרֶץ וְכָל־צְבָאָם: 2:2 וַיְכַל אֱלֹהִים בַּיּוֹם הַשְּׁבִיעִי מְלַאכְתּוֹ אֲשֶׁר עָשָׂה וַיִּשְׁבֹּת בַּיּוֹם הַשְּׁבִיעִי מִכָּל־מְלַאכְתּוֹ אֲשֶׁר עָשָׂה: 2:3 וַיְבָרֶךְ אֱלֹהִים אֶת־יוֹם הַשְּׁבִיעִי וַיְקַדֵּשׁ אֹתוֹ כִּי בוֹ שָׁבַת מִכָּל־מְלַאכְתּוֹ אֲשֶׁר־בָּרָא אֱלֹהִים לַעֲשׂוֹת: פ

==2:4 אֵלֶּה תוֹלְדוֹת הַשָּׁמַיִם וְהָאָרֶץ בְּהִבָּרְאָם בְּיוֹם עֲשׂוֹת יְהוָה אֱלֹהִים אֶרֶץ וְשָׁמָיִם: 2:5 וְכֹל ׀ שִׂיחַ הַשָּׂדֶה טֶרֶם יִהְיֶה בָאָרֶץ וְכָל־עֵשֶׂב הַשָּׂדֶה טֶרֶם יִצְמָח כִּי לֹא הִמְטִיר יְהוָה אֱלֹהִים עַל־הָאָרֶץ וְאָדָם אַיִן לַעֲבֹד אֶת־הָאֲדָמָה: 2:6 וְאֵד יַעֲלֶה מִן־הָאָרֶץ וְהִשְׁקָה אֶת־כָּל־פְּנֵי־הָאֲדָמָה: 2:7 וַיִּיצֶר יְהוָה אֱלֹהִים אֶת־הָאָדָם עָפָר מִן־הָאֲדָמָה וַיִּפַּח בְּאַפָּיו נִשְׁמַת חַיִּים וַיְהִי הָאָדָם לְנֶפֶשׁ חַיָּה: 2:8 וַיִּטַּע יְהוָה אֱלֹהִים גַּן־בְעֵדֶן מִקֶּדֶם וַיָּשֶׂם שָׁם אֶת־הָאָדָם אֲשֶׁר יָצָר:==

==2:9 וַיַּצְמַח יְהוָה אֱלֹהִים מִן־הָאֲדָמָה כָּל־עֵץ נֶחְמָד לְמַרְאֶה וְטוֹב לְמַאֲכָל וְעֵץ הַחַיִּים בְּתוֹךְ הַגָּן וְעֵץ הַדַּעַת טוֹב וָרָע: 2:15 וַיִּקַּח יְהוָה אֱלֹהִים אֶת־הָאָדָם וַיַּנִּחֵהוּ בְגַן־עֵדֶן לְעָבְדָהּ וּלְשָׁמְרָהּ: 2:16 וַיְצַו יְהוָה אֱלֹהִים עַל־הָאָדָם לֵאמֹר מִכֹּל עֵץ־הַגָּן אָכֹל תֹּאכֵל:==

GENESIS 1–2: J + P – CONTINUED

2:17 but of the Tree of the Knowledge of Good and Evil, you shall not eat of it; for on the day that you eat of it you will surely die."

2:18 Yahweh God said, "It is not good that the man is alone; I will make a suitable helper for him." 2:19 Yahweh God formed all animals of the field, and every bird of the sky, out of the ground, and brought them to the man to see what he would call them. Whatever the man called every living creature, that was its name. 2:20 The man gave names to all livestock, and to the birds of the sky, and to every animal of the field; but for the man no suitable helper was found. 2:21 Yahweh God caused a deep sleep to fall upon the man, and he slept; and he took one of his ribs, and closed up the flesh in its place. 2:22 He fashioned the rib, which He (Yahweh God) had taken from the man, into a woman, and brought her to the man. 2:23 The man said, "This is now a bone of my bones, and flesh of my flesh. She will be called 'woman,' because she was taken from man." 2:24 It is for this reason that man leaves his father and his mother, and cleaves to his wife, and they become one flesh. 2:25 They were both naked, the man and his wife, and were not ashamed.

What P Adds

In his creation story, P responds to J's earlier account, attempting to sculpt it in important ways. One logical difficulty that P tries to resolve is how human beings could have multiplied if Adam and Eve were the only couple and they only gave birth to sons. This problem is solved by hinting that, in fact, many couples were created at once, and by implying through the genealogies of Chapters 5 and 11 that the reason that God is particularly interested in Adam and Eve is that they begin the line that will eventually lead to the Israelites.

J's account in Chapter 2 places limits on the Lord's power. J implies that the Lord did not plant the Tree of Knowledge or the Tree of Life, the two most important trees in the Garden of Eden, and his account alludes only indirectly to the Lord's role in the creation of heaven and earth. Chapter 2 also implies that the Lord doesn't know how Adam will relate to the animals or who will fill the role of Adam's mate. In P, however, God's power is unlimited: he creates heaven and earth with his words (in J, the earth already exists, and the Lord God creates only living things) and distinguishes between light and darkness. According to P, all of the trees in the world were created by God ("Then God said, 'Let the earth sprout vegetation…' And it was so. The earth brought forth vegetation."), in order to undermine J's version of events in which two mysterious trees, the Tree of Life and the Tree of Knowledge were not created by the deity. P's God has a plan for human beings from the outset, and thus creates male and female human beings and commands them to procreate (in J the Lord God only creates man from the outset, initially, without a companion).

GENESIS 1–2: J + P (HEBREW) – CONTINUED

2:17 וּמֵעֵ֗ץ הַדַּ֙עַת֙ ט֣וֹב וָרָ֔ע לֹ֥א תֹאכַ֖ל מִמֶּ֑נּוּ כִּ֗י בְּי֛וֹם אֲכָלְךָ֥ מִמֶּ֖נּוּ מ֥וֹת תָּמֽוּת: 2:18 וַיֹּ֙אמֶר֙ יְהוָ֣ה אֱלֹהִ֔ים לֹא־ט֛וֹב הֱי֥וֹת הָֽאָדָ֖ם לְבַדּ֑וֹ אֶֽעֱשֶׂהּ־לּ֥וֹ עֵ֖זֶר כְּנֶגְדּֽוֹ: 2:19 וַיִּצֶר֩ יְהוָ֨ה אֱלֹהִ֜ים מִן־הָֽאֲדָמָ֗ה כָּל־חַיַּ֤ת הַשָּׂדֶה֙ וְאֵת֙ כָּל־ע֣וֹף הַשָּׁמַ֔יִם וַיָּבֵא֙ אֶל־הָ֣אָדָ֔ם לִרְא֖וֹת מַה־יִּקְרָא־ל֑וֹ וְכֹל֩ אֲשֶׁ֨ר יִקְרָא־ל֧וֹ הָֽאָדָ֛ם נֶ֥פֶשׁ חַיָּ֖ה ה֥וּא שְׁמֽוֹ: 2:20 וַיִּקְרָ֨א הָֽאָדָ֜ם שֵׁמ֗וֹת לְכָל־הַבְּהֵמָה֙ וּלְע֣וֹף הַשָּׁמַ֔יִם וּלְכֹ֖ל חַיַּ֣ת הַשָּׂדֶ֑ה וּלְאָדָ֕ם לֹֽא־מָצָ֥א עֵ֖זֶר כְּנֶגְדּֽוֹ: 2:21 וַיַּפֵּל֩ יְהוָ֨ה אֱלֹהִ֧ים ׀ תַּרְדֵּמָ֛ה עַל־הָאָדָ֖ם וַיִּישָׁ֑ן וַיִּקַּ֗ח אַחַת֙ מִצַּלְעֹתָ֔יו וַיִּסְגֹּ֥ר בָּשָׂ֖ר תַּחְתֶּֽנָּה: 2:22 וַיִּ֩בֶן֩ יְהוָ֨ה אֱלֹהִ֧ים ׀ אֶֽת־הַצֵּלָ֛ע אֲשֶׁר־לָקַ֥ח מִן־הָֽאָדָ֖ם לְאִשָּׁ֑ה וַיְבִאֶ֖הָ אֶל־הָֽאָדָֽם: 2:23 וַיֹּאמֶר֮ הָֽאָדָם֒ זֹ֣את הַפַּ֗עַם עֶ֚צֶם מֵֽעֲצָמַ֔י וּבָשָׂ֖ר מִבְּשָׂרִ֑י לְזֹאת֙ יִקָּרֵ֣א אִשָּׁ֔ה כִּ֥י מֵאִ֖ישׁ לֻֽקֳחָה־זֹּֽאת: 2:24 עַל־כֵּן֙ יַֽעֲזָב־אִ֔ישׁ אֶת־אָבִ֖יו וְאֶת־אִמּ֑וֹ וְדָבַ֣ק בְּאִשְׁתּ֔וֹ וְהָי֖וּ לְבָשָׂ֥ר אֶחָֽד: 2:25 וַיִּֽהְי֤וּ שְׁנֵיהֶם֙ עֲרוּמִּ֔ים הָֽאָדָ֖ם וְאִשְׁתּ֑וֹ וְלֹ֖א יִתְבֹּשָֽׁשׁוּ:

It is important to note that in this narrative, P lays the foundation for his most important law—the imperative to observe the Sabbath—by stating that working for six days and resting on the seventh was God's timeline for creation, and thus that it is incumbent upon human beings to follow God's example. Following God's rest, P has to transition from his account to the earlier J account, a feat which he manages quite well. In the first half of verse 4, P states that what follows is a history (Toldot) of earth upon its creation, and history means people (the term Toldot, roughly rendered as history, otherwise appears only in human contexts throughout the Bible). Thus, in P's combined version, J's account of Chapter 2 is meant to narrow our focus and concentrate on particular creatures, most importantly the creation of human beings, which are only dealt with in a few short verses in P's Chapter 1. We thus can forgive The Lord God for creating people before trees and animals contrary to P's Chapter 1, for in J's Chapter 2, man is at the center of the story. This way of reading the texts together blurs the differences between the accounts listed above, and allows us to read the Genesis account as one.

GENESIS 1–2: CANON (J + P + B)

1:1 In the beginning when God created the heavens and the earth, 1:2 the earth was a formless void, and darkness covered the face of the deep, while a wind from God swept over the face of the waters. 1:3 Then God said, "Let there be light;" and there was light. 1:4 And God saw that the light was good; and God separated the light from the darkness. 1:5 God called the light Day, and the darkness he called Night. And there was evening and there was morning, the first day.

1:6 And God said, "Let there be a plane in the midst of the waters, and let it distinguish between water and water." 1:7 So God made the plane and separated the waters that were under the plane from the waters that were above the plane. And it was so. 1:8 God called the plane Sky. And there was evening and there was morning, the second day.

1:9 And God said, "Let the waters under the sky be gathered together into one place, and let the dry land appear." And it was so. 1:10 God called the dry land Earth, and the waters that were gathered together he called Seas. And God saw that it was good. 1:11 Then God said, "Let the earth sprout vegetation: plants with seed, and fruit trees of every kind on earth that bear fruit with the seed in it." And it was so. 1:12 The earth brought forth vegetation: plants yielding seed of every kind, and trees of every kind bearing fruit with the seed in it. And God saw that it was good. 1:13 And there was evening and there was morning, the third day.

1:14 And God said, "Let there be lights upon the surface of the sky to separate the day from the night; and let them be signs for seasons and for days and years, 1:15 and let them be luminaries upon the surface of the sky to light up the earth." And it was so.

GENESIS 1–2: CANON (J + P + B) HEBREW

1:1 בְּרֵאשִׁ֖ית בָּרָ֣א אֱלֹהִ֑ים אֵ֥ת הַשָּׁמַ֖יִם וְאֵ֥ת הָאָֽרֶץ׃ 1:2 וְהָאָ֗רֶץ הָיְתָ֥ה תֹ֙הוּ֙ וָבֹ֔הוּ וְחֹ֖שֶׁךְ עַל־פְּנֵ֣י תְה֑וֹם וְר֣וּחַ אֱלֹהִ֔ים מְרַחֶ֖פֶת עַל־פְּנֵ֥י הַמָּֽיִם׃ 1:3 וַיֹּ֥אמֶר אֱלֹהִ֖ים יְהִ֣י א֑וֹר וַֽיְהִי־אֽוֹר׃ 1:4 וַיַּ֧רְא אֱלֹהִ֛ים אֶת־הָא֖וֹר כִּי־ט֑וֹב וַיַּבְדֵּ֣ל אֱלֹהִ֔ים בֵּ֥ין הָא֖וֹר וּבֵ֥ין הַחֹֽשֶׁךְ׃ 1:5 וַיִּקְרָ֨א אֱלֹהִ֤ים ׀ לָאוֹר֙ י֔וֹם וְלַחֹ֖שֶׁךְ קָ֣רָא לָ֑יְלָה וַֽיְהִי־עֶ֥רֶב וַֽיְהִי־בֹ֖קֶר י֥וֹם אֶחָֽד׃ פ

1:6 וַיֹּ֣אמֶר אֱלֹהִ֔ים יְהִ֥י רָקִ֖יעַ בְּת֣וֹךְ הַמָּ֑יִם וִיהִ֣י מַבְדִּ֔יל בֵּ֥ין מַ֖יִם לָמָֽיִם׃ 1:7 וַיַּ֣עַשׂ אֱלֹהִים֮ אֶת־הָרָקִיעַ֒ וַיַּבְדֵּ֗ל בֵּ֤ין הַמַּ֙יִם֙ אֲשֶׁר֙ מִתַּ֣חַת לָרָקִ֔יעַ וּבֵ֣ין הַמַּ֔יִם אֲשֶׁ֖ר מֵעַ֣ל לָרָקִ֑יעַ וַֽיְהִי־כֵֽן׃ 1:8 וַיִּקְרָ֧א אֱלֹהִ֛ים לָֽרָקִ֖יעַ שָׁמָ֑יִם וַֽיְהִי־עֶ֥רֶב וַֽיְהִי־בֹ֖קֶר י֥וֹם שֵׁנִֽי׃ פ

1:9 וַיֹּ֣אמֶר אֱלֹהִ֗ים יִקָּו֨וּ הַמַּ֜יִם מִתַּ֤חַת הַשָּׁמַ֙יִם֙ אֶל־מָק֣וֹם אֶחָ֔ד וְתֵרָאֶ֖ה הַיַּבָּשָׁ֑ה וַֽיְהִי־כֵֽן׃ 1:10 וַיִּקְרָ֨א אֱלֹהִ֤ים ׀ לַיַּבָּשָׁה֙ אֶ֔רֶץ וּלְמִקְוֵ֥ה הַמַּ֖יִם קָרָ֣א יַמִּ֑ים וַיַּ֥רְא אֱלֹהִ֖ים כִּי־טֽוֹב׃ 1:11 וַיֹּ֣אמֶר אֱלֹהִ֗ים תַּֽדְשֵׁ֤א הָאָ֙רֶץ֙ דֶּ֗שֶׁא עֵ֚שֶׂב מַזְרִ֣יעַ זֶ֔רַע עֵ֣ץ פְּרִ֞י עֹ֤שֶׂה פְּרִי֙ לְמִינ֔וֹ אֲשֶׁ֥ר זַרְעוֹ־ב֖וֹ עַל־הָאָ֑רֶץ וַֽיְהִי־כֵֽן׃ 1:12 וַתּוֹצֵ֨א הָאָ֜רֶץ דֶּ֠שֶׁא עֵ֣שֶׂב מַזְרִ֤יעַ זֶ֙רַע֙ לְמִינֵ֔הוּ וְעֵ֧ץ עֹֽשֶׂה־פְּרִ֛י אֲשֶׁ֥ר זַרְעוֹ־ב֖וֹ לְמִינֵ֑הוּ וַיַּ֥רְא אֱלֹהִ֖ים כִּי־טֽוֹב׃ 1:13 וַֽיְהִי־עֶ֥רֶב וַֽיְהִי־בֹ֖קֶר י֥וֹם שְׁלִישִֽׁי׃ פ

1:14 וַיֹּ֣אמֶר אֱלֹהִ֗ים יְהִ֤י מְאֹרֹת֙ בִּרְקִ֣יעַ הַשָּׁמַ֔יִם לְהַבְדִּ֕יל בֵּ֥ין הַיּ֖וֹם וּבֵ֣ין הַלָּ֑יְלָה וְהָי֤וּ לְאֹתֹת֙ וּלְמ֣וֹעֲדִ֔ים וּלְיָמִ֖ים וְשָׁנִֽים׃ 1:15 וְהָי֤וּ לִמְאוֹרֹת֙ בִּרְקִ֣יעַ הַשָּׁמַ֔יִם לְהָאִ֖יר עַל־הָאָ֑רֶץ וַֽיְהִי־כֵֽן׃ 1:16 וַיַּ֣עַשׂ אֱלֹהִ֔ים אֶת־שְׁנֵ֥י הַמְּאֹרֹ֖ת הַגְּדֹלִ֑ים אֶת־הַמָּא֤וֹר הַגָּדֹל֙ לְמֶמְשֶׁ֣לֶת הַיּ֔וֹם וְאֶת־הַמָּא֤וֹר הַקָּטֹן֙ לְמֶמְשֶׁ֣לֶת הַלַּ֔יְלָה וְאֵ֖ת הַכּוֹכָבִֽים׃

GENESIS 1–2: CANON (J + P + B) – CONTINUED

1:16 God made the two great luminaries—the greater luminary to rule the day and the lesser luminary to rule the night—and the stars. 1:17 God placed them upon the surface of the sky to give light upon the earth, 1:18 to rule over the day and over the night, and to separate light from darkness. And God saw that it was good. 1:19 And there was evening and there was morning, the fourth day.

1:20 And God said, "Let the waters bring forth swarms of living creatures, and let birds fly above the earth across the sky's surface." 1:21 So God created the great sea monsters and every living creature that moves, of all types, that swarm in the waters and every winged bird of every kind. And God saw that it was good. 1:22 God blessed them, saying, "Be fruitful and multiply and fill the waters in the seas, and let birds multiply upon the earth." 1:23 And there was evening and there was morning, the fifth day.

1:24 And God said, "Let the earth bring forth living creatures of all types: cattle and creeping things and wild animals of the earth of all types." And it was so. 1:25 God made wild animals of the earth of all types, and the cattle of all types, and everything that creeps upon the ground of all types. And God saw that it was good.

1:26 Then God said, "Let us make humankind in our image, according to our likeness; and let them have dominion over the fish of the sea, and over the birds of the air, and over the cattle, and over all the wild animals of the earth, and over every creeping thing that creeps upon the earth." 1:27 So God created humankind in his image; he created them in the image of God; he created them male and female. 1:28 God blessed them, and God said to them, "Be fruitful and multiply, and fill the earth and subdue it; and have dominion over the fish of the sea and over the birds of the air and over every living thing that moves upon the earth." 1:29 God said, "See, I have given you every plant with seeds that is upon the face of all the earth, and every tree with seed in its fruit, as food for you. 1:30 And to every beast of the earth, and to every bird of the air, and to everything that creeps on the earth, everything that has the breath of life, I have given every sprouting plant as food." And it was so. 1:31 God saw everything that he had made, and indeed, it was very good. And there was evening and there was morning, the sixth day.

2:1 The heavens and the earth were finished, and all their vast array. 2:2 On the seventh day God finished his work which he had made; and he rested on the seventh day from all his work which he had made. 2:3 God blessed the seventh day, and made it holy, because he rested in it from all his work which he had created and made.

GENESIS 1–2: CANON (J + P + B) HEBREW – CONTINUED

1:17 וַיִּתֵּ֥ן אֹתָ֛ם אֱלֹהִ֖ים בִּרְקִ֣יעַ הַשָּׁמָ֑יִם לְהָאִ֖יר עַל־הָאָֽרֶץ׃ 1:18 וְלִמְשֹׁל֙ בַּיּ֣וֹם וּבַלַּ֔יְלָה וּֽלְהַבְדִּ֔יל בֵּ֥ין הָא֖וֹר וּבֵ֣ין הַחֹ֑שֶׁךְ וַיַּ֥רְא אֱלֹהִ֖ים כִּי־טֽוֹב׃ 1:19 וַֽיְהִי־עֶ֥רֶב וַֽיְהִי־בֹ֖קֶר י֥וֹם רְבִיעִֽי׃ פ

1:20 וַיֹּ֣אמֶר אֱלֹהִ֔ים יִשְׁרְצ֣וּ הַמַּ֔יִם שֶׁ֖רֶץ נֶ֣פֶשׁ חַיָּ֑ה וְעוֹף֙ יְעוֹפֵ֣ף עַל־הָאָ֔רֶץ עַל־פְּנֵ֖י רְקִ֥יעַ הַשָּׁמָֽיִם׃ 1:21 וַיִּבְרָ֣א אֱלֹהִ֔ים אֶת־הַתַּנִּינִ֖ם הַגְּדֹלִ֑ים וְאֵ֣ת כָּל־נֶ֣פֶשׁ הַֽחַיָּ֣ה ׀ הָֽרֹמֶ֡שֶׂת אֲשֶׁר֩ שָׁרְצ֨וּ הַמַּ֜יִם לְמִֽינֵהֶ֗ם וְאֵ֨ת כָּל־ע֤וֹף כָּנָף֙ לְמִינֵ֔הוּ וַיַּ֥רְא אֱלֹהִ֖ים כִּי־טֽוֹב׃ 1:22 וַיְבָ֧רֶךְ אֹתָ֛ם אֱלֹהִ֖ים לֵאמֹ֑ר פְּר֣וּ וּרְב֗וּ וּמִלְא֤וּ אֶת־הַמַּ֨יִם֙ בַּיַּמִּ֔ים וְהָע֖וֹף יִ֥רֶב בָּאָֽרֶץ׃ 1:23 וַֽיְהִי־עֶ֥רֶב וַֽיְהִי־בֹ֖קֶר י֥וֹם חֲמִישִֽׁי׃ פ

1:24 וַיֹּ֣אמֶר אֱלֹהִ֗ים תּוֹצֵ֨א הָאָ֜רֶץ נֶ֤פֶשׁ חַיָּה֙ לְמִינָ֔הּ בְּהֵמָ֥ה וָרֶ֛מֶשׂ וְחַֽיְתוֹ־אֶ֖רֶץ לְמִינָ֑הּ וַֽיְהִי־כֵֽן׃ 1:25 וַיַּ֣עַשׂ אֱלֹהִים֩ אֶת־חַיַּ֨ת הָאָ֜רֶץ לְמִינָ֗הּ וְאֶת־הַבְּהֵמָה֙ לְמִינָ֔הּ וְאֵ֛ת כָּל־רֶ֥מֶשׂ הָֽאֲדָמָ֖ה לְמִינֵ֑הוּ וַיַּ֥רְא אֱלֹהִ֖ים כִּי־טֽוֹב׃ 1:26 וַיֹּ֣אמֶר אֱלֹהִ֔ים נַֽעֲשֶׂ֥ה אָדָ֛ם בְּצַלְמֵ֖נוּ כִּדְמוּתֵ֑נוּ וְיִרְדּוּ֩ בִדְגַ֨ת הַיָּ֜ם וּבְע֣וֹף הַשָּׁמַ֗יִם וּבַבְּהֵמָה֙ וּבְכָל־הָאָ֔רֶץ וּבְכָל־הָרֶ֖מֶשׂ הָֽרֹמֵ֥שׂ עַל־הָאָֽרֶץ׃ 1:27 וַיִּבְרָ֨א אֱלֹהִ֤ים ׀ אֶת־הָֽאָדָם֙ בְּצַלְמ֔וֹ בְּצֶ֥לֶם אֱלֹהִ֖ים בָּרָ֣א אֹת֑וֹ זָכָ֥ר וּנְקֵבָ֖ה בָּרָ֥א אֹתָֽם׃ 1:28 וַיְבָ֣רֶךְ אֹתָם֮ אֱלֹהִים֒ וַיֹּ֨אמֶר לָהֶ֜ם אֱלֹהִ֗ים פְּר֥וּ וּרְב֛וּ וּמִלְא֥וּ אֶת־הָאָ֖רֶץ וְכִבְשֻׁ֑הָ וּרְד֞וּ בִּדְגַ֤ת הַיָּם֙ וּבְע֣וֹף הַשָּׁמַ֔יִם וּבְכָל־חַיָּ֖ה הָֽרֹמֶ֥שֶׂת עַל־הָאָֽרֶץ׃ 1:29 וַיֹּ֣אמֶר אֱלֹהִ֗ים הִנֵּה֩ נָתַ֨תִּי לָכֶ֜ם אֶת־כָּל־עֵ֣שֶׂב ׀ זֹרֵ֣עַ זֶ֗רַע אֲשֶׁר֙ עַל־פְּנֵ֣י כָל־הָאָ֔רֶץ וְאֶת־כָּל־הָעֵ֛ץ אֲשֶׁר־בּ֥וֹ פְרִי־עֵ֖ץ זֹרֵ֣עַ זָ֑רַע לָכֶ֥ם יִֽהְיֶ֖ה לְאָכְלָֽה׃ 1:30 וּֽלְכָל־חַיַּ֣ת הָ֠אָרֶץ וּלְכָל־ע֨וֹף הַשָּׁמַ֜יִם וּלְכֹ֣ל ׀ רוֹמֵ֣שׂ עַל־הָאָ֗רֶץ אֲשֶׁר־בּוֹ֙ נֶ֣פֶשׁ חַיָּ֔ה אֶת־כָּל־יֶ֥רֶק עֵ֖שֶׂב לְאָכְלָ֑ה וַֽיְהִי־כֵֽן׃ 1:31 וַיַּ֤רְא אֱלֹהִים֙ אֶת־כָּל־אֲשֶׁ֣ר עָשָׂ֔ה וְהִנֵּה־ט֖וֹב מְאֹ֑ד וַֽיְהִי־עֶ֥רֶב וַֽיְהִי־בֹ֖קֶר י֥וֹם הַשִּׁשִּֽׁי׃ פ

2:1 וַיְכֻלּ֛וּ הַשָּׁמַ֥יִם וְהָאָ֖רֶץ וְכָל־צְבָאָֽם׃ 2:2 וַיְכַ֤ל אֱלֹהִים֙ בַּיּ֣וֹם הַשְּׁבִיעִ֔י מְלַאכְתּ֖וֹ אֲשֶׁ֣ר עָשָׂ֑ה וַיִּשְׁבֹּת֙ בַּיּ֣וֹם הַשְּׁבִיעִ֔י מִכָּל־מְלַאכְתּ֖וֹ אֲשֶׁ֥ר עָשָֽׂה׃ 2:3 וַיְבָ֤רֶךְ אֱלֹהִים֙ אֶת־י֣וֹם הַשְּׁבִיעִ֔י וַיְקַדֵּ֖שׁ אֹת֑וֹ כִּ֣י ב֤וֹ שָׁבַת֙ מִכָּל־מְלַאכְתּ֔וֹ אֲשֶׁר־בָּרָ֥א אֱלֹהִ֖ים לַעֲשֽׂוֹת׃ פ

GENESIS 1–2: CANON (J + P + B) – CONTINUED

2:4 This is the history of the heavens and of the earth when they were created: in the day that Yahweh God made the earth and the heavens, 2:5 no plant of the field was yet in the earth, and no herbs of the field had sprouted yet; for Yahweh God had not caused it to rain upon the earth. There was no one to till the ground, 2:6 but a mist arose from the earth, and watered the entire ground. 2:7 Yahweh God fashioned a man from the earth upon the ground, and breathed the breath of life into his nostrils; and man became a living thing. 2:8 Yahweh God planted a garden eastward, in Eden, and there he placed the man whom he had formed. 2:9 Yahweh God caused every tree that is pleasant to the sight and good for food to grow out of the ground; and the Tree of Life was in the midst of the garden, and the Tree of the Knowledge of Good and Evil. 2:10 A river flowed out of Eden to water the garden; and from there it branched, and became four tributaries. 2:11 The name of the first was Pishon, which flowed around the whole land of Havilah, where there was gold; 2:12 and the gold of that land was good. There was also aromatic resin and onyx stones there. 2:13 The name of the second river was Gihon, the same river that flowed around the whole land of Cush. 2:14 The name of the third river was Hiddekel, which flowed to the east of Assyria. The fourth river was the Euphrates. 2:15 Yahweh God took the man, and put him into the garden of Eden to tend to it and to preserve it. 2:16 Yahweh God commanded the man, thusly, "you may freely eat of every tree of the garden; 2:17 but of the Tree of the Knowledge of Good and Evil, you shall not eat of it; for on the day that you eat of it you will surely die."

2:18 Yahweh God said, "It is not good that the man is alone; I will make a suitable helper for him." 2:19 Yahweh God formed all animals of the field, and every bird of the sky, out of the ground, and brought them to the man to see what he would call them. Whatever the man called every living creature, that was its name. 2:20 The man gave names to all livestock, and to the birds of the sky, and to every animal of the field; but for the man no suitable helper was found. 2:21 Yahweh God caused a deep sleep to fall upon the man, and he slept; and he took one of his ribs, and closed up the flesh in its place. 2:22 He fashioned the rib, which He (Yahweh God) had taken from the man, into a woman, and brought her to the man. 2:23 The man said, "This is now a bone of my bones, and flesh of my flesh. She will be called 'woman,' because she was taken from man." 2:24 It is for this reason that man leaves his father and his mother, and cleaves to his wife, and they become one flesh. 2:25 They were both naked, the man and his wife, and were not ashamed.

GENESIS 1–2: CANON (J + P + B) HEBREW – CONTINUED

2:4 אֵ֣לֶּה תוֹלְד֧וֹת הַשָּׁמַ֛יִם וְהָאָ֖רֶץ בְּהִבָּֽרְאָ֑ם בְּי֗וֹם עֲשׂ֛וֹת יְהוָ֥ה אֱלֹהִ֖ים אֶ֥רֶץ וְשָׁמָֽיִם: 2:5 וְכֹ֣ל ׀ שִׂ֣יחַ הַשָּׂדֶ֗ה טֶ֚רֶם יִֽהְיֶ֣ה בָאָ֔רֶץ וְכָל־עֵ֥שֶׂב הַשָּׂדֶ֖ה טֶ֣רֶם יִצְמָ֑ח כִּי֩ לֹ֨א הִמְטִ֜יר יְהוָ֤ה אֱלֹהִים֙ עַל־הָאָ֔רֶץ וְאָדָ֣ם אַ֔יִן לַֽעֲבֹ֖ד אֶת־הָֽאֲדָמָֽה: 2:6 וְאֵ֖ד יַֽעֲלֶ֣ה מִן־הָאָ֑רֶץ וְהִשְׁקָ֖ה אֶֽת־כָּל־פְּנֵֽי־הָֽאֲדָמָֽה: 2:7 וַיִּיצֶר֩ יְהוָ֨ה אֱלֹהִ֜ים אֶת־הָֽאָדָ֗ם עָפָר֙ מִן־הָ֣אֲדָמָ֔ה וַיִּפַּ֥ח בְּאַפָּ֖יו נִשְׁמַ֣ת חַיִּ֑ים וַֽיְהִ֥י הָֽאָדָ֖ם לְנֶ֥פֶשׁ חַיָּֽה: 2:8 וַיִּטַּ֞ע יְהוָ֧ה אֱלֹהִ֛ים גַּן־בְּעֵ֖דֶן מִקֶּ֑דֶם וַיָּ֣שֶׂם שָׁ֔ם אֶת־הָֽאָדָ֖ם אֲשֶׁ֥ר יָצָֽר: 2:9 וַיַּצְמַ֞ח יְהוָ֤ה אֱלֹהִים֙ מִן־הָ֣אֲדָמָ֔ה כָּל־עֵ֛ץ נֶחְמָ֥ד לְמַרְאֶ֖ה וְט֣וֹב לְמַֽאֲכָ֑ל וְעֵ֤ץ הַֽחַיִּים֙ בְּת֣וֹךְ הַגָּ֔ן וְעֵ֕ץ הַדַּ֖עַת ט֥וֹב וָרָֽע: 2:10 וְנָהָר֙ יֹצֵ֣א מֵעֵ֔דֶן לְהַשְׁק֖וֹת אֶת־הַגָּ֑ן וּמִשָּׁם֙ יִפָּרֵ֔ד וְהָיָ֖ה לְאַרְבָּעָ֥ה רָאשִֽׁים: 2:11 שֵׁ֥ם הָֽאֶחָ֖ד פִּישׁ֑וֹן ה֣וּא הַסֹּבֵ֗ב אֵ֚ת כָּל־אֶ֣רֶץ הַֽחֲוִילָ֔ה אֲשֶׁר־שָׁ֖ם הַזָּהָֽב: 2:12 וּֽזֲהַ֛ב הָאָ֥רֶץ הַהִ֖וא ט֑וֹב שָׁ֥ם הַבְּדֹ֖לַח וְאֶ֥בֶן הַשֹּֽׁהַם: 2:13 וְשֵֽׁם־הַנָּהָ֥ר הַשֵּׁנִ֖י גִּיח֑וֹן ה֣וּא הַסּוֹבֵ֔ב אֵ֖ת כָּל־אֶ֥רֶץ כּֽוּשׁ: 2:14 וְשֵׁ֨ם הַנָּהָ֤ר הַשְּׁלִישִׁי֙ חִדֶּ֔קֶל ה֥וּא הַֽהֹלֵ֖ךְ קִדְמַ֣ת אַשּׁ֑וּר וְהַנָּהָ֥ר הָֽרְבִיעִ֖י ה֥וּא פְרָֽת:

2:15 וַיִּקַּ֛ח יְהוָ֥ה אֱלֹהִ֖ים אֶת־הָֽאָדָ֑ם וַיַּנִּחֵ֣הוּ בְגַן־עֵ֔דֶן לְעָבְדָ֖הּ וּלְשָׁמְרָֽהּ: 2:16 וַיְצַו֙ יְהוָ֣ה אֱלֹהִ֔ים עַל־הָֽאָדָ֖ם לֵאמֹ֑ר מִכֹּ֥ל עֵֽץ־הַגָּ֖ן אָכֹ֥ל תֹּאכֵֽל: 2:17 וּמֵעֵ֗ץ הַדַּ֨עַת֙ ט֣וֹב וָרָ֔ע לֹ֥א תֹאכַ֖ל מִמֶּ֑נּוּ כִּ֗י בְּי֛וֹם אֲכָלְךָ֥ מִמֶּ֖נּוּ מ֥וֹת תָּמֽוּת: 2:18 וַיֹּ֨אמֶר֙ יְהוָ֣ה אֱלֹהִ֔ים לֹא־ט֛וֹב הֱי֥וֹת הָֽאָדָ֖ם לְבַדּ֑וֹ אֶֽעֱשֶׂהּ־לּ֥וֹ עֵ֖זֶר כְּנֶגְדּֽוֹ: 2:19 וַיִּצֶר֩ יְהוָ֨ה אֱלֹהִ֜ים מִן־הָֽאֲדָמָ֗ה כָּל־חַיַּ֤ת הַשָּׂדֶה֙ וְאֵת֙ כָּל־ע֣וֹף הַשָּׁמַ֔יִם וַיָּבֵא֙ אֶל־הָ֣אָדָ֔ם לִרְא֖וֹת מַה־יִּקְרָא־ל֑וֹ וְכֹל֩ אֲשֶׁ֨ר יִקְרָא־ל֧וֹ הָֽאָדָ֛ם נֶ֥פֶשׁ חַיָּ֖ה ה֥וּא שְׁמֽוֹ: 2:20 וַיִּקְרָ֨א הָֽאָדָ֜ם שֵׁמ֗וֹת לְכָל־הַבְּהֵמָה֙ וּלְע֣וֹף הַשָּׁמַ֔יִם וּלְכֹ֖ל חַיַּ֣ת הַשָּׂדֶ֑ה וּלְאָדָ֕ם לֹֽא־מָצָ֥א עֵ֖זֶר כְּנֶגְדּֽוֹ: 2:21 וַיַּפֵּל֩ יְהוָ֨ה אֱלֹהִ֧ים ׀ תַּרְדֵּמָ֛ה עַל־הָֽאָדָ֖ם וַיִּישָׁ֑ן וַיִּקַּ֗ח אַחַת֙ מִצַּלְעֹתָ֔יו וַיִּסְגֹּ֥ר בָּשָׂ֖ר תַּחְתֶּֽנָּה: 2:22 וַיִּבֶן֩ יְהוָ֨ה אֱלֹהִ֧ים ׀ אֶֽת־הַצֵּלָ֛ע אֲשֶׁר־לָקַ֥ח מִן־הָֽאָדָ֖ם לְאִשָּׁ֑ה וַיְבִאֶ֖הָ אֶל־הָֽאָדָֽם: 2:23 וַיֹּאמֶר֘ הָֽאָדָם֒ זֹ֣את הַפַּ֗עַם עֶ֚צֶם מֵֽעֲצָמַ֔י וּבָשָׂ֖ר מִבְּשָׂרִ֑י לְזֹאת֙ יִקָּרֵ֣א אִשָּׁ֔ה כִּ֥י מֵאִ֖ישׁ לֻֽקֳחָה־זֹּֽאת: 2:24 עַל־כֵּן֙ יַֽעֲזָב־אִ֔ישׁ אֶת־אָבִ֖יו וְאֶת־אִמּ֑וֹ וְדָבַ֣ק בְּאִשְׁתּ֔וֹ וְהָי֖וּ לְבָשָׂ֥ר אֶחָֽד: 2:25 וַיִּֽהְי֤וּ שְׁנֵיהֶם֙ עֲרוּמִּ֔ים הָֽאָדָ֖ם וְאִשְׁתּ֑וֹ וְלֹ֖א יִתְבֹּשָֽׁשׁוּ:

What B adds

B interrupts the flow of Chapter 2, which focuses on Adam and his function in the Garden of Eden, to give us a bird's-eye view of the Garden, placing it geographically as lying at the nexus of four rivers. These details are part and parcel of B's agenda to broaden the scope of the text by adding details that go beyond those that relate only to Israel. Now if we ever go in search of Eden, we will know where it is!

THE CREATION STORY: GENESIS 3

A snake, the slyest of all creatures, comes to the woman and tells her that despite God's warning, she would not die if she were to eat from the Tree of Knowledge. The woman believes him, and she and Adam both eat from the tree. They then hear the Lord walking in the garden, and, ashamed of their own nakedness, hide among the branches of the tree. The Lord finds them and punishes their defiance by relegating Adam to a life of toil tilling the earth, imposing upon the woman the hardships of bearing children, and condemning the snake to crawl in the dust. The chapter ends with the Lord banishing them all from the Garden of Eden.

GENESIS 3: CANON (J)

3:1 Now the serpent was slyer than any wild animal which Yahweh God had made. He said to the woman, "Did God really say, 'You shall not eat of any tree of the garden?'"

3:2 The woman said to the serpent, "Of the fruit of the trees of the garden we may eat, 3 but of the fruit of the tree which is in the middle of the garden, God has said, 'You shall not eat of it, neither shall you touch it, lest you die.'"

3:4 The serpent said to the woman, "You won't die, 3:5 for God knows that on the day you eat it, your eyes will open, and you will be like God, and know good and evil."

3:6 When the woman saw that the tree's (fruit) was edible, and that it was delightful to the eyes, and that it was pleasantly stimulating, she took of its fruit, and ate it; and she gave some to her husband with her, and he ate. 3:7 The eyes of both of them were opened, and they knew that they were naked. They sewed fig leaves together, and made themselves aprons. 3:8 They heard the voice of Yahweh God walking in the garden in the middle of the day, and the man and his wife hid themselves from the presence of Yahweh God among the trees of the garden.

GENESIS 3: CANON (J) HEBREW

3:1 וְהַנָּחָשׁ֙ הָיָ֣ה עָר֔וּם מִכֹּל֙ חַיַּ֣ת הַשָּׂדֶ֔ה אֲשֶׁ֥ר עָשָׂ֖ה יְהוָ֣ה אֱלֹהִ֑ים וַיֹּ֙אמֶר֙ אֶל־הָ֣אִשָּׁ֔ה אַ֚ף כִּֽי־אָמַ֣ר אֱלֹהִ֔ים לֹ֣א תֹֽאכְל֔וּ מִכֹּ֖ל עֵ֥ץ הַגָּֽן׃ 3:2 וַתֹּ֥אמֶר הָֽאִשָּׁ֖ה אֶל־הַנָּחָ֑שׁ מִפְּרִ֥י עֵֽץ־הַגָּ֖ן נֹאכֵֽל׃ 3:3 וּמִפְּרִ֣י הָעֵץ֮ אֲשֶׁ֣ר בְּתוֹךְ־הַגָּן֒ אָמַ֣ר אֱלֹהִ֗ים לֹ֤א תֹֽאכְלוּ֙ מִמֶּ֔נּוּ וְלֹ֥א תִגְּע֖וּ בּ֑וֹ פֶּן־תְּמֻתֽוּן׃ 3:4 וַיֹּ֥אמֶר הַנָּחָ֖שׁ אֶל־הָֽאִשָּׁ֑ה לֹֽא־מ֖וֹת תְּמֻתֽוּן׃ 3:5 כִּ֚י יֹדֵ֣עַ אֱלֹהִ֔ים כִּ֗י בְּיוֹם֙ אֲכָלְכֶ֣ם מִמֶּ֔נּוּ וְנִפְקְח֖וּ עֵֽינֵיכֶ֑ם וִהְיִיתֶם֙ כֵּֽאלֹהִ֔ים יֹדְעֵ֖י ט֥וֹב וָרָֽע׃ 3:6 וַתֵּ֣רֶא הָֽאִשָּׁ֡ה כִּ֣י טוֹב֩ הָעֵ֨ץ לְמַאֲכָ֜ל וְכִ֧י תַֽאֲוָה־ה֣וּא לָעֵינַ֗יִם וְנֶחְמָ֤ד הָעֵץ֙ לְהַשְׂכִּ֔יל וַתִּקַּ֥ח מִפִּרְי֖וֹ וַתֹּאכַ֑ל וַתִּתֵּ֧ן גַּם־לְאִישָׁ֛הּ עִמָּ֖הּ וַיֹּאכַֽל׃ 3:7 וַתִּפָּקַ֙חְנָה֙ עֵינֵ֣י שְׁנֵיהֶ֔ם וַיֵּ֣דְע֔וּ כִּ֥י עֵֽירֻמִּ֖ם הֵ֑ם וַֽיִּתְפְּרוּ֙ עֲלֵ֣ה תְאֵנָ֔ה וַיַּעֲשׂ֥וּ לָהֶ֖ם חֲגֹרֹֽת׃ 3:8 וַֽיִּשְׁמְע֞וּ אֶת־ק֨וֹל יְהוָ֧ה אֱלֹהִ֛ים מִתְהַלֵּ֥ךְ בַּגָּ֖ן לְר֣וּחַ הַיּ֑וֹם וַיִּתְחַבֵּ֨א הָֽאָדָ֜ם וְאִשְׁתּ֗וֹ מִפְּנֵי֙ יְהוָ֣ה אֱלֹהִ֔ים בְּת֖וֹךְ עֵ֥ץ הַגָּֽן׃

GENESIS 3: CANON (J) – CONTINUED

3:9 Yahweh God called to the man, and said to him, "Where are you?" 3:10 The man said, "I heard your voice in the garden, and I was afraid, because I was naked; and I hid myself." 3:11 God said, "Who told you that you were naked? Have you eaten from the tree that I commanded you not to eat from?"

3:12 The man said, "The woman whom you gave me to be with, she gave me of the tree, and I ate (from the fruit)." 3:13 Yahweh God said to the woman, "What is this you have done?" The woman said, "The serpent deceived me, and I ate (from the fruit)."

3:14 Yahweh God said to the serpent,"Because you have done this, you are cursed more than all livestock and wild animals. On your belly you shall crawl, and you shall eat dust all the days of your life. 3:15 I will cause there to be enmity between you and the woman, and between your offspring and her offspring. He will strike your head, and you will strike his heel."

3:16 To the woman he said, "I will increase your travails whilst you are in childbirth. Bearing children will be painful. You will covet your husband, and he will rule over you."

3:17 To Adam he said, "Because you listened to your wife and ate of the tree of which I commanded you, saying, 'You shall not eat of it,' the ground is cursed because of you. You will eat of it all the days of your life. 3:18 It will yield thorns and thistles to you; and you will eat the grass of the field. 3:19 You will eat bread by the sweat of your brow, until you return to the ground, for it is there you originated. For you are dust, and to dust you shall return."

3:20 The man called his wife Eve, because she was the mother of all living things. 3:21 Yahweh God made coats from (animal) skins for Adam and for his wife, and clothed them.

3:22 Yahweh God said, "Behold, the man has become like one of us, knowing good and evil. Now, lest he reach out, and take of the Tree of Life, and eat, and live forever…" 3:23 Therefore Yahweh God banished him from the garden of Eden, to till the ground from whence he originated. 3:24 He drove out the man; and he placed cherubim and a flaming sword which turned every way to guard the way to the Tree of Life.

GENESIS 3: CANON (J) HEBREW – CONTINUED

3:9 וַיִּקְרָ֛א יְהוָ֥ה אֱלֹהִ֖ים אֶל־הָֽאָדָ֑ם וַיֹּ֥אמֶר ל֖וֹ אַיֶּֽכָּה: 3:10 וַיֹּ֕אמֶר אֶת־קֹלְךָ֥ שָׁמַ֖עְתִּי בַּגָּ֑ן וָאִירָ֛א כִּֽי־עֵירֹ֥ם אָנֹ֖כִי וָאֵחָבֵֽא: 3:11 וַיֹּ֕אמֶר מִ֚י הִגִּ֣יד לְךָ֔ כִּ֥י עֵירֹ֖ם אָ֑תָּה הֲמִן־הָעֵ֗ץ אֲשֶׁ֧ר צִוִּיתִ֛יךָ לְבִלְתִּ֥י אֲכָל־מִמֶּ֖נּוּ אָכָֽלְתָּ: 3:12 וַיֹּ֖אמֶר הָֽאָדָ֑ם הָֽאִשָּׁה֙ אֲשֶׁ֣ר נָתַ֣תָּה עִמָּדִ֔י הִ֛וא נָֽתְנָה־לִּ֥י מִן־הָעֵ֖ץ וָאֹכֵֽל: 3:13 וַיֹּ֨אמֶר יְהוָ֧ה אֱלֹהִ֛ים לָֽאִשָּׁ֖ה מַה־זֹּ֣את עָשִׂ֑ית וַתֹּ֙אמֶר֙ הָֽאִשָּׁ֔ה הַנָּחָ֥שׁ הִשִּׁיאַ֖נִי וָאֹכֵֽל: 3:14 וַיֹּאמֶר֩ יְהֹוָ֨ה אֱלֹהִ֥ים ׀ אֶֽל־הַנָּחָשׁ֮ כִּ֣י עָשִׂ֣יתָ זֹּאת֒ אָר֤וּר אַתָּה֙ מִכָּל־הַבְּהֵמָ֔ה וּמִכֹּ֖ל חַיַּ֣ת הַשָּׂדֶ֑ה עַל־גְּחֹנְךָ֣ תֵלֵ֔ךְ וְעָפָ֥ר תֹּאכַ֖ל כָּל־יְמֵ֥י חַיֶּֽיךָ: 3:15 וְאֵיבָ֣ה ׀ אָשִׁ֗ית בֵּֽינְךָ֙ וּבֵ֣ין הָֽאִשָּׁ֔ה וּבֵ֥ין זַרְעֲךָ֖ וּבֵ֣ין זַרְעָ֑הּ ה֚וּא יְשׁוּפְךָ֣ רֹ֔אשׁ וְאַתָּ֖ה תְּשׁוּפֶ֥נּוּ עָקֵֽב: ס

3:16 אֶֽל־הָאִשָּׁ֣ה אָמַ֗ר הַרְבָּ֤ה אַרְבֶּה֙ עִצְּבוֹנֵ֣ךְ וְהֵֽרֹנֵ֔ךְ בְּעֶ֖צֶב תֵּֽלְדִ֣י בָנִ֑ים וְאֶל־אִישֵׁךְ֙ תְּשׁ֣וּקָתֵ֔ךְ וְה֖וּא יִמְשָׁל־בָּֽךְ: ס

3:17 וּלְאָדָ֣ם אָמַ֗ר כִּֽי־שָׁמַעְתָּ֮ לְק֣וֹל אִשְׁתֶּךָ֒ וַתֹּ֙אכַל֙ מִן־הָעֵ֔ץ אֲשֶׁ֤ר צִוִּיתִ֙יךָ֙ לֵאמֹ֔ר לֹ֥א תֹאכַ֖ל מִמֶּ֑נּוּ אֲרוּרָ֤ה הָֽאֲדָמָה֙ בַּֽעֲבוּרֶ֔ךָ בְּעִצָּבוֹן֙ תֹּֽאכֲלֶ֔נָּה כֹּ֖ל יְמֵ֥י חַיֶּֽיךָ: 3:18 וְק֥וֹץ וְדַרְדַּ֖ר תַּצְמִ֣יחַֽ לָ֑ךְ וְאָכַלְתָּ֖ אֶת־עֵ֥שֶׂב הַשָּׂדֶֽה: 3:19 בְּזֵעַ֤ת אַפֶּ֙יךָ֙ תֹּ֣אכַל לֶ֔חֶם עַ֤ד שֽׁוּבְךָ֙ אֶל־הָ֣אֲדָמָ֔ה כִּ֥י מִמֶּ֖נָּה לֻקָּ֑חְתָּ כִּֽי־עָפָ֣ר אַ֔תָּה וְאֶל־עָפָ֖ר תָּשֽׁוּב: 3:20 וַיִּקְרָ֧א הָֽאָדָ֛ם שֵׁ֥ם אִשְׁתּ֖וֹ חַוָּ֑ה כִּ֛י הִ֥וא הָֽיְתָ֖ה אֵ֥ם כָּל־חָֽי: 3:21 וַיַּעַשׂ֩ יְהוָ֨ה אֱלֹהִ֜ים לְאָדָ֧ם וּלְאִשְׁתּ֛וֹ כָּתְנ֥וֹת ע֖וֹר וַיַּלְבִּשֵֽׁם: פ

3:22 וַיֹּ֣אמֶר ׀ יְהוָ֣ה אֱלֹהִ֗ים הֵ֤ן הָֽאָדָם֙ הָיָה֙ כְּאַחַ֣ד מִמֶּ֔נּוּ לָדַ֖עַת ט֣וֹב וָרָ֑ע וְעַתָּ֣ה ׀ פֶּן־יִשְׁלַ֣ח יָד֗וֹ וְלָקַח֙ גַּ֚ם מֵעֵ֣ץ הַֽחַיִּ֔ים וְאָכַ֖ל וָחַ֥י לְעֹלָֽם: 3:23 וַֽיְשַׁלְּחֵ֛הוּ יְהוָ֥ה אֱלֹהִ֖ים מִגַּן־עֵ֑דֶן לַֽעֲבֹד֙ אֶת־הָ֣אֲדָמָ֔ה אֲשֶׁ֥ר לֻקַּ֖ח מִשָּֽׁם: 3:24 וַיְגָ֖רֶשׁ אֶת־הָֽאָדָ֑ם וַיַּשְׁכֵּן֩ מִקֶּ֨דֶם לְגַן־עֵ֜דֶן אֶת־הַכְּרֻבִ֗ים וְאֵ֨ת לַ֤הַט הַחֶ֙רֶב֙ הַמִּתְהַפֶּ֔כֶת לִשְׁמֹ֕ר אֶת־דֶּ֖רֶךְ עֵ֥ץ הַֽחַיִּֽים: ס

The depiction of God in this chapter is quintessentially J. The Lord God is afraid of what Adam might do now that he has eaten from the Tree of Knowledge—which, according to Chapter 2, existed in the Garden of Eden independent of the Lord God's will—and thus He banishes Adam and Eve from the Garden and places a guard at its entrance. The Lord's fear may be difficult for modern readers of the Bible to grasp. If the Lord is all-powerful, then what does He have to fear from human beings? For J, the answer is that the Lord is not all-powerful. Only a minority of Biblical authors viewed monotheism in the same way we understand it today, and more than one Biblical author was simply not monotheistic. J's understanding of the Lord is perhaps the furthest from modern concepts of monotheism. According to J, the Lord God was just like many of the other deities portrayed in Greek and Mesopotamian myth: undeniably potent, but not actually omnipotent, and psychologically and perhaps even physiologically similar to human beings.

Following his account of the expulsion from the Garden, J has Adam name the first woman Eve ("Chavvah" in Hebrew). The text states explicitly that the reason for this is that "she was the mother of all living things" ("chay" is the Hebrew word for "life"), but in Biblical Hebrew, her name has another, much more sinister connotation: that of a snake. In two other languages closely related to Hebrew, Arabic and Aramaic, the words for snake ("chawi" and "chaviyah," respectively) are much closer to the name "Chavvah" than is the Hebrew word "chay." This association highlights Eve's role in the first couple's fall from grace, suggesting that although she was a victim of the snake's deception, she may also have preyed upon Adam's naïveté in the same way that the actual snake had preyed upon hers. This linguistic move is typical of J, who often tries to pull his readers in two different directions as a way to heighten narrative tension.

THE CREATION STORY: GENESIS 4–5

The newly exiled Adam and Eve produce two children: Cain and Abel. Cain becomes a farmer, and Abel a shepherd. Each of them brings a sacrifice to the Lord: Cain offers fruit, while Abel sacrifices the choicest of his lambs. The Lord accepts Abel's sacrifice, but does not accept Cain's. Consumed with anger, Cain lures his brother out into the field and kills him. The Lord responds by banishing Cain from the land of his youth, but also protects him against possible retribution by marking him. Cain goes on to father a dynasty that leads to Lemech, who also engages in an act of indiscriminate murder, and whose children become the first human inventors. Adam and Eve then give birth to another son, Seth, who also fathers a dynasty that leads to a man named Lemech, and to Lemech's son, Noah.

GENESIS 4–5: THE J KERNEL

4:1 The man knew his wife Eve. She conceived, and gave birth to Cain, and said, "I have created a man with Yahweh." 4:2 Again she gave birth, to Cain's brother, Abel. Abel was a keeper of sheep, but Cain was a tiller of soil. 4:3 After a time, Cain brought an offering to Yahweh from the fruit of the field. 4:4 Abel also brought of the firstborn of his flock and of their fat. Yahweh held Abel and his offering in high regard, 4:5 but didn't regard Cain and his offering. Cain was very angry, and his face fell. 4:6 Yahweh said to Cain, "Why are you angry and why has your face fallen? 4:7 If you behave uprightly (then all the better). If you don't behave uprightly, sin crouches at the door. It desires you, but you can rule over it." 4:8 Cain said to Abel, his brother, ("Let's go into the field.") It happened that when they were in the field, Cain rose up against Abel, his brother, and killed him.

4:9 Yahweh said to Cain, "Where is Abel, your brother?"
He said, "I don't know. Am I my brother's keeper?"

4:10 Yahweh said, "What have you done? The voice of your brother's blood cries to me from the ground.

GENESIS 4–5: THE J KERNEL (HEBREW)

4:1 וְהָאָדָם יָדַע אֶת־חַוָּה אִשְׁתּוֹ וַתַּהַר וַתֵּלֶד אֶת־קַיִן וַתֹּאמֶר קָנִיתִי אִישׁ אֶת־יְהוָה: 4:2 וַתֹּסֶף לָלֶדֶת אֶת־אָחִיו אֶת־הָבֶל וַיְהִי־הֶבֶל רֹעֵה צֹאן וְקַיִן הָיָה עֹבֵד אֲדָמָה: 4:3 וַיְהִי מִקֵּץ יָמִים וַיָּבֵא קַיִן מִפְּרִי הָאֲדָמָה מִנְחָה לַיהוָה: 4:4 וְהֶבֶל הֵבִיא גַם־הוּא מִבְּכֹרוֹת צֹאנוֹ וּמֵחֶלְבֵהֶן וַיִּשַׁע יְהוָה אֶל־הֶבֶל וְאֶל־מִנְחָתוֹ: 4:5 וְאֶל־קַיִן וְאֶל־מִנְחָתוֹ לֹא שָׁעָה וַיִּחַר לְקַיִן מְאֹד וַיִּפְּלוּ פָּנָיו: 4:6 וַיֹּאמֶר יְהוָה אֶל־קָיִן לָמָּה חָרָה לָךְ וְלָמָּה נָפְלוּ פָנֶיךָ: 4:7 הֲלוֹא אִם־תֵּיטִיב שְׂאֵת וְאִם לֹא תֵיטִיב לַפֶּתַח חַטָּאת רֹבֵץ וְאֵלֶיךָ תְּשׁוּקָתוֹ וְאַתָּה תִּמְשָׁל־בּוֹ: 4:8 וַיֹּאמֶר קַיִן אֶל־הֶבֶל אָחִיו וַיְהִי בִּהְיוֹתָם בַּשָּׂדֶה וַיָּקָם קַיִן אֶל־הֶבֶל אָחִיו וַיַּהַרְגֵהוּ: 4:9 וַיֹּאמֶר יְהוָה אֶל־קַיִן אֵי הֶבֶל אָחִיךָ וַיֹּאמֶר לֹא יָדַעְתִּי הֲשֹׁמֵר אָחִי אָנֹכִי: 4:10 וַיֹּאמֶר מֶה עָשִׂיתָ קוֹל דְּמֵי אָחִיךָ צֹעֲקִים אֵלַי מִן־הָאֲדָמָה:

GENESIS 4–5: THE J KERNEL – CONTINUED

4:11 Now you are cursed because of the ground, which has opened its mouth to receive your brother's blood from your hand. 4:12 From this point forward, when you till the ground, it won't yield its fruit to you. You shall be a peripatetic wanderer upon the earth." 4:13 Cain said to Yahweh, "My punishment is greater than I can bear. 4:14 Behold, you have driven me out today from (settling upon) the face of the earth. I will be hidden from your face, and I will be a fugitive and a wanderer upon the earth. It will happen that whoever finds me will kill me." 4:15 Yahweh said to him, "Therefore whoever slays Cain, vengeance will be taken on him sevenfold." Yahweh appointed a sign for Cain, lest any finding him should strike him.

4:16 Cain went out from Yahweh's presence, and lived in the land of Nod, east of Eden. 4:17 Cain knew his wife. She conceived, and gave birth to Enoch. He built a city, and named the city, after his son, Enoch. 4:18 To Enoch was born Irad. Irad fathered Mehujael. Mehujael fathered Methushael. Methushael fathered Lamech.

4:19 Lamech took two wives: the name of the one was Adah, and the name of the other Zillah. 4:20 Adah gave birth to Jabal, who was the progenitor of those who dwell in tents and tend livestock. 4:21 His brother's name was Jubal, the progenitor of all who play the harp and pipe. 4:22 Zillah also gave birth to Tubal Cain, the forger of every cutting implement of brass and iron. Tubal Cain's sister was Naamah.

4:23 Lamech said to his wives, "Adah and Zillah, hear my voice. Wives of Lamech, listen to my words, for I have slain a man for wounding me, a young man for bruising me. 4:24 If Cain will be avenged seven times, surely Lamech (shall be avenged) seventy-seven times." 5:28 Lamech fathered a son, 5:29 and he named him Noah, saying, "He will comfort us in our work and in the toil of our hands, for Yahweh has cursed the earth."

In J's contribution to Genesis 4, Cain kills his brother Abel in cold blood. This act can reasonably be expected to lead to some sort of retribution, and, *prima facie*, it seems that Cain is indeed punished: Yahweh pronounces that "when you till the ground, it won't yield its fruit to you" (4:11), and that Cain will be forced to wander in order to scratch out his sustenance. Examining the punishment more closely, however, reveals that it is in fact only an echo of the more harshly worded curse that the Lord had pronounced upon Adam (see 3:17–19: "The ground is cursed because of you… It will yield thorns and thistles to you… You will eat bread by the sweat of your brow, until you return to the ground").

GENESIS 4–5: THE J KERNEL (HEBREW) – CONTINUED

4:11 וְעַתָּה אָרוּר אָתָּה מִן־הָאֲדָמָה אֲשֶׁר פָּצְתָה אֶת־פִּיהָ לָקַחַת אֶת־דְּמֵי אָחִיךָ מִיָּדֶךָ: 4:12 כִּי תַעֲבֹד אֶת־הָאֲדָמָה לֹא־תֹסֵף תֵּת־כֹּחָהּ לָךְ נָע וָנָד תִּהְיֶה בָאָרֶץ: 4:13 וַיֹּאמֶר קַיִן אֶל־יְהוָה גָּדוֹל עֲוֹנִי מִנְּשֹׂא: 4:14 הֵן גֵּרַשְׁתָּ אֹתִי הַיּוֹם מֵעַל פְּנֵי הָאֲדָמָה וּמִפָּנֶיךָ אֶסָּתֵר וְהָיִיתִי נָע וָנָד בָּאָרֶץ וְהָיָה כָל־מֹצְאִי יַהַרְגֵנִי: 4:15 וַיֹּאמֶר לוֹ יְהוָה לָכֵן כָּל־הֹרֵג קַיִן שִׁבְעָתַיִם יֻקָּם וַיָּשֶׂם יְהוָה לְקַיִן אוֹת לְבִלְתִּי הַכּוֹת־אֹתוֹ כָּל־מֹצְאוֹ: 4:16 וַיֵּצֵא קַיִן מִלִּפְנֵי יְהוָה וַיֵּשֶׁב בְּאֶרֶץ־נוֹד קִדְמַת־עֵדֶן: 4:17 וַיֵּדַע קַיִן אֶת־אִשְׁתּוֹ וַתַּהַר וַתֵּלֶד אֶת־חֲנוֹךְ וַיְהִי בֹּנֶה עִיר וַיִּקְרָא שֵׁם הָעִיר כְּשֵׁם בְּנוֹ חֲנוֹךְ: 4:18 וַיִּוָּלֵד לַחֲנוֹךְ אֶת־עִירָד וְעִירָד יָלַד אֶת־מְחוּיָאֵל וּמְחִיּיָאֵל יָלַד אֶת־מְתוּשָׁאֵל וּמְתוּשָׁאֵל יָלַד אֶת־לָמֶךְ: 4:19 וַיִּקַּח־לוֹ לֶמֶךְ שְׁתֵּי נָשִׁים שֵׁם הָאַחַת עָדָה וְשֵׁם הַשֵּׁנִית צִלָּה:

4:20 וַתֵּלֶד עָדָה אֶת־יָבָל הוּא הָיָה אֲבִי יֹשֵׁב אֹהֶל וּמִקְנֶה: 4:21 וְשֵׁם אָחִיו יוּבָל הוּא הָיָה אֲבִי כָּל־תֹּפֵשׂ כִּנּוֹר וְעוּגָב: 4:22 וְצִלָּה גַם־הִוא יָלְדָה אֶת־תּוּבַל קַיִן לֹטֵשׁ כָּל־חֹרֵשׁ נְחֹשֶׁת וּבַרְזֶל וַאֲחוֹת תּוּבַל־קַיִן נַעֲמָה: 4:23 וַיֹּאמֶר לֶמֶךְ לְנָשָׁיו עָדָה וְצִלָּה שְׁמַעַן קוֹלִי נְשֵׁי לֶמֶךְ הַאְזֵנָּה אִמְרָתִי כִּי אִישׁ הָרַגְתִּי לְפִצְעִי וְיֶלֶד לְחַבֻּרָתִי: 4:24 כִּי שִׁבְעָתַיִם יֻקַּם־קָיִן וְלֶמֶךְ שִׁבְעִים וְשִׁבְעָה:

5:28 וַיְחִי־לֶמֶךְ בֵּן: 5:29 וַיִּקְרָא אֶת־שְׁמוֹ נֹחַ לֵאמֹר זֶה יְנַחֲמֵנוּ מִמַּעֲשֵׂנוּ וּמֵעִצְּבוֹן יָדֵינוּ מִן־הָאֲדָמָה אֲשֶׁר אֵרְרָהּ יְהוָה:

The mild language used in the description of Cain's sentence stands in marked contrast to the graphic description of Cain's culpability: "The blood of your brother screams to me from the earth" (4:10). Furthermore, it would seem that Cain's sentence is never really carried out, since he is described not as wandering endlessly, but rather as "settling" in the land of Nod (4:16) and building the first city there (4:17). This is an obvious piece of wordplay on the content of the punishment—the name "Nod" derives from the Hebrew verb "nadad," meaning "to wander." Even if Cain's sentence had been carried out, it is clear that according to the Pentateuchal law codes, this punishment would be too lenient to fit the crime. Exile is named as a possible punishment for killing in the Pentateuchal law codes, but only in cases where the killing is accidental; the penalty for murder is always death.

The leniency the Lord shows to Cain in sentencing him to exile is not even the most mystifying element of J's account. The Lord's promise to protect Cain from retribution, by providing him with the proverbial mark that ensures a sevenfold revenge upon anyone who kills him, borders on the extraordinary. It seems only natural that people would wish to kill Cain, and they would be entirely justified in doing so according to the law codes of the time. No protection is provided to a person who deliberately kills his or her fellow; in fact, it is the *responsibility* of the victim's closest living relative to kill the murderer. The Lord's bizarre protection of Cain leads Lemech, Cain's descendant, to brag that if Cain would have been avenged sevenfold for his death, then he (Lemech), who also is guilty of murder, should be avenged seventy-seven fold in the event of his untimely demise. Lemech's pronouncement can be understood as a mockery of Yahweh's promise to Cain to keep him from harm.

The matter becomes even more critical if one accepts my hypothesis, which I share with Israel Knohl, that according to J, Cain, not Seth, was the father of humanity. Consider that in the canonical narrative, we never hear what happens to Cain's progeny; after Lemech and his children, the list simply ends, and we are presumably meant to think that Cain's descendants died in the flood. After J's genealogical list, we are given the short narrative of Lemech and his wives (4:18–24), followed by B's note of Seth's birth (4:25) and the Priestly genealogy of the subsequent chapter (5:1–27). This genealogy ends with a presumably different, Priestly Lemech fathering Noah (5:28–29). The etymology of Noah's name is not Priestly, however, but Yahwistic— Lemech says of Noah that "he will comfort us in our work and in the toil of our hands, for Yahweh has cursed the earth" ("noah" means "comfortable" in Hebrew), a clear reference to J's curses upon Adam and Cain. Note also that while the rest of Genesis 5 uses the name Elohim, the Priestly name for the deity, verse 29 uses Yahweh, J's name for the deity. It would seem, then, that according to J, after the birth of the first Lemech's other children, that same Lemech fathered Noah. Thus, when Noah is saved in the flood, Cain, through him, becomes the father of humanity.

How can J submit that Cain, the quintessential murderer, was the progenitor of humankind? Although it may not be possible to answer this question, it is clear that this is not the first time in the J text that people who deserve to die are preserved. Consider the Lord's warning to Adam that on the day he ate from the Tree of

Knowledge, he would surely die. This promise was clearly not carried out (unless you consider his death 930 years later in the P text to be an enactment of this promise, and you accept the psalmic idea that one thousand years are the same as one day in the eyes of God [Psalms 90:4]). In Genesis 3, Eve's sin not only does not lead to her death, but is in fact the catalyst for all of human history. Without Eve's sin, the text implies that the two humans would have lived eternally in perfect harmony in the Garden of Eden. Similarly, Cain's fratricide marks the antediluvian generation that descends from him as evil, thus setting the stage for the cataclysmic flood that immediately follows. Although Noah is called righteous and is saved, the Lord resignedly concludes after the flood, "I will never again curse the ground because of human beings, because the ruminations of human beings' hearts is evil from their youth" (8:21).

GENESIS 4–5: J + P

4:1 The man knew his wife Eve. She conceived, and gave birth to Cain, and said, "I have created a man with Yahweh." 4:2 Again she gave birth, to Cain's brother, Abel. Abel was a keeper of sheep, but Cain was a tiller of soil. 4:3 After a time, Cain brought an offering to Yahweh from the fruit of the field. 4:4 Abel also brought of the firstborn of his flock and of their fat. Yahweh held Abel and his offering in high regard, 4:5 but didn't regard Cain and his offering. Cain was very angry, and his face fell. 4:6 Yahweh said to Cain, "Why are you angry and why has your face fallen? 4:7 If you behave uprightly (then all the better). If you don't behave uprightly, sin crouches at the door. It desires you, but you can rule over it." 4:8 Cain said to Abel, his brother, ("Let's go into the field.") It happened that when they were in the field, Cain rose up against Abel, his brother, and killed him.

4:9 Yahweh said to Cain, "Where is Abel, your brother?" He said, "I don't know. Am I my brother's keeper?" 4:10 Yahweh said, "What have you done? The voice of your brother's blood cries to me from the ground. 4:11 Now you are cursed because of the ground, which has opened its mouth to receive your brother's blood from your hand. 4:12 From this point forward, when you till the ground, it won't yield its fruit to you. You shall be a peripatetic wanderer upon the earth." 4:13 Cain said to Yahweh, "My punishment is greater than I can bear. 4:14 Behold, you have driven me out today from (settling upon) the face of the earth. I will be hidden from your face, and I will be a fugitive and a wanderer upon the earth. It will happen that whoever finds me will kill me." 4:15 Yahweh said to him, "Therefore whoever slays Cain, vengeance will be taken on him sevenfold." Yahweh appointed a sign for Cain, lest any finding him should strike him.

4:16 Cain went out from Yahweh's presence, and lived in the land of Nod, east of Eden. 4:17 Cain knew his wife. She conceived, and gave birth to Enoch. He built a city, and named the city, after his son, Enoch. 4:18 To Enoch was born Irad. Irad fathered Mehujael. Mehujael fathered Methushael. Methushael fathered Lamech. 4:19 Lamech took two wives: the name of the one was Adah, and the name of the other Zillah. 4:20 Adah gave birth to Jabal, who was the progenitor of those who dwell in tents and tend livestock. 4:21 His brother's name was Jubal, the progenitor of all who play the harp and pipe. 4:22 Zillah also gave birth to Tubal Cain, the forger of every cutting implement of brass and iron. Tubal Cain's sister was Naamah. 4:23 Lamech said to his wives,"Adah and Zillah, hear my voice. Wives of Lamech, listen to my words, for I have slain a man for wounding me, a young man for bruising me. 4:24 If Cain will be avenged seven times, surely Lamech (shall be avenged) seventy-seven times."

5:1 This is an account of Adam's generations. In the day that God created man, he made him in God's likeness. 5:2 He created them male and female, and blessed them, and called them "humans" on the day when they were created.

GENESIS 4–5: J + P (HEBREW)

4:1 וְהָאָדָם יָדַע אֶת־חַוָּה אִשְׁתּוֹ וַתַּהַר וַתֵּלֶד אֶת־קַיִן וַתֹּאמֶר קָנִיתִי אִישׁ אֶת־יְהוָה: 4:2 וַתֹּסֶף לָלֶדֶת אֶת־אָחִיו אֶת־הָבֶל וַיְהִי־הֶבֶל רֹעֵה צֹאן וְקַיִן הָיָה עֹבֵד אֲדָמָה: 4:3 וַיְהִי מִקֵּץ יָמִים וַיָּבֵא קַיִן מִפְּרִי הָאֲדָמָה מִנְחָה לַיהוָה: 4:4 וְהֶבֶל הֵבִיא גַם־הוּא מִבְּכֹרוֹת צֹאנוֹ וּמֵחֶלְבֵהֶן וַיִּשַׁע יְהוָה אֶל־הֶבֶל וְאֶל־מִנְחָתוֹ: 4:5 וְאֶל־קַיִן וְאֶל־מִנְחָתוֹ לֹא שָׁעָה וַיִּחַר לְקַיִן מְאֹד וַיִּפְּלוּ פָּנָיו: 4:6 וַיֹּאמֶר יְהוָה אֶל־קָיִן לָמָּה חָרָה לָךְ וְלָמָּה נָפְלוּ פָנֶיךָ: 4:7 הֲלוֹא אִם־תֵּיטִיב שְׂאֵת וְאִם לֹא תֵיטִיב לַפֶּתַח חַטָּאת רֹבֵץ וְאֵלֶיךָ תְּשׁוּקָתוֹ וְאַתָּה תִּמְשָׁל־בּוֹ: 4:8 וַיֹּאמֶר קַיִן אֶל־הֶבֶל אָחִיו וַיְהִי בִּהְיוֹתָם בַּשָּׂדֶה וַיָּקָם קַיִן אֶל־הֶבֶל אָחִיו וַיַּהַרְגֵהוּ: 4:9 וַיֹּאמֶר יְהוָה אֶל־קַיִן אֵי הֶבֶל אָחִיךָ וַיֹּאמֶר לֹא יָדַעְתִּי הֲשֹׁמֵר אָחִי אָנֹכִי: 4:10 וַיֹּאמֶר מֶה עָשִׂיתָ קוֹל דְּמֵי אָחִיךָ צֹעֲקִים אֵלַי מִן־הָאֲדָמָה: 4:11 וְעַתָּה אָרוּר אָתָּה מִן־הָאֲדָמָה אֲשֶׁר פָּצְתָה אֶת־פִּיהָ לָקַחַת אֶת־דְּמֵי אָחִיךָ מִיָּדֶךָ: 4:12 כִּי תַעֲבֹד אֶת־הָאֲדָמָה לֹא־תֹסֵף תֵּת־כֹּחָהּ לָךְ נָע וָנָד תִּהְיֶה בָאָרֶץ: 4:13 וַיֹּאמֶר קַיִן אֶל־יְהוָה גָּדוֹל עֲוֹנִי מִנְּשֹׂא: 4:14 הֵן גֵּרַשְׁתָּ אֹתִי הַיּוֹם מֵעַל פְּנֵי הָאֲדָמָה וּמִפָּנֶיךָ אֶסָּתֵר וְהָיִיתִי נָע וָנָד בָּאָרֶץ וְהָיָה כָל־מֹצְאִי יַהַרְגֵנִי:

4:16 וַיֵּצֵא קַיִן מִלִּפְנֵי יְהוָה וַיֵּשֶׁב בְּאֶרֶץ־נוֹד קִדְמַת־עֵדֶן: 4:17 וַיֵּדַע קַיִן אֶת־אִשְׁתּוֹ וַתַּהַר וַתֵּלֶד אֶת־חֲנוֹךְ וַיְהִי בֹּנֶה עִיר וַיִּקְרָא שֵׁם הָעִיר כְּשֵׁם בְּנוֹ חֲנוֹךְ: 4:18 וַיִּוָּלֵד לַחֲנוֹךְ אֶת־עִירָד וְעִירָד יָלַד אֶת־מְחוּיָאֵל וּמְחִיָּיאֵל יָלַד אֶת־מְתוּשָׁאֵל וּמְתוּשָׁאֵל יָלַד אֶת־לָמֶךְ: 4:19 וַיִּקַּח־לוֹ לֶמֶךְ שְׁתֵּי נָשִׁים שֵׁם הָאַחַת עָדָה וְשֵׁם הַשֵּׁנִית צִלָּה: 4:20 וַתֵּלֶד עָדָה אֶת־יָבָל הוּא הָיָה אֲבִי יֹשֵׁב אֹהֶל וּמִקְנֶה: 4:21 וְשֵׁם אָחִיו יוּבָל הוּא הָיָה אֲבִי כָּל־תֹּפֵשׂ כִּנּוֹר וְעוּגָב: 4:22 וְצִלָּה גַם־הִוא יָלְדָה אֶת־תּוּבַל קַיִן לֹטֵשׁ כָּל־חֹרֵשׁ נְחֹשֶׁת וּבַרְזֶל וַאֲחוֹת תּוּבַל־קַיִן נַעֲמָה: 4:23 וַיֹּאמֶר לֶמֶךְ לְנָשָׁיו עָדָה וְצִלָּה שְׁמַעַן קוֹלִי נְשֵׁי לֶמֶךְ הַאְזֵנָּה אִמְרָתִי כִּי אִישׁ הָרַגְתִּי לְפִצְעִי וְיֶלֶד לְחַבֻּרָתִי: 4:24 כִּי שִׁבְעָתַיִם יֻקַּם־קָיִן וְלֶמֶךְ שִׁבְעִים וְשִׁבְעָה:

5:1 זֶה סֵפֶר תּוֹלְדֹת אָדָם בְּיוֹם בְּרֹא אֱלֹהִים אָדָם בִּדְמוּת אֱלֹהִים עָשָׂה אֹתוֹ: 5:2 זָכָר וּנְקֵבָה בְּרָאָם וַיְבָרֶךְ אֹתָם וַיִּקְרָא אֶת־שְׁמָם אָדָם בְּיוֹם הִבָּרְאָם: ס

GENESIS 4–5: J + P – CONTINUED

5:3 Adam lived one hundred and thirty years, and fathered a son in his own likeness, and in his own image, and named him Seth. 5:4 The days of Adam after he'd fathered Seth were eight hundred years, and he sired sons and daughters.

5:5 All the years that Adam lived amounted to nine hundred and thirty years; then he died.

5:6 Seth lived one hundred and five years, and fathered Enosh. 5:7 Seth lived eight hundred and seven years after he'd fathered Enosh, and sired sons and daughters.

5:8 All the years of Seth's (life) were nine hundred and twelve years; then he died.

5:9 Enosh lived ninety years, and fathered Kenan. 5:10 Enosh lived eight hundred and fifteen years after he'd fathered Kenan, and sired sons and daughters.

5:11 All the years of Enosh's (life) were nine hundred and five years; then he died.

5:12 Kenan lived seventy years, and fathered Mahalalel. 5:13 Kenan lived eight hundred and forty years after he'd fathered Mahalalel, and sired sons and daughters,

5:14 All the years of Kenan's (life) were nine hundred and ten years; then he died.

5:15 Mahalalel lived sixty-five years, and fathered Jared. 5:16 Mahalalel lived eight hundred and thirty years after he'd fathered Jared, and sired sons and daughters.

5:17 All the years of Mahalalel's (life) were eight hundred and ninety-five years; then he died.

5:18 Jared lived one hundred and sixty-two years, and fathered Enoch. 5:19 Jared lived eight hundred years after he'd fathered Enoch, and sired sons and daughters.

5:20 All the years of Jared's (life) were nine hundred and sixty-two years; then he died.

5:21 Enoch lived sixty-five years, and fathered Methuselah. 5:22 Enoch walked with God for three hundred years after he'd fathered Methuselah, and sired sons and daughters. 5:23 All the years of Enoch's (life) were three hundred and sixty-five years.

5:24 Enoch walked with God, and he disappeared, for God took him.

GENESIS 4–5: J + P (HEBREW) – CONTINUED

5:3 וַיְחִי אָדָם שְׁלֹשִׁים וּמְאַת שָׁנָה וַיּוֹלֶד בִּדְמוּתוֹ כְּצַלְמוֹ וַיִּקְרָא אֶת־שְׁמוֹ שֵׁת: 5:4 וַיִּהְיוּ יְמֵי־אָדָם אַחֲרֵי הוֹלִידוֹ אֶת־שֵׁת שְׁמֹנֶה מֵאֹת שָׁנָה וַיּוֹלֶד בָּנִים וּבָנוֹת: 5:5 וַיִּהְיוּ כָּל־יְמֵי אָדָם אֲשֶׁר־חַי תְּשַׁע מֵאוֹת שָׁנָה וּשְׁלֹשִׁים שָׁנָה וַיָּמֹת: ס

5:6 וַיְחִי־שֵׁת חָמֵשׁ שָׁנִים וּמְאַת שָׁנָה וַיּוֹלֶד אֶת־אֱנוֹשׁ: 5:7 וַיְחִי־שֵׁת אַחֲרֵי הוֹלִידוֹ אֶת־אֱנוֹשׁ שֶׁבַע שָׁנִים וּשְׁמֹנֶה מֵאוֹת שָׁנָה וַיּוֹלֶד בָּנִים וּבָנוֹת: 5:8 וַיִּהְיוּ כָּל־יְמֵי־שֵׁת שְׁתֵּים עֶשְׂרֵה שָׁנָה וּתְשַׁע מֵאוֹת שָׁנָה וַיָּמֹת: ס

5:9 וַיְחִי אֱנוֹשׁ תִּשְׁעִים שָׁנָה וַיּוֹלֶד אֶת־קֵינָן: 5:10 וַיְחִי אֱנוֹשׁ אַחֲרֵי הוֹלִידוֹ אֶת־קֵינָן חֲמֵשׁ עֶשְׂרֵה שָׁנָה וּשְׁמֹנֶה מֵאוֹת שָׁנָה וַיּוֹלֶד בָּנִים וּבָנוֹת: 5:11 וַיִּהְיוּ כָּל־יְמֵי אֱנוֹשׁ חָמֵשׁ שָׁנִים וּתְשַׁע מֵאוֹת שָׁנָה וַיָּמֹת: ס

5:12 וַיְחִי קֵינָן שִׁבְעִים שָׁנָה וַיּוֹלֶד אֶת־מַהֲלַלְאֵל: 5:13 וַיְחִי קֵינָן אַחֲרֵי הוֹלִידוֹ אֶת־מַהֲלַלְאֵל אַרְבָּעִים שָׁנָה וּשְׁמֹנֶה מֵאוֹת שָׁנָה וַיּוֹלֶד בָּנִים וּבָנוֹת: 5:14 וַיִּהְיוּ כָּל־יְמֵי קֵינָן עֶשֶׂר שָׁנִים וּתְשַׁע מֵאוֹת שָׁנָה וַיָּמֹת: ס

5:12 וַיְחִי קֵינָן שִׁבְעִים שָׁנָה וַיּוֹלֶד אֶת־מַהֲלַלְאֵל: 5:13 וַיְחִי קֵינָן אַחֲרֵי הוֹלִידוֹ אֶת־מַהֲלַלְאֵל אַרְבָּעִים שָׁנָה וּשְׁמֹנֶה מֵאוֹת שָׁנָה וַיּוֹלֶד בָּנִים וּבָנוֹת: 5:14 וַיִּהְיוּ כָּל־יְמֵי קֵינָן עֶשֶׂר שָׁנִים וּתְשַׁע מֵאוֹת שָׁנָה וַיָּמֹת: ס

5:15 וַיְחִי מַהֲלַלְאֵל חָמֵשׁ שָׁנִים וְשִׁשִּׁים שָׁנָה וַיּוֹלֶד אֶת־יָרֶד: 5:16 וַיְחִי מַהֲלַלְאֵל אַחֲרֵי הוֹלִידוֹ אֶת־יֶרֶד שְׁלֹשִׁים שָׁנָה וּשְׁמֹנֶה מֵאוֹת שָׁנָה וַיּוֹלֶד בָּנִים וּבָנוֹת: 5:17 וַיִּהְיוּ כָּל־יְמֵי מַהֲלַלְאֵל חָמֵשׁ וְתִשְׁעִים שָׁנָה וּשְׁמֹנֶה מֵאוֹת שָׁנָה וַיָּמֹת: ס

5:18 וַיְחִי־יֶרֶד שְׁתַּיִם וְשִׁשִּׁים שָׁנָה וּמְאַת שָׁנָה וַיּוֹלֶד אֶת־חֲנוֹךְ: 5:19 וַיְחִי־יֶרֶד אַחֲרֵי הוֹלִידוֹ אֶת־חֲנוֹךְ שְׁמֹנֶה מֵאוֹת שָׁנָה וַיּוֹלֶד בָּנִים וּבָנוֹת: 5:20 וַיִּהְיוּ כָּל־יְמֵי־יֶרֶד שְׁתַּיִם וְשִׁשִּׁים שָׁנָה וּתְשַׁע מֵאוֹת שָׁנָה וַיָּמֹת: פ

5:21 וַיְחִי חֲנוֹךְ חָמֵשׁ וְשִׁשִּׁים שָׁנָה וַיּוֹלֶד אֶת־מְתוּשָׁלַח: 5:22 וַיִּתְהַלֵּךְ חֲנוֹךְ אֶת־הָאֱלֹהִים אַחֲרֵי הוֹלִידוֹ אֶת־מְתוּשֶׁלַח שְׁלֹשׁ מֵאוֹת שָׁנָה וַיּוֹלֶד בָּנִים וּבָנוֹת: 5:23 וַיְהִי כָּל־יְמֵי חֲנוֹךְ חָמֵשׁ וְשִׁשִּׁים שָׁנָה וּשְׁלֹשׁ מֵאוֹת שָׁנָה: 5:24 וַיִּתְהַלֵּךְ חֲנוֹךְ אֶת־הָאֱלֹהִים וְאֵינֶנּוּ כִּי־לָקַח אֹתוֹ אֱלֹהִים: פ

GENESIS 4–5: J + P – CONTINUED

5:25 Methuselah lived one hundred and eighty-seven years, and fathered Lamech. 5:26 Methuselah lived seven hundred and eighty-two years after he'd fathered Lamech, and sired sons and daughters.

5:27 All the years of Methuselah's (life) were nine hundred and sixty-nine years; then he died.

==5:28 Lamech== lived one hundred and eighty-two years, and ==fathered a son, 5:29 and he named him Noah, saying, "He will comfort us in our work and in the toil of our hands, for Yahweh has cursed the earth."== 5:30 Lamech lived five hundred and ninety-five years after he'd fathered Noah, and sired sons and daughters.

5:31 All the years of Lamech's (life) were seven hundred seventy-seven years; then he died.

5:32 Noah was five hundred years old, and Noah fathered Shem, Ham, and Japheth.

What P Adds

P's genealogy in Genesis 5 is a reworking of J's genealogy from Genesis 4. P essentially borrows all of his names from J: Cain becomes Kenan, Mehujael becomes Mahalalel, Irad becomes Jared, Enoch remains Enoch, and Methushael becomes Methuselah. In the process, P cuts off Noah's birth from its original Yahwistic context, and thereby cuts off Cain from his place in Biblical history. This result is not at all accidental. P invents Seth, and the subsequent genealogy through him, in order to prevent the first murderer from being rewarded with the honor of becoming the father of humanity.

GENESIS 4–5: J + P (HEBREW) – CONTINUED

5:25 וַיְחִי מְתוּשֶׁלַח שֶׁבַע וּשְׁמֹנִים שָׁנָה וּמְאַת שָׁנָה וַיּוֹלֶד אֶת־לָמֶךְ: 5:26 וַיְחִי מְתוּשֶׁלַח אַחֲרֵי הוֹלִידוֹ אֶת־לֶמֶךְ שְׁתַּיִם וּשְׁמוֹנִים שָׁנָה וּשְׁבַע מֵאוֹת שָׁנָה וַיּוֹלֶד בָּנִים וּבָנוֹת: 5:27 וַיִּהְיוּ כָּל־יְמֵי מְתוּשֶׁלַח תֵּשַׁע וְשִׁשִּׁים שָׁנָה וּתְשַׁע מֵאוֹת שָׁנָה וַיָּמֹת: פ

5:28 וַיְחִי־לֶמֶךְ שְׁתַּיִם וּשְׁמֹנִים שָׁנָה וּמְאַת שָׁנָה וַיּוֹלֶד בֵּן: 5:29 וַיִּקְרָא אֶת־שְׁמוֹ נֹחַ לֵאמֹר זֶה יְנַחֲמֵנוּ מִמַּעֲשֵׂנוּ וּמֵעִצְּבוֹן יָדֵינוּ מִן־הָאֲדָמָה אֲשֶׁר אֵרְרָהּ יְהוָה: 5:30 וַיְחִי־לֶמֶךְ אַחֲרֵי הוֹלִידוֹ אֶת־נֹחַ חָמֵשׁ וְתִשְׁעִים שָׁנָה וַחֲמֵשׁ מֵאֹת שָׁנָה וַיּוֹלֶד בָּנִים וּבָנוֹת: 5:31 וַיְהִי כָּל־יְמֵי־לֶמֶךְ שֶׁבַע וְשִׁבְעִים שָׁנָה וּשְׁבַע מֵאוֹת שָׁנָה וַיָּמֹת: ס

5:32 וַיְהִי־נֹחַ בֶּן־חֲמֵשׁ מֵאוֹת שָׁנָה וַיּוֹלֶד נֹחַ אֶת־שֵׁם אֶת־חָם וְאֶת־יָפֶת:

GENESIS 4–5: CANON (J + P + B)

4:1 The man knew his wife Eve. She conceived, and gave birth to Cain, and said, "I have created a man with Yahweh." 4:2 Again she gave birth, to Cain's brother, Abel. Abel was a keeper of sheep, but Cain was a tiller of soil. 4:3 After a time, Cain brought an offering to Yahweh from the fruit of the field. 4:4 Abel also brought of the firstborn of his flock and of their fat. Yahweh held Abel and his offering in high regard, 4:5 but didn't regard Cain and his offering. Cain was very angry, and his face fell. 4:6 Yahweh said to Cain, "Why are you angry and why has your face fallen? 4:7 If you behave uprightly (then all the better). If you don't behave uprightly, sin crouches at the door. It desires you, but you can rule over it." 4:8 Cain said to Abel, his brother, ("Let's go into the field.") It happened that when they were in the field, Cain rose up against Abel, his brother, and killed him.

4:9 Yahweh said to Cain, "Where is Abel, your brother?" He said, "I don't know. Am I my brother's keeper?" 4:10 Yahweh said, "What have you done? The voice of your brother's blood cries to me from the ground. 4:11 Now you are cursed because of the ground, which has opened its mouth to receive your brother's blood from your hand. 4:12 From this point forward, when you till the ground, it won't yield its fruit to you. You shall be a peripatetic wanderer upon the earth." 4:13 Cain said to Yahweh, "My punishment is greater than I can bear. 4:14 Behold, you have driven me out today from (settling upon) the face of the earth. I will be hidden from your face, and I will be a fugitive and a wanderer upon the earth. It will happen that whoever finds me will kill me." 4:15 Yahweh said to him, "Therefore whoever slays Cain, vengeance will be taken on him sevenfold." Yahweh appointed a sign for Cain, lest any finding him should strike him.

4:16 Cain went out from Yahweh's presence, and lived in the land of Nod, east of Eden. 4:17 Cain knew his wife. She conceived, and gave birth to Enoch. He built a city, and named the city, after his son, Enoch. 4:18 To Enoch was born Irad. Irad fathered Mehujael. Mehujael fathered Methushael. Methushael fathered Lamech.

4:19 Lamech took two wives: the name of the one was Adah, and the name of the other Zillah. 4:20 Adah gave birth to Jabal, who was the progenitor of those who dwell in tents and tend livestock. 4:21 His brother's name was Jubal, the progenitor of all who play the harp and pipe. 4:22 Zillah also gave birth to Tubal Cain, the forger of every cutting implement of brass and iron. Tubal Cain's sister was Naamah. 4:23 Lamech said to his wives, "Adah and Zillah, hear my voice. Wives of Lamech, listen to my words, for I have slain a man for wounding me, a young man for bruising me. 4:24 If Cain will be avenged seven times, surely Lamech (shall be avenged) seventy-seven times."

GENESIS 4–5: CANON (J + P + B) HEBREW

4:1 וְהָאָדָם יָדַע אֶת־חַוָּה אִשְׁתּוֹ וַתַּהַר וַתֵּלֶד אֶת־קַיִן וַתֹּאמֶר קָנִיתִי אִישׁ אֶת־יְהוָה: 4:2 וַתֹּסֶף לָלֶדֶת אֶת־אָחִיו אֶת־הָבֶל וַיְהִי־הֶבֶל רֹעֵה צֹאן וְקַיִן הָיָה עֹבֵד אֲדָמָה: 4:3 וַיְהִי מִקֵּץ יָמִים וַיָּבֵא קַיִן מִפְּרִי הָאֲדָמָה מִנְחָה לַיהוָה: 4:4 וְהֶבֶל הֵבִיא גַם־הוּא מִבְּכֹרוֹת צֹאנוֹ וּמֵחֶלְבֵהֶן וַיִּשַׁע יְהוָה אֶל־הֶבֶל וְאֶל־מִנְחָתוֹ: 4:5 וְאֶל־קַיִן וְאֶל־מִנְחָתוֹ לֹא שָׁעָה וַיִּחַר לְקַיִן מְאֹד וַיִּפְּלוּ פָּנָיו: 4:6 וַיֹּאמֶר יְהוָה אֶל־קָיִן לָמָּה חָרָה לָךְ וְלָמָּה נָפְלוּ פָנֶיךָ: 4:7 הֲלוֹא אִם־תֵּיטִיב שְׂאֵת וְאִם לֹא תֵיטִיב לַפֶּתַח חַטָּאת רֹבֵץ וְאֵלֶיךָ תְּשׁוּקָתוֹ וְאַתָּה תִּמְשָׁל־בּוֹ: 4:8 וַיֹּאמֶר קַיִן אֶל־הֶבֶל אָחִיו וַיְהִי בִּהְיוֹתָם בַּשָּׂדֶה וַיָּקָם קַיִן אֶל־הֶבֶל אָחִיו וַיַּהַרְגֵהוּ:

4:9 וַיֹּאמֶר יְהוָה אֶל־קַיִן אֵי הֶבֶל אָחִיךָ וַיֹּאמֶר לֹא יָדַעְתִּי הֲשֹׁמֵר אָחִי אָנֹכִי: 4:10 וַיֹּאמֶר מֶה עָשִׂיתָ קוֹל דְּמֵי אָחִיךָ צֹעֲקִים אֵלַי מִן־הָאֲדָמָה: 4:11 וְעַתָּה אָרוּר אָתָּה מִן־הָאֲדָמָה אֲשֶׁר פָּצְתָה אֶת־פִּיהָ לָקַחַת אֶת־דְּמֵי אָחִיךָ מִיָּדֶךָ: 4:12 כִּי תַעֲבֹד אֶת־הָאֲדָמָה לֹא־תֹסֵף תֵּת־כֹּחָהּ לָךְ נָע וָנָד תִּהְיֶה בָאָרֶץ: 4:13 וַיֹּאמֶר קַיִן אֶל־יְהוָה גָּדוֹל עֲוֹנִי מִנְּשֹׂא: 4:14 הֵן גֵּרַשְׁתָּ אֹתִי הַיּוֹם מֵעַל פְּנֵי הָאֲדָמָה וּמִפָּנֶיךָ אֶסָּתֵר וְהָיִיתִי נָע וָנָד בָּאָרֶץ וְהָיָה כָל־מֹצְאִי יַהַרְגֵנִי:

4:16 וַיֵּצֵא קַיִן מִלִּפְנֵי יְהוָה וַיֵּשֶׁב בְּאֶרֶץ־נוֹד קִדְמַת־עֵדֶן: 4:17 וַיֵּדַע קַיִן אֶת־אִשְׁתּוֹ וַתַּהַר וַתֵּלֶד אֶת־חֲנוֹךְ וַיְהִי בֹּנֶה עִיר וַיִּקְרָא שֵׁם הָעִיר כְּשֵׁם בְּנוֹ חֲנוֹךְ: 4:18 וַיִּוָּלֵד לַחֲנוֹךְ אֶת־עִירָד וְעִירָד יָלַד אֶת־מְחוּיָאֵל וּמְחִיָּיאֵל יָלַד אֶת־מְתוּשָׁאֵל וּמְתוּשָׁאֵל יָלַד אֶת־לָמֶךְ:

4:19 וַיִּקַּח־לוֹ לֶמֶךְ שְׁתֵּי נָשִׁים שֵׁם הָאַחַת עָדָה וְשֵׁם הַשֵּׁנִית צִלָּה: 4:20 וַתֵּלֶד עָדָה אֶת־יָבָל הוּא הָיָה אֲבִי יֹשֵׁב אֹהֶל וּמִקְנֶה: 4:21 וְשֵׁם אָחִיו יוּבָל הוּא הָיָה אֲבִי כָּל־תֹּפֵשׂ כִּנּוֹר וְעוּגָב: 4:22 וְצִלָּה גַם־הִוא יָלְדָה אֶת־תּוּבַל קַיִן לֹטֵשׁ כָּל־חֹרֵשׁ נְחֹשֶׁת וּבַרְזֶל וַאֲחוֹת תּוּבַל־קַיִן נַעֲמָה: 4:23 וַיֹּאמֶר לֶמֶךְ לְנָשָׁיו עָדָה וְצִלָּה שְׁמַעַן קוֹלִי נְשֵׁי לֶמֶךְ הַאְזֵנָּה אִמְרָתִי כִּי אִישׁ הָרַגְתִּי לְפִצְעִי וְיֶלֶד לְחַבֻּרָתִי: 4:24 כִּי שִׁבְעָתַיִם יֻקַּם־קָיִן וְלֶמֶךְ שִׁבְעִים וְשִׁבְעָה:

GENESIS 4–5: CANON (J + P + B) – CONTINUED

==4:25 Adam knew his wife again. She gave birth to a son, and named him Seth, "for God has granted me another child instead of Abel, whom Cain killed." 4:26 Seth as well was granted progeny, and he named him Enosh. Then men began to call on Yahweh's name.==

5:1 This is an account of Adam's generations. In the day that God created man, he made him in God's likeness. 5:2 He created them male and female, and blessed them, and called them "humans" on the day when they were created. 5:3 Adam lived one hundred and thirty years, and fathered a son in his own likeness, and in his own image, and named him Seth. 5:4 The days of Adam after he'd fathered Seth were eight hundred years, and he sired sons and daughters. 5:5 All the years that Adam lived amounted to nine hundred and thirty years; then he died.

5:6 Seth lived one hundred and five years, and fathered Enosh. 5:7 Seth lived eight hundred and seven years after he'd fathered Enosh, and sired sons and daughters. 5:8 All the years of Seth's (life) were nine hundred and twelve years; then he died.

5:9 Enosh lived ninety years, and fathered Kenan. 5:10 Enosh lived eight hundred and fifteen years after he'd fathered Kenan, and sired sons and daughters. 5:11 All the years of Enosh's (life) were nine hundred and five years; then he died.

5:12 Kenan lived seventy years, and fathered Mahalalel. 5:13 Kenan lived eight hundred and forty years after he'd fathered Mahalalel, and sired sons and daughters, 5:14 and all the years of Kenan's (life) were nine hundred and ten years; then he died.

5:15 Mahalalel lived sixty-five years, and fathered Jared. 5:16 Mahalalel lived eight hundred and thirty years after he'd fathered Jared, and sired sons and daughters. 5:17 All the years of Mahalalel's (life) were eight hundred and ninety-five years; then he died.

5:18 Jared lived one hundred and sixty-two years, and fathered Enoch. 5:19 Jared lived eight hundred years after he'd fathered Enoch, and sired sons and daughters. 5:20 All the years of Jared's (life) were nine hundred and sixty-two years; then he died.

5:21 Enoch lived sixty-five years, and fathered Methuselah. 5:22 Enoch walked with God for three hundred years after he'd fathered Methuselah, and sired sons and daughters. 5:23 All the years of Enoch's (life) were three hundred and sixty-five years. 5:24 Enoch walked with God, and he disappeared, for God took him.

GENESIS 4–5: CANON (J + P + B) HEBREW – CONTINUED

4:25 וַיֵּ֨דַע אָדָ֥ם עוֹד֙ אֶת־אִשְׁתּ֔וֹ וַתֵּ֣לֶד בֵּ֔ן וַתִּקְרָ֥א אֶת־שְׁמ֖וֹ שֵׁ֑ת כִּ֣י שָֽׁת־לִ֤י אֱלֹהִים֙ זֶ֣רַע אַחֵ֔ר תַּ֥חַת הֶ֖בֶל כִּ֥י הֲרָג֥וֹ קָֽיִן׃ 4:26 וּלְשֵׁ֤ת גַּם־הוּא֙ יֻלַּד־בֵּ֔ן וַיִּקְרָ֥א אֶת־שְׁמ֖וֹ אֱנ֑וֹשׁ אָ֣ז הוּחַ֔ל לִקְרֹ֖א בְּשֵׁ֥ם יְהוָֽה׃

5:1 זֶ֣ה סֵ֔פֶר תּוֹלְדֹ֖ת אָדָ֑ם בְּי֗וֹם בְּרֹ֤א אֱלֹהִים֙ אָדָ֔ם בִּדְמ֥וּת אֱלֹהִ֖ים עָשָׂ֥ה אֹתֽוֹ׃ 5:2 זָכָ֥ר וּנְקֵבָ֖ה בְּרָאָ֑ם וַיְבָ֣רֶךְ אֹתָ֗ם וַיִּקְרָ֤א אֶת־שְׁמָם֙ אָדָ֔ם בְּי֖וֹם הִבָּֽרְאָֽם׃ 5:3 וַֽיְחִ֣י אָדָ֗ם שְׁלֹשִׁ֤ים וּמְאַת֙ שָׁנָ֔ה וַיּ֥וֹלֶד בִּדְמוּת֖וֹ כְּצַלְמ֑וֹ וַיִּקְרָ֥א אֶת־שְׁמ֖וֹ שֵֽׁת׃ 5:4 וַיִּֽהְי֣וּ יְמֵי־אָדָ֗ם אַֽחֲרֵי֙ הוֹלִיד֣וֹ אֶת־שֵׁ֔ת שְׁמֹנֶ֥ה מֵאֹ֖ת שָׁנָ֑ה וַיּ֥וֹלֶד בָּנִ֖ים וּבָנֽוֹת׃ 5:5 וַיִּֽהְי֞וּ כָּל־יְמֵ֤י אָדָם֙ אֲשֶׁר־חַ֔י תְּשַׁ֤ע מֵאוֹת֙ שָׁנָ֔ה וּשְׁלֹשִׁ֖ים שָׁנָ֑ה וַיָּמֹֽת׃ ס

5:6 וַֽיְחִי־שֵׁ֕ת חָמֵ֥שׁ שָׁנִ֖ים וּמְאַ֣ת שָׁנָ֑ה וַיּ֖וֹלֶד אֶת־אֱנֽוֹשׁ׃ 5:7 וַֽיְחִי־שֵׁ֗ת אַֽחֲרֵי֙ הוֹלִיד֣וֹ אֶת־אֱנ֔וֹשׁ שֶׁ֣בַע שָׁנִ֔ים וּשְׁמֹנֶ֥ה מֵא֖וֹת שָׁנָ֑ה וַיּ֥וֹלֶד בָּנִ֖ים וּבָנֽוֹת׃ 5:8 וַיִּֽהְיוּ֙ כָּל־יְמֵי־שֵׁ֔ת שְׁתֵּ֤ים עֶשְׂרֵה֙ שָׁנָ֔ה וּתְשַׁ֥ע מֵא֖וֹת שָׁנָ֑ה וַיָּמֹֽת׃ ס

5:9 וַֽיְחִ֥י אֱנ֖וֹשׁ תִּשְׁעִ֣ים שָׁנָ֑ה וַיּ֖וֹלֶד אֶת־קֵינָֽן׃ 5:10 וַֽיְחִ֣י אֱנ֗וֹשׁ אַֽחֲרֵי֙ הוֹלִיד֣וֹ אֶת־קֵינָ֔ן חֲמֵ֤שׁ עֶשְׂרֵה֙ שָׁנָ֔ה וּשְׁמֹנֶ֥ה מֵא֖וֹת שָׁנָ֑ה וַיּ֥וֹלֶד בָּנִ֖ים וּבָנֽוֹת׃ 5:11 וַיִּֽהְיוּ֙ כָּל־יְמֵ֣י אֱנ֔וֹשׁ חָמֵ֣שׁ שָׁנִ֔ים וּתְשַׁ֥ע מֵא֖וֹת שָׁנָ֑ה וַיָּמֹֽת׃ ס

5:12 וַֽיְחִ֥י קֵינָ֖ן שִׁבְעִ֣ים שָׁנָ֑ה וַיּ֖וֹלֶד אֶת־מַֽהֲלַלְאֵֽל׃ 5:13 וַיְחִ֣י קֵינָ֗ן אַֽחֲרֵי֙ הוֹלִיד֣וֹ אֶת־מַֽהֲלַלְאֵ֔ל אַרְבָּעִ֣ים שָׁנָ֔ה וּשְׁמֹנֶ֥ה מֵא֖וֹת שָׁנָ֑ה וַיּ֥וֹלֶד בָּנִ֖ים וּבָנֽוֹת׃ 5:14 וַיִּֽהְיוּ֙ כָּל־יְמֵ֣י קֵינָ֔ן עֶ֣שֶׂר שָׁנִ֔ים וּתְשַׁ֥ע מֵא֖וֹת שָׁנָ֑ה וַיָּמֹֽת׃ ס

5:15 וַֽיְחִ֣י מַֽהֲלַלְאֵ֔ל חָמֵ֥שׁ שָׁנִ֖ים וְשִׁשִּׁ֣ים שָׁנָ֑ה וַיּ֖וֹלֶד אֶת־יָֽרֶד׃ 5:16 וַֽיְחִ֣י מַֽהֲלַלְאֵ֗ל אַֽחֲרֵי֙ הוֹלִיד֣וֹ אֶת־יֶ֔רֶד שְׁלֹשִׁ֥ים שָׁנָ֖ה וּשְׁמֹנֶ֣ה מֵא֣וֹת שָׁנָ֑ה וַיּ֥וֹלֶד בָּנִ֖ים וּבָנֽוֹת׃ 5:17 וַיִּֽהְיוּ֙ כָּל־יְמֵ֣י מַֽהֲלַלְאֵ֔ל חָמֵ֤שׁ וְתִשְׁעִים֙ שָׁנָ֔ה וּשְׁמֹנֶ֥ה מֵא֖וֹת שָׁנָ֑ה וַיָּמֹֽת׃ס

5:18 וַֽיְחִי־יֶ֕רֶד שְׁתַּ֧יִם וְשִׁשִּׁ֛ים שָׁנָ֖ה וּמְאַ֣ת שָׁנָ֑ה וַיּ֖וֹלֶד אֶת־חֲנֽוֹךְ׃ 5:19 וַֽיְחִי־יֶ֗רֶד אַֽחֲרֵי֙ הוֹלִיד֣וֹ אֶת־חֲנ֔וֹךְ שְׁמֹנֶ֥ה מֵא֖וֹת שָׁנָ֑ה וַיּ֥וֹלֶד בָּנִ֖ים וּבָנֽוֹת׃ 5:20 וַיִּֽהְיוּ֙ כָּל־יְמֵי־יֶ֔רֶד שְׁתַּ֤יִם וְשִׁשִּׁים֙ שָׁנָ֔ה וּתְשַׁ֥ע מֵא֖וֹת שָׁנָ֑ה וַיָּמֹֽת׃ פ

5:21 וַֽיְחִ֣י חֲנ֔וֹךְ חָמֵ֥שׁ וְשִׁשִּׁ֖ים שָׁנָ֑ה וַיּ֖וֹלֶד אֶת־מְתוּשָֽׁלַח׃ 5:22 וַיִּתְהַלֵּ֨ךְ חֲנ֤וֹךְ אֶת־הָֽאֱלֹהִים֙ אַֽחֲרֵ֣י הוֹלִיד֣וֹ אֶת־מְתוּשֶׁ֔לַח שְׁלֹ֥שׁ מֵא֖וֹת שָׁנָ֑ה וַיּ֥וֹלֶד בָּנִ֖ים וּבָנֽוֹת׃ 5:23 וַיְהִ֖י כָּל־יְמֵ֣י חֲנ֑וֹךְ חָמֵ֤שׁ וְשִׁשִּׁים֙ שָׁנָ֔ה וּשְׁלֹ֥שׁ מֵא֖וֹת שָׁנָֽה׃ 5:24 וַיִּתְהַלֵּ֥ךְ חֲנ֖וֹךְ אֶת־הָֽאֱלֹהִ֑ים וְאֵינֶ֕נּוּ כִּֽי־לָקַ֥ח אֹת֖וֹ אֱלֹהִֽים׃ פ

GENESIS 4–5: CANON (J + P + B) – CONTINUED

5:25 Methuselah lived one hundred and eighty-seven years, and fathered Lamech. 5:26 Methuselah lived seven hundred and eighty-two years after he'd fathered Lamech, and sired sons and daughters. 5:27 All the years of Methuselah's (life) were nine hundred and sixty-nine years; then he died.

==5:28 Lamech== lived one hundred and eighty-two years, and ==fathered a son, 5:29 and he named him Noah, saying, "He will comfort us in our work and in the toil of our hands, for Yahweh has cursed the earth."== 5:30 Lamech lived five hundred and ninety-five years after he'd fathered Noah, and sired sons and daughters. 5:31 All the years of Lamech's (life) were seven hundred seventy-seven years; then he died. 5:32 Noah was five hundred years old, and Noah fathered Shem, Ham, and Japheth.

What B adds

Chapter 4 ends with a curious note regarding Adam and Eve. This is a complete non-sequitor—by this point, the story has already moved away from Adam and Eve, seven generations into the future. It is likely that these verses are B's attempt to make the birth of Seth part of the overall story, instead of just a name on a Priestly genealogical list (note also B's use of the passive form "yulad" [was born to], which is a feature of his genealogies throughout the Pentateuch). He claims that Adam and Eve conceived Seth after losing Abel and thus were consoled. Seth then fathers Enosh, who, in addition to not being a murderer like his uncle Cain, is the first worshipper of Yahweh. B adds this information to justify P's choice of Seth as the father of humanity.

GENESIS 4–5: CANON (J + P + B) HEBREW – CONTINUED

5:25 וַיְחִי מְתוּשֶׁלַח שֶׁבַע וּשְׁמֹנִים שָׁנָה וּמְאַת שָׁנָה וַיּוֹלֶד אֶת־לָמֶךְ: 5:26 וַיְחִי מְתוּשֶׁלַח אַחֲרֵי הוֹלִידוֹ אֶת־לֶמֶךְ שְׁתַּיִם וּשְׁמוֹנִים שָׁנָה וּשְׁבַע מֵאוֹת שָׁנָה וַיּוֹלֶד בָּנִים וּבָנוֹת: 5:27 וַיִּהְיוּ כָּל־יְמֵי מְתוּשֶׁלַח תֵּשַׁע וְשִׁשִּׁים שָׁנָה וּתְשַׁע מֵאוֹת שָׁנָה וַיָּמֹת: פ

5:28 וַיְחִי־לֶמֶךְ שְׁתַּיִם וּשְׁמֹנִים שָׁנָה וּמְאַת שָׁנָה וַיּוֹלֶד בֵּן: 5:29 וַיִּקְרָא אֶת־שְׁמוֹ נֹחַ לֵאמֹר זֶה יְנַחֲמֵנוּ מִמַּעֲשֵׂנוּ וּמֵעִצְּבוֹן יָדֵינוּ מִן־הָאֲדָמָה אֲשֶׁר אֵרְרָהּ יְהוָה: 5:30 וַיְחִי־לֶמֶךְ אַחֲרֵי הוֹלִידוֹ אֶת־נֹחַ חָמֵשׁ וְתִשְׁעִים שָׁנָה וַחֲמֵשׁ מֵאֹת שָׁנָה וַיּוֹלֶד בָּנִים וּבָנוֹת: 5:31 וַיְהִי כָּל־יְמֵי־לֶמֶךְ שֶׁבַע וְשִׁבְעִים שָׁנָה וּשְׁבַע מֵאוֹת שָׁנָה וַיָּמֹת: 5:32 וַיְהִי־נֹחַ בֶּן־חֲמֵשׁ מֵאוֹת שָׁנָה וַיּוֹלֶד נֹחַ אֶת־שֵׁם אֶת־חָם וְאֶת־יָפֶת:

THE CREATION STORY: GENESIS 6

Genesis 6 begins with the mysterious episode of the sons of God descending from heaven and fathering children with human wives, giving birth to demigods or heroes. The Lord then sees how evil humans have become and decides to kill them all with a flood, except for Noah, whom he commands to build an ark according to a specific design. Noah is also instructed to take two pairs of each animal in the world and preserve them aboard the ark for the duration of the flood.

GENESIS 6: THE J KERNEL

> 6:5 Yahweh saw that the wickedness of the human being was great upon the earth, and all the thoughts emanating from his heart were only evil all the time. 6:6 Yahweh regretted that he had made human beings upon the earth, and it grieved his heart. 6:7 Yahweh said, "I will destroy the humans whom I have created from the face of the earth; men, along with animals, creeping things, and the birds of the sky; for I regret having made them."

> 6:8 But Noah found favor in Yahweh's eyes.

According to J all of humanity is evil (see vss. 5–7), marked as they are by their murderous forefather Cain. Perhaps Noah finds favor in Yahweh's eyes (vs. 8) and is righteous compared to his generation (Gen. 7:1), but he is not exempt from this moral pronouncement, as his drunkenness and nakedness in Chapter 9 will demonstrate.

GENESIS 6: THE J KERNEL (HEBREW)

6:5 וַיַּרְא יְהוָה כִּי רַבָּה רָעַת הָאָדָם בָּאָרֶץ וְכָל־יֵצֶר מַחְשְׁבֹת לִבּוֹ רַק רַע כָּל־הַיּוֹם: 6:6 וַיִּנָּחֶם יְהוָה כִּי־עָשָׂה אֶת־הָאָדָם בָּאָרֶץ וַיִּתְעַצֵּב אֶל־לִבּוֹ: 6:7 וַיֹּאמֶר יְהוָה אֶמְחֶה אֶת־הָאָדָם אֲשֶׁר־בָּרָאתִי מֵעַל פְּנֵי הָאֲדָמָה מֵאָדָם עַד־בְּהֵמָה עַד־רֶמֶשׂ וְעַד־עוֹף הַשָּׁמָיִם כִּי נִחַמְתִּי כִּי עֲשִׂיתִם: 6:8 וְנֹחַ מָצָא חֵן בְּעֵינֵי יְהוָה: פ

GENESIS 6: J + P – CONTINUED

<mark>6:5 Yahweh saw that the wickedness of the human being was great upon the earth, and all the thoughts emanating from his heart were only evil all the time. 6:6 Yahweh regretted that he had made human beings upon the earth, and it grieved his heart. 6:7 Yahweh said, "I will destroy the humans whom I have created from the face of the earth; men, along with animals, creeping things, and the birds of the sky; for I regret having made them." 6:8 But Noah found favor in Yahweh's eyes.</mark>

6:9 These are the generations of Noah. Noah was a righteous man, blameless among the people of his time. Noah walked with God. 6:10 Noah fathered three sons: Shem, Ham, and Japheth. 6:11 The earth was corrupt before God, and the earth was filled with violence. 6:12 God saw the earth, that it was corrupt, for all flesh on earth had become corrupt.

6:13 God said to Noah, "The end of all flesh has come for I (have decreed it), since the earth is filled with violence because of them. Behold, I will destroy them with the earth. 6:14 Make an ark of gopher wood. You shall partition the ark, and shall seal it inside and outside with pitch. 6:15 This is how you shall make it. The length of the ark will be three hundred cubits, its breadth fifty cubits, and its height thirty cubits. 6:16 You shall construct a window for the ark, which you shall place a cubit above. You shall set the door of the ship in its side. You shall make it with lower, second, and third decks. 6:17 I will then bring a flood of waters upon this earth, to destroy all breathing creatures from under the sky. Everything that is upon the earth will die. 6:18 But I will establish my covenant with you. You shall come into the ship, you, your sons, your wife, and your sons' wives with you. 6:19 Of every living thing of all flesh, you shall bring two of every sort into the ship, to keep them alive with you. They shall be male and female. 6:20 Of species of birds, of species of livestock, of every species of creepers upon the ground, two of every sort shall come with you, to keep them alive. 6:21 Take with you of all food that is eaten, and gather it to yourself; and it will sustain both you and them." 6:22 Thus Noah did. As God had commanded him, so he did.

What P Adds

The supplementary character of the Priestly section of Genesis 6 is readily apparent. Verse 9 marks an abrupt switch from the use of "the Lord" (J's name for the deity) in previous verses to "God" (P's preferred name). P's claim in verse 9 that Noah was chosen because he was "righteous" and "blameless" is a response to J's vaguer statement that Noah found favor in the eyes of Yahweh. For the Priestly author, who is deeply invested in morality, how could Noah have found favor with God if not by being righteous?

GENESIS 6: J + P (HEBREW) – CONTINUED

==6:5 וַיַּ֣רְא יְהוָ֔ה כִּ֥י רַבָּ֛ה רָעַ֥ת הָאָדָ֖ם בָּאָ֑רֶץ וְכָל־יֵ֙צֶר֙ מַחְשְׁבֹ֣ת לִבּ֔וֹ רַ֥ק רַ֖ע כָּל־הַיּֽוֹם: 6:6 וַיִּנָּ֣חֶם יְהוָ֔ה כִּֽי־עָשָׂ֥ה אֶת־הָֽאָדָ֖ם בָּאָ֑רֶץ וַיִּתְעַצֵּ֖ב אֶל־לִבּֽוֹ: 6:7 וַיֹּ֣אמֶר יְהוָ֗ה אֶמְחֶ֨ה אֶת־הָאָדָ֤ם אֲשֶׁר־בָּרָ֙אתִי֙ מֵעַל֙ פְּנֵ֣י הָֽאֲדָמָ֔ה מֵֽאָדָם֙ עַד־בְּהֵמָ֔ה עַד־רֶ֖מֶשׂ וְעַד־ע֣וֹף הַשָּׁמָ֑יִם כִּ֥י נִחַ֖מְתִּי כִּ֥י עֲשִׂיתִֽם: 6:8 וְנֹ֕חַ מָ֥צָא חֵ֖ן בְּעֵינֵ֥י יְהוָֽה: פ==

6:9 אֵ֚לֶּה תּוֹלְדֹ֣ת נֹ֔חַ נֹ֗חַ אִ֥ישׁ צַדִּ֛יק תָּמִ֥ים הָיָ֖ה בְּדֹֽרֹתָ֑יו אֶת־הָֽאֱלֹהִ֖ים הִֽתְהַלֶּךְ־נֹֽחַ: 6:10 וַיּ֥וֹלֶד נֹ֖חַ שְׁלֹשָׁ֣ה בָנִ֑ים אֶת־שֵׁ֖ם אֶת־חָ֥ם וְאֶת־יָֽפֶת: 6:11 וַתִּשָּׁחֵ֥ת הָאָ֖רֶץ לִפְנֵ֣י הָֽאֱלֹהִ֑ים וַתִּמָּלֵ֥א הָאָ֖רֶץ חָמָֽס: 6:12 וַיַּ֧רְא אֱלֹהִ֛ים אֶת־הָאָ֖רֶץ וְהִנֵּ֣ה נִשְׁחָ֑תָה כִּֽי־הִשְׁחִ֧ית כָּל־בָּשָׂ֛ר אֶת־דַּרְכּ֖וֹ עַל־הָאָֽרֶץ: ס

6:13 וַיֹּ֨אמֶר אֱלֹהִ֜ים לְנֹ֗חַ קֵ֤ץ כָּל־בָּשָׂר֙ בָּ֣א לְפָנַ֔י כִּֽי־מָלְאָ֥ה הָאָ֛רֶץ חָמָ֖ס מִפְּנֵיהֶ֑ם וְהִנְנִ֥י מַשְׁחִיתָ֖ם אֶת־הָאָֽרֶץ: 6:14 עֲשֵׂ֤ה לְךָ֙ תֵּבַ֣ת עֲצֵי־גֹ֔פֶר קִנִּ֖ים תַּֽעֲשֶׂ֣ה אֶת־הַתֵּבָ֑ה וְכָֽפַרְתָּ֥ אֹתָ֛הּ מִבַּ֥יִת וּמִח֖וּץ בַּכֹּֽפֶר: 6:15 וְזֶ֕ה אֲשֶׁ֥ר תַּֽעֲשֶׂ֖ה אֹתָ֑הּ שְׁלֹ֧שׁ מֵא֣וֹת אַמָּ֗ה אֹ֚רֶךְ הַתֵּבָ֔ה חֲמִשִּׁ֤ים אַמָּה֙ רָחְבָּ֔הּ וּשְׁלֹשִׁ֥ים אַמָּ֖ה קֽוֹמָתָֽהּ: 6:16 צֹ֣הַר ׀ תַּֽעֲשֶׂ֣ה לַתֵּבָ֗ה וְאֶל־אַמָּה֙ תְּכַלֶּ֣נָּה מִלְמַ֔עְלָה וּפֶ֥תַח הַתֵּבָ֖ה בְּצִדָּ֣הּ תָּשִׂ֑ים תַּחְתִּיִּ֛ם שְׁנִיִּ֥ם וּשְׁלִשִׁ֖ים תַּֽעֲשֶֽׂהָ: 6:17 וַֽאֲנִ֗י הִנְנִי֩ מֵבִ֨יא אֶת־הַמַּבּ֥וּל מַ֙יִם֙ עַל־הָאָ֔רֶץ לְשַׁחֵ֣ת כָּל־בָּשָׂ֗ר אֲשֶׁר־בּוֹ֙ ר֣וּחַ חַיִּ֔ים מִתַּ֖חַת הַשָּׁמָ֑יִם כֹּ֥ל אֲשֶׁר־בָּאָ֖רֶץ יִגְוָֽע: 6:18 וַהֲקִמֹתִ֥י אֶת־בְּרִיתִ֖י אִתָּ֑ךְ וּבָאתָ֙ אֶל־הַתֵּבָ֔ה אַתָּ֕ה וּבָנֶ֛יךָ וְאִשְׁתְּךָ֥ וּנְשֵֽׁי־בָנֶ֖יךָ אִתָּֽךְ: 6:19 וּמִכָּל־הָ֠חַי מִֽכָּל־בָּשָׂ֞ר שְׁנַ֧יִם מִכֹּ֛ל תָּבִ֥יא אֶל־הַתֵּבָ֖ה לְהַחֲיֹ֣ת אִתָּ֑ךְ זָכָ֥ר וּנְקֵבָ֖ה יִֽהְיֽוּ: 6:20 מֵהָע֣וֹף לְמִינֵ֗הוּ וּמִן־הַבְּהֵמָה֙ לְמִינָ֔הּ מִכֹּ֛ל רֶ֥מֶשׂ הָֽאֲדָמָ֖ה לְמִינֵ֑הוּ שְׁנַ֧יִם מִכֹּ֛ל יָבֹ֥אוּ אֵלֶ֖יךָ לְהַֽחֲיֽוֹת: 6:21 וְאַתָּ֣ה קַח־לְךָ֗ מִכָּל־מַֽאֲכָל֙ אֲשֶׁ֣ר יֵֽאָכֵ֔ל וְאָֽסַפְתָּ֖ אֵלֶ֑יךָ וְהָיָ֥ה לְךָ֛ וְלָהֶ֖ם לְאָכְלָֽה: 6:22 וַיַּ֖עַשׂ נֹ֑חַ כְּ֠כֹל אֲשֶׁ֨ר צִוָּ֥ה אֹת֛וֹ אֱלֹהִ֖ים כֵּ֥ן עָשָֽׂה: ס

P also provides a building plan for the ark (reminiscent of his orderly and detailed account of creation in Gen. 1), which J neglected to do, and even reminds Noah to pack food. These details may seem truistic, but the Priestly source wants to emphasize that every action that Noah takes is according to God's command, which is, for P, the essence of righteousness. P also makes this point by using the formula "as God had commanded him, so he did" in verse 22, a phrase that will occur many dozens of times in Priestly texts (see Exodus 39–40 in particular). This formula is not exclusive to P, but it is most prevalent in this source. It is a reflection of the high value that P places upon following the divine plan.

Another important difference between the sources is the number of animals that Noah is supposed to take with him onto the ark. The Yahwistic source in Genesis 7 makes a distinction between pure and non-pure animals that the Priestly source does not, commanding that Noah should bring seven pairs of each pure animal and only two pairs of each non-pure animal. The narrative function of these extra pure animals is to provide fuel for Noah's sacrifice to God in Genesis 8:20, since according to J, the deluge is only forty days long. The Priestly source corrects the Yahwistic narrative by stating that Noah should bring two pairs of each animal onto the ark, regardless of whether the animal is pure or non-pure, and cements this correction by offering it three times: twice in Genesis 7, and above in 6:20, which is meant to trump J's command to Noah by appearing before it. What is at stake in this matter for the Priestly source? In my opinion, P regards the Yahwistic tradition as anachronistic, since for P, the laws regarding the purity of animals are not given until Sinai (for J, it seems that purity and non-purity are intrinsic categories). P is aware of the ramifications of this correction, and thus provides sufficient time during the deluge—one year—for the animals to reproduce, thereby providing Noah with the animals he needs for his thanksgiving offering.

GENESIS 6: CANON (J + P + B)

6:1 It happened, that when people began to multiply upon the face of the earth, daughters were born to them. 6:2 God's sons saw that the daughters of the humans were beautiful, and they took wives for themselves from anywhere they chose. 6:3 Yahweh said, "My Spirit will not strive with man forever, for he is flesh; and thus his days will be one hundred twenty years." 6:4 The Nephilim were in the earth in those days, and also after that, when God's sons copulated with men's daughters, who bore them children. Those were the mighty heroes of old, men of renown.

6:5 Yahweh saw that the wickedness of the human being was great upon the earth, and all the thoughts emanating from his heart were only evil all the time. 6:6 Yahweh regretted that he had made human beings upon the earth, and it grieved his heart. 6:7 Yahweh said, "I will destroy the humans whom I have created from the face of the earth; men, along with animals, creeping things, and the birds of the sky; for I regret having made them." 8 But Noah found favor in Yahweh's eyes.

GENESIS 6: CANON (J + P + B) HEBREW

6:1 וַֽיְהִי֙ כִּֽי־הֵחֵ֣ל הָֽאָדָ֔ם לָרֹ֖ב עַל־פְּנֵ֣י הָֽאֲדָמָ֑ה וּבָנ֖וֹת יֻלְּד֥וּ לָהֶֽם׃ 6:2 וַיִּרְא֤וּ בְנֵי־הָֽאֱלֹהִים֙ אֶת־בְּנ֣וֹת הָֽאָדָ֔ם כִּ֥י טֹבֹ֖ת הֵ֑נָּה וַיִּקְח֤וּ לָהֶם֙ נָשִׁ֔ים מִכֹּ֖ל אֲשֶׁ֥ר בָּחָֽרוּ׃ 6:3 וַיֹּ֣אמֶר יְהוָ֗ה לֹֽא־יָד֨וֹן רוּחִ֤י בָֽאָדָם֙ לְעֹלָ֔ם בְּשַׁגַּ֖ם ה֣וּא בָשָׂ֑ר וְהָי֣וּ יָמָ֔יו מֵאָ֥ה וְעֶשְׂרִ֖ים שָׁנָֽה׃ 6:4 הַנְּפִלִ֞ים הָי֣וּ בָאָרֶץ֮ בַּיָּמִ֣ים הָהֵם֒ וְגַ֣ם אַֽחֲרֵי־כֵ֗ן אֲשֶׁ֨ר יָבֹ֜אוּ בְּנֵ֤י הָֽאֱלֹהִים֙ אֶל־בְּנ֣וֹת הָֽאָדָ֔ם וְיָלְד֖וּ לָהֶ֑ם הֵ֧מָּה הַגִּבֹּרִ֛ים אֲשֶׁ֥ר מֵעוֹלָ֖ם אַנְשֵׁ֥י הַשֵּֽׁם׃ פ

6:5 וַיַּ֣רְא יְהוָ֔ה כִּ֥י רַבָּ֛ה רָעַ֥ת הָאָדָ֖ם בָּאָ֑רֶץ וְכָל־יֵ֨צֶר֙ מַחְשְׁבֹ֣ת לִבּ֔וֹ רַ֥ק רַ֖ע כָּל־הַיּֽוֹם׃ 6:6 וַיִּנָּ֣חֶם יְהוָ֔ה כִּֽי־עָשָׂ֥ה אֶת־הָֽאָדָ֖ם בָּאָ֑רֶץ וַיִּתְעַצֵּ֖ב אֶל־לִבּֽוֹ׃ 6:7 וַיֹּ֣אמֶר יְהוָ֗ה אֶמְחֶ֨ה אֶת־הָאָדָ֤ם אֲשֶׁר־בָּרָ֨אתִי֙ מֵעַל֙ פְּנֵ֣י הָֽאֲדָמָ֔ה מֵֽאָדָם֙ עַד־בְּהֵמָ֔ה עַד־רֶ֖מֶשׂ וְעַד־ע֣וֹף הַשָּׁמָ֑יִם כִּ֥י נִחַ֖מְתִּי כִּ֥י עֲשִׂיתִֽם׃ 6:8 וְנֹ֕חַ מָ֥צָא חֵ֖ן בְּעֵינֵ֥י יְהוָֽה׃ פ

GENESIS 6: CANON (J + P + B) – CONTINUED

6:9 These are the generations of Noah. Noah was a righteous man, blameless among the people of his time. Noah walked with God. 6:10 Noah fathered three sons: Shem, Ham, and Japheth. 6:11 The earth was corrupt before God, and the earth was filled with violence. 6:12 God saw the earth, that it was corrupt, for all flesh on earth had become corrupt.

6:13 God said to Noah, "The end of all flesh has come for I (have decreed it), since the earth is filled with violence because of them. Behold, I will destroy them with the earth. 6:14 Make an ark of gopher wood. You shall partition the ark, and shall seal it inside and outside with pitch. 6:15 This is how you shall make it. The length of the ark will be three hundred cubits, its breadth fifty cubits, and its height thirty cubits. 6:16 You shall construct a window for the ark, which you shall place a cubit above. You shall set the door of the ship in its side. You shall make it with lower, second, and third decks.

6:17 I will then bring a flood of waters upon this earth, to destroy all breathing creatures from under the sky. Everything that is upon the earth will die. 6:18 But I will establish my covenant with you. You shall come into the ship, you, your sons, your wife, and your sons' wives with you. 6:19 Of every living thing of all flesh, you shall bring two of every sort into the ship, to keep them alive with you. They shall be male and female. 6:20 Of species of birds, of species of livestock, of every species of creepers upon the ground, two of every sort shall come with you, to keep them alive. 6:21 Take with you of all food that is eaten, and gather it to yourself; and it will sustain both you and them." 6:22 Thus Noah did. As God had commanded him, so he did.

What B adds

Verses 1–4 add the very racy myth of the fallen angels to the flood account. This section is clearly distinct from the rest of the chapter. For one thing, it seems strange that God would choose this moment to limit the lifespan of human beings, given that he is about to destroy them all. Moreover, this limited lifespan does not accord with Noah's lifespan of 600 years in the subsequent chapter, nor with the lifespans of his children in Genesis 11. The fallen angel myth is also contrary (directly opposed, in fact) to the monotheistic tenor of the Genesis narratives in both J and P, and their decided lack of an angelic hierarchy or demigod figures. In fact, God is not described as having sons in any other part of the Pentateuch, let alone sons who have sex with human beings.

GENESIS 6: CANON (J + P + B) HEBREW – CONTINUED

6:9 אֵ֚לֶּה תּוֹלְדֹ֣ת נֹ֔חַ נֹ֗חַ אִ֥ישׁ צַדִּ֛יק תָּמִ֥ים הָיָ֖ה בְּדֹרֹתָ֑יו אֶת־הָֽאֱלֹהִ֖ים הִֽתְהַלֶּךְ־נֹֽחַ׃ 6:10 וַיּ֥וֹלֶד נֹ֖חַ שְׁלֹשָׁ֣ה בָנִ֑ים אֶת־שֵׁ֖ם אֶת־חָ֥ם וְאֶת־יָֽפֶת׃ 6:11 וַתִּשָּׁחֵ֥ת הָאָ֖רֶץ לִפְנֵ֣י הָאֱלֹהִ֑ים וַתִּמָּלֵ֥א הָאָ֖רֶץ חָמָֽס׃ 6:12 וַיַּ֧רְא אֱלֹהִ֛ים אֶת־הָאָ֖רֶץ וְהִנֵּ֣ה נִשְׁחָ֑תָה כִּֽי־הִשְׁחִ֧ית כָּל־בָּשָׂ֛ר אֶת־דַּרְכּ֖וֹ עַל־הָאָֽרֶץ׃ ס

6:13 וַיֹּ֨אמֶר אֱלֹהִ֜ים לְנֹ֗חַ קֵ֤ץ כָּל־בָּשָׂר֙ בָּ֣א לְפָנַ֔י כִּֽי־מָלְאָ֥ה הָאָ֛רֶץ חָמָ֖ס מִפְּנֵיהֶ֑ם וְהִנְנִ֥י מַשְׁחִיתָ֖ם אֶת־הָאָֽרֶץ׃ 6:14 עֲשֵׂ֤ה לְךָ֙ תֵּבַ֣ת עֲצֵי־גֹ֔פֶר קִנִּ֖ים תַּֽעֲשֶׂ֣ה אֶת־הַתֵּבָ֑ה וְכָֽפַרְתָּ֥ אֹתָ֛הּ מִבַּ֥יִת וּמִח֖וּץ בַּכֹּֽפֶר׃ 6:15 וְזֶ֕ה אֲשֶׁ֥ר תַּֽעֲשֶׂ֖ה אֹתָ֑הּ שְׁלֹ֧שׁ מֵא֣וֹת אַמָּ֗ה אֹ֚רֶךְ הַתֵּבָ֔ה חֲמִשִּׁ֤ים אַמָּה֙ רָחְבָּ֔הּ וּשְׁלֹשִׁ֥ים אַמָּ֖ה קֽוֹמָתָֽהּ׃ 6:16 צֹ֣הַר ׀ תַּֽעֲשֶׂ֣ה לַתֵּבָ֗ה וְאֶל־אַמָּה֙ תְּכַלֶ֣נָּה מִלְמַ֔עְלָה וּפֶ֥תַח הַתֵּבָ֖ה בְּצִדָּ֣הּ תָּשִׂ֑ים תַּחְתִּיִּ֛ם שְׁנִיִּ֥ם וּשְׁלִשִׁ֖ים תַּֽעֲשֶֽׂהָ׃ 6:17 וַאֲנִ֗י הִנְנִי֩ מֵבִ֨יא אֶת־הַמַּבּ֥וּל מַ֨יִם֙ עַל־הָאָ֔רֶץ לְשַׁחֵ֣ת כָּל־בָּשָׂ֗ר אֲשֶׁר־בּוֹ֙ ר֣וּחַ חַיִּ֔ים מִתַּ֖חַת הַשָּׁמָ֑יִם כֹּ֥ל אֲשֶׁר־בָּאָ֖רֶץ יִגְוָֽע׃ 6:18 וַהֲקִמֹתִ֥י אֶת־בְּרִיתִ֖י אִתָּ֑ךְ וּבָאתָ֙ אֶל־הַתֵּבָ֔ה אַתָּ֕ה וּבָנֶי֛ךָ וְאִשְׁתְּךָ֥ וּנְשֵֽׁי־בָנֶ֖יךָ אִתָּֽךְ׃ 6:19 וּמִכָּל־הָ֠חַי מִֽכָּל־בָּשָׂ֞ר שְׁנַ֧יִם מִכֹּ֛ל תָּבִ֥יא אֶל־הַתֵּבָ֖ה לְהַחֲיֹ֣ת אִתָּ֑ךְ זָכָ֥ר וּנְקֵבָ֖ה יִֽהְיֽוּ׃ 6:20 מֵהָע֣וֹף לְמִינֵ֗הוּ וּמִן־הַבְּהֵמָה֙ לְמִינָ֔הּ מִכֹּ֛ל רֶ֥מֶשׂ הָֽאֲדָמָ֖ה לְמִינֵ֑הוּ שְׁנַ֧יִם מִכֹּ֛ל יָבֹ֥אוּ אֵלֶ֖יךָ לְהַֽחֲיֽוֹת׃ 6:21 וְאַתָּ֣ה קַח־לְךָ֗ מִכָּל־מַֽאֲכָל֙ אֲשֶׁ֣ר יֵֽאָכֵ֔ל וְאָסַפְתָּ֖ אֵלֶ֑יךָ וְהָיָ֥ה לְךָ֛ וְלָהֶ֖ם לְאָכְלָֽה׃ 6:22 וַיַּ֖עַשׂ נֹ֑חַ כְּ֠כֹל אֲשֶׁ֨ר צִוָּ֥ה אֹת֛וֹ אֱלֹהִ֖ים כֵּ֥ן עָשָֽׂה׃ ס

It thus makes sense to attribute this myth to the Bridger, a post-exilic author, later than both J and P, who included elements like these to add an international flavor to Biblical stories and make them relevant to a wider, non-Judaic audience. His distinctive disregard for Israelite theological norms is found here and in his other additions, including in Exodus 4, in which an angel tries to kill Moses. Further evidence for B's authorship of this section is that his typical signature, a passive form of the verb "yalad" ("to give birth"), appears in verse 1.

THE CREATION STORY: GENESIS 7

The Lord repeats His command to Noah to build the ark, this time adding a distinction between pure and impure animals, commanding Noah to bring with him seven pairs of all pure animals and two pairs of everything else. God opens up the heavens and the earth, unleashing heavy rains and waters from the depths. After forty days, the rains stop, but the water level continues to rise for a further 150 days. The water covers even the highest mountains, and all creatures on earth are killed.

GENESIS 7: THE J KERNEL

7:1 Yahweh said to Noah, "Come with all of your household into the ark, for I have seen that you are righteous before me in this generation. 7:2 You shall take seven pairs of every clean animal with you, the male and its female mate. Of the animals that are not clean, take two (each), of the male and its female mate. 7:3 Also of the birds of the sky, seven and seven, male and female, to keep seed alive on the surface of all the earth. 7:4 In seven days, I will cause it to rain on the earth for forty days and forty nights. Every living thing that I have made, I will destroy from the face of the earth."

7:5 Noah did everything that Yahweh commanded him.

7:7 Noah went into the ship with his sons, his wife, and his sons' wives, anticipating the waters of the flood. 7:10 Seven days later, the waters of the flood swept over the earth. 7:12 It rained on the earth for forty days and forty nights.

7:16 And Yahweh shut him in. 7:19 The waters swelled exceedingly on the earth. All the high mountains that were under the whole sky were covered. 7:23 He blotted out every living thing that was on the face of the earth, including people, livestock, creeping things, and birds of the sky.

GENESIS 7: THE J KERNEL (HEBREW)

7:1 וַיֹּאמֶר יְהוָה֙ לְנֹ֔חַ בֹּֽא־אַתָּ֥ה וְכָל־בֵּיתְךָ֖ אֶל־הַתֵּבָ֑ה כִּֽי־אֹתְךָ֥ רָאִ֛יתִי צַדִּ֥יק לְפָנַ֖י בַּדּ֥וֹר הַזֶּֽה: 7:2 מִכֹּ֣ל ׀ הַבְּהֵמָ֣ה הַטְּהוֹרָ֗ה תִּֽקַּח־לְךָ֛ שִׁבְעָ֥ה שִׁבְעָ֖ה אִ֣ישׁ וְאִשְׁתּ֑וֹ וּמִן־הַבְּהֵמָ֡ה אֲ֠שֶׁר לֹ֣א טְהֹרָ֥ה הִ֛וא שְׁנַ֖יִם אִ֥ישׁ וְאִשְׁתּֽוֹ: 7:3 גַּ֣ם מֵע֧וֹף הַשָּׁמַ֛יִם שִׁבְעָ֥ה שִׁבְעָ֖ה זָכָ֣ר וּנְקֵבָ֑ה לְחַיּ֥וֹת זֶ֖רַע עַל־פְּנֵ֥י כָל־הָאָֽרֶץ: 7:4 כִּי֩ לְיָמִ֨ים ע֜וֹד שִׁבְעָ֗ה אָֽנֹכִי֙ מַמְטִ֣יר עַל־הָאָ֔רֶץ אַרְבָּעִ֣ים י֔וֹם וְאַרְבָּעִ֖ים לָ֑יְלָה וּמָחִ֗יתִי אֶֽת־כָּל־הַיְקוּם֙ אֲשֶׁ֣ר עָשִׂ֔יתִי מֵעַ֖ל פְּנֵ֥י הָֽאֲדָמָֽה: 7:5 וַיַּ֖עַשׂ נֹ֑חַ כְּכֹ֥ל אֲשֶׁר־צִוָּ֖הוּ יְהוָֽה: 7:7 וַיָּ֣בֹא נֹ֔חַ וּ֠בָנָיו וְאִשְׁתּ֧וֹ וּנְשֵֽׁי־בָנָ֛יו אִתּ֖וֹ אֶל־הַתֵּבָ֑ה מִפְּנֵ֖י מֵ֥י הַמַּבּֽוּל: 7:10 וַֽיְהִ֖י לְשִׁבְעַ֣ת הַיָּמִ֑ים וּמֵ֣י הַמַּבּ֔וּל הָי֖וּ עַל־הָאָֽרֶץ: 7:12 וַֽיְהִ֥י הַגֶּ֖שֶׁם עַל־הָאָ֑רֶץ אַרְבָּעִ֣ים י֔וֹם וְאַרְבָּעִ֖ים לָֽיְלָה: 7:16 וַיִּסְגֹּ֥ר יְהוָ֖ה בַּֽעֲדֽוֹ: 7:19 וְהַמַּ֗יִם גָּֽבְר֛וּ מְאֹ֥ד מְאֹ֖ד עַל־הָאָ֑רֶץ וַיְכֻסּ֗וּ כָּל־הֶֽהָרִים֙ הַגְּבֹהִ֔ים אֲשֶׁר־תַּ֖חַת כָּל־הַשָּׁמָֽיִם: 7:23 וַיִּ֜מַח אֶֽת־כָּל־הַיְק֣וּם ׀ אֲשֶׁ֣ר ׀ עַל־פְּנֵ֣י הָֽאֲדָמָ֗ה מֵֽאָדָ֤ם עַד־בְּהֵמָה֙ עַד־רֶ֣מֶשׂ֙ וְעַד־ע֣וֹף הַשָּׁמַ֔יִם וַיִּמָּח֖וּ מִן־הָאָ֑רֶץ וַיִּשָּׁ֧אֶר אַךְ־נֹ֛חַ וַֽאֲשֶׁ֥ר אִתּ֖וֹ בַּתֵּבָֽה:

J's flood narrative is among the more laconic of his accounts in Genesis; the story only gets really interesting after Noah leaves the ark, at which point he essentially bribes the Lord with sacrifices to never again wipe out His creations. The very abrupt switches from Yahweh to Elohim, most apparent in verse 16, help to sharpen the distinctions between the J kernel and P's additions. Note also the different verbs used in J and P for the destruction of life. J tells us in verse 23, and earlier in 6:7, that God "blotted out" every living thing. For P, the description of life's termination is typically less anthropomorphic, and the words used are passive—the animals simply "die" or "perish," without any mention of direct action on God's part. This is consistent with P's portrayal of God as more remote and less human than He is in J.

GENESIS 7: CANON (J + P)

7:1 Yahweh said to Noah, "Come with all of your household into the ark, for I have seen that you are righteous before me in this generation. 7:2 You shall take seven pairs of every clean animal with you, the male and its female mate. Of the animals that are not clean, take two (each), of the male and its female mate. 7:3 Also of the birds of the sky, seven and seven, male and female, to keep seed alive on the surface of all the earth. 7:4 In seven days, I will cause it to rain on the earth for forty days and forty nights. Every living thing that I have made, I will destroy from the face of the earth."

7:5 Noah did everything that Yahweh commanded him.

7:6 Noah was six hundred years old when the flood of waters swept over the earth. 7:7 Noah went into the ship with his sons, his wife, and his sons' wives, anticipating the waters of the flood. 7:8 Clean animals, animals that are not clean, birds, and everything that creeps on the ground 7:9 went by pairs to Noah into the ark, male and female, as God had commanded Noah. 7:10 Seven days later, the waters of the flood swept over the earth. 7:11 In the six hundredth year of Noah's life, in the second month, on the seventeenth day of the month, on the same day all the fountains of the great deep burst forth, and the sky's apertures were opened. 7:12 It rained on the earth for forty days and forty nights.

7:13 On the same day Noah, and Shem, Ham, and Japheth, the sons of Noah, and Noah's wife, and his sons' three wives, entered into the ark with them; 7:14 they, and every animal according to its species, all the livestock according to their species, every creeping thing that creeps on the earth according to its species, and every bird according to its species, every bird of every sort. 7:15 They went to Noah into the ark, by pairs, all flesh with the breath of life in them. 7:16 Those who went in, male and female of all flesh, went in as God had commanded him; and Yahweh shut him in.

GENESIS 7: CANON (J + P) HEBREW

7:1 ‏וַיֹּאמֶר יְהוָה לְנֹחַ בֹּא־אַתָּה וְכָל־בֵּיתְךָ אֶל־הַתֵּבָה כִּי־אֹתְךָ רָאִיתִי צַדִּיק לְפָנַי בַּדּוֹר הַזֶּה: 7:2 מִכֹּל ׀ הַבְּהֵמָה הַטְּהוֹרָה תִּקַּח־לְךָ שִׁבְעָה שִׁבְעָה אִישׁ וְאִשְׁתּוֹ וּמִן־הַבְּהֵמָה אֲשֶׁר לֹא טְהֹרָה הִוא שְׁנַיִם אִישׁ וְאִשְׁתּוֹ: 7:3 גַּם מֵעוֹף הַשָּׁמַיִם שִׁבְעָה שִׁבְעָה זָכָר וּנְקֵבָה לְחַיּוֹת זֶרַע עַל־פְּנֵי כָל־הָאָרֶץ: 7:4 כִּי לְיָמִים עוֹד שִׁבְעָה אָנֹכִי מַמְטִיר עַל־הָאָרֶץ אַרְבָּעִים יוֹם וְאַרְבָּעִים לָיְלָה וּמָחִיתִי אֶת־כָּל־הַיְקוּם אֲשֶׁר עָשִׂיתִי מֵעַל פְּנֵי הָאֲדָמָה: 7:5 וַיַּעַשׂ נֹחַ כְּכֹל אֲשֶׁר־צִוָּהוּ יְהוָה: 7:6 וְנֹחַ בֶּן־שֵׁשׁ מֵאוֹת שָׁנָה וְהַמַּבּוּל הָיָה מַיִם עַל־הָאָרֶץ: 7:7 וַיָּבֹא נֹחַ וּבָנָיו וְאִשְׁתּוֹ וּנְשֵׁי־בָנָיו אִתּוֹ אֶל־הַתֵּבָה מִפְּנֵי מֵי הַמַּבּוּל: 7:8 מִן־הַבְּהֵמָה הַטְּהוֹרָה וּמִן־הַבְּהֵמָה אֲשֶׁר אֵינֶנָּה טְהֹרָה וּמִן־הָעוֹף וְכֹל אֲשֶׁר־רֹמֵשׂ עַל־הָאֲדָמָה: 7:9 שְׁנַיִם שְׁנַיִם בָּאוּ אֶל־נֹחַ אֶל־הַתֵּבָה זָכָר וּנְקֵבָה כַּאֲשֶׁר צִוָּה אֱלֹהִים אֶת־נֹחַ: 7:10 וַיְהִי לְשִׁבְעַת הַיָּמִים וּמֵי הַמַּבּוּל הָיוּ עַל־הָאָרֶץ: 7:11 בִּשְׁנַת שֵׁשׁ־מֵאוֹת שָׁנָה לְחַיֵּי־נֹחַ בַּחֹדֶשׁ הַשֵּׁנִי בְּשִׁבְעָה־עָשָׂר יוֹם לַחֹדֶשׁ בַּיּוֹם הַזֶּה נִבְקְעוּ כָּל־מַעְיְנֹת תְּהוֹם רַבָּה וַאֲרֻבֹּת הַשָּׁמַיִם נִפְתָּחוּ: 7:12 וַיְהִי הַגֶּשֶׁם עַל־הָאָרֶץ אַרְבָּעִים יוֹם וְאַרְבָּעִים לָיְלָה: 7:13 בְּעֶצֶם הַיּוֹם הַזֶּה בָּא נֹחַ וְשֵׁם־וְחָם וָיֶפֶת בְּנֵי־נֹחַ וְאֵשֶׁת נֹחַ וּשְׁלֹשֶׁת נְשֵׁי־בָנָיו אִתָּם אֶל־הַתֵּבָה: 7:14 הֵמָּה וְכָל־הַחַיָּה לְמִינָהּ וְכָל־הַבְּהֵמָה לְמִינָהּ וְכָל־הָרֶמֶשׂ הָרֹמֵשׂ עַל־הָאָרֶץ לְמִינֵהוּ וְכָל־הָעוֹף לְמִינֵהוּ כֹּל צִפּוֹר כָּל־כָּנָף: 7:15 וַיָּבֹאוּ אֶל־נֹחַ אֶל־הַתֵּבָה שְׁנַיִם שְׁנַיִם מִכָּל־הַבָּשָׂר אֲשֶׁר־בּוֹ רוּחַ חַיִּים: 7:16 וְהַבָּאִים זָכָר וּנְקֵבָה מִכָּל־בָּשָׂר בָּאוּ כַּאֲשֶׁר צִוָּה אֹתוֹ אֱלֹהִים וַיִּסְגֹּר יְהוָה בַּעֲדוֹ:

GENESIS 7: CANON (J + P) – CONTINUED

7:17 The flood lasted for forty days on the earth. The waters increased, and lifted up the ark, and it rose above the earth. 7:18 The waters swelled, and increased greatly on the earth; and the ark floated on the surface of the waters. ==7:19 The waters swelled exceedingly on the earth. All the high mountains that were under the whole sky were covered.== 7:20 The waters rose fifteen cubits upward, and the mountains were covered. 7:21 All flesh that moved upon the earth died, including birds, livestock, animals, every creeping thing that creeps upon the earth, and every person. 7:22 All in whose nostrils was the animating breath of life, all who were on dry land, died. ==7:23 He blotted out every living thing that was on the face of the earth, including people, livestock, creeping things, and birds of the sky.== They were destroyed from the earth. Only Noah was left, and those who were with him in the ark. 7:24 The waters increased upon the earth for one hundred fifty days.

What P Adds

One of the most striking divergences between P and J in this chapter is in the length of the flood. According to J, the flood lasts for forty days (see vss. 4 and 12), after which the waters begin to subside. According to P, however, the flood lasts for an entire year, and is comprised of six distinct stages that are meticulously chronicled in this chapter and the next. P integrates J's forty days of rain into his account by making them the first stage of the flood. Following the rain, there is an "increase of water upon the earth" from unspecified sources that lasts 150 days, after which the water level finally begins to go down.

P and J also disagree, here and in Genesis 6, about the number of animals entering the ark. In 6:19–20 and in 7:8–9, P insists that only two pairs of each animal are brought onto the ark, implying that the dichotomy between pure and impure does not apply (in contradiction to J in vss. 2 and 3). Not to leave this detail to chance, P repeats his version of events at greater length in verses 13–15. After the threefold repetitions of P's universal two-by-two idea, only a discerning reader would recall that this isn't the only version of events. Another divergence not left to chance is in the number of Noah's sons, whose names P lists again in verse 13. This repetition is meant to undermine J's figure of four sons in Genesis 9.

Overall, the flood story offers a prime example of P's penchant for detail. P twice mentions Noah's age (vss. 6 and 11), and twice the number of animals going into the ark (vss. 8 and 13–15); adds the date of the flood (vs. 11), his version of the number of Noah's children (vs. 13), and an exact figure for the water level (vs. 20); and repeats the duration of the rain (vs. 17) in counterpoint to his total length for the flood (vs. 24). This barrage of data, which the human mind is hardwired to accept over approximate figures or narrative descriptions, effectively overwhelms J's original text.

GENESIS 7: CANON (J + P) HEBREW – CONTINUED

7:17 וַיְהִי הַמַּבּוּל אַרְבָּעִים יוֹם עַל־הָאָרֶץ וַיִּרְבּוּ הַמַּיִם וַיִּשְׂאוּ אֶת־הַתֵּבָה וַתָּרָם מֵעַל הָאָרֶץ: 7:18 וַיִּגְבְּרוּ הַמַּיִם וַיִּרְבּוּ מְאֹד עַל־הָאָרֶץ וַתֵּלֶךְ הַתֵּבָה עַל־פְּנֵי הַמָּיִם: <mark>7:19 וְהַמַּיִם גָּבְרוּ מְאֹד מְאֹד עַל־הָאָרֶץ וַיְכֻסּוּ כָּל־הֶהָרִים הַגְּבֹהִים אֲשֶׁר־תַּחַת כָּל־הַשָּׁמָיִם:</mark> 7:20 חֲמֵשׁ עֶשְׂרֵה אַמָּה מִלְמַעְלָה גָּבְרוּ הַמָּיִם וַיְכֻסּוּ הֶהָרִים: 7:21 וַיִּגְוַע כָּל־בָּשָׂר ׀ הָרֹמֵשׂ עַל־הָאָרֶץ בָּעוֹף וּבַבְּהֵמָה וּבַחַיָּה וּבְכָל־הַשֶּׁרֶץ הַשֹּׁרֵץ עַל־הָאָרֶץ וְכֹל הָאָדָם: 7:22 כֹּל אֲשֶׁר נִשְׁמַת־רוּחַ חַיִּים בְּאַפָּיו מִכֹּל אֲשֶׁר בֶּחָרָבָה מֵתוּ: <mark>7:23 וַיִּמַח אֶת־כָּל־הַיְקוּם ׀ אֲשֶׁר ׀ עַל־פְּנֵי הָאֲדָמָה מֵאָדָם עַד־בְּהֵמָה עַד־רֶמֶשׂ וְעַד־עוֹף הַשָּׁמַיִם וַיִּמָּחוּ מִן־הָאָרֶץ וַיִשָּׁאֶר אַךְ־נֹחַ וַאֲשֶׁר אִתּוֹ בַּתֵּבָה:</mark> 7:24 וַיִּגְבְּרוּ הַמַּיִם עַל־הָאָרֶץ חֲמִשִּׁים וּמְאַת יוֹם:

That being said, P also inserts a piece of poetry here, which could easily be overlooked by the reader of P who is accustomed to numerical data and lists. "On that day," P writes, "all the fountains of the great deep burst forth, and the sky's apertures were opened" (vs. 11). Here, P references the mythic reservoir that he first mentions in his account of the first day of creation (in J, there is no mention of these depths), and emphasizes that although these reservoirs may have predated the world, they are still solidly under God's control.

THE CREATION STORY: GENESIS 8

The waters finally begin to subside, and Noah sends out first a raven, and then a dove to search for dry land. When the dove returns with an olive branch in her mouth, Noah knows that the flood has truly ended. After Noah leaves the ark, he sacrifices some of the pure animals to the Lord, and the Lord, pleased with Noah's offering, promises to never again bring a flood that would destroy all living things.

GENESIS 8: THE J KERNEL

8:6 It happened that after forty days, Noah opened the window of the ark which he had made, 8:7 and he sent out a raven. It went back and forth, until the waters dried up from the earth. 8:8 He sent out a dove, to see if the waters were abated from the face the earth, 8:9 but the dove found no place to rest her feet, and she returned to him, to the ark; for the waters were upon the surface of the entire earth. He put out his hand, and took her, and brought her to him into the ark. 8:10 He waited yet another seven days, and once again he sent the dove out of the ark. 8:11 The dove came back to him at evening, and, behold, in her mouth was a plucked olive leaf. So Noah knew that the waters were abated from the earth. 8:12 He waited yet another seven days, and sent out the dove; but she didn't return to him again.

8:18 Noah with his sons, his wife, and his sons' wives with him 8:19 went out of the ark.

8:20 Noah built an altar to Yahweh, and took of every clean animal, and of every clean bird, and offered burnt offerings on the altar. 8:21 Yahweh smelled the pleasant aroma. Yahweh said in his heart, "I will never again curse the ground because of human beings, because the ruminations of human beings' hearts is evil from their youth; neither will I ever again strike everything living, as I have done. 8:22 While the earth endures, seed time and harvest, and cold and heat, and summer and winter, and day and night shall not cease."

GENESIS 8: THE J KERNEL (HEBREW)

8:6 וַיְהִ֕י מִקֵּ֖ץ אַרְבָּעִ֣ים י֑וֹם וַיִּפְתַּ֣ח נֹ֔חַ אֶת־חַלּ֥וֹן הַתֵּבָ֖ה אֲשֶׁ֥ר עָשָֽׂה: 8:7 וַיְשַׁלַּ֖ח אֶת־הָֽעֹרֵ֑ב וַיֵּצֵ֤א יָצוֹא֙ וָשׁ֔וֹב עַד־יְבֹ֥שֶׁת הַמַּ֖יִם מֵעַ֥ל הָאָֽרֶץ: 8:8 וַיְשַׁלַּ֥ח אֶת־הַיּוֹנָ֖ה מֵאִתּ֑וֹ לִרְאוֹת֙ הֲקַ֣לּוּ הַמַּ֔יִם מֵעַ֖ל פְּנֵ֥י הָֽאֲדָמָֽה: 8:9 וְלֹֽא־מָצְאָה֩ הַיּוֹנָ֨ה מָנ֜וֹחַ לְכַף־רַגְלָ֗הּ וַתָּ֤שָׁב אֵלָיו֙ אֶל־הַתֵּבָ֔ה כִּי־מַ֖יִם עַל־פְּנֵ֣י כָל־הָאָ֑רֶץ וַיִּשְׁלַ֤ח יָדוֹ֙ וַיִּקָּחֶ֔הָ וַיָּבֵ֥א אֹתָ֛הּ אֵלָ֖יו אֶל־הַתֵּבָֽה: 8:10 וַיָּ֣חֶל ע֔וֹד שִׁבְעַ֥ת יָמִ֖ים אֲחֵרִ֑ים וַיֹּ֛סֶף שַׁלַּ֥ח אֶת־הַיּוֹנָ֖ה מִן־הַתֵּבָֽה: 8:11 וַתָּבֹ֨א אֵלָ֤יו הַיּוֹנָה֙ לְעֵ֣ת עֶ֔רֶב וְהִנֵּ֥ה עֲלֵה־זַ֖יִת טָרָ֣ף בְּפִ֑יהָ וַיֵּ֣דַע נֹ֔חַ כִּי־קַ֥לּוּ הַמַּ֖יִם מֵעַ֥ל הָאָֽרֶץ: 8:12 וַיִּיָּ֣חֶל ע֔וֹד שִׁבְעַ֥ת יָמִ֖ים אֲחֵרִ֑ים וַיְשַׁלַּח֙ אֶת־הַיּוֹנָ֔ה וְלֹֽא־יָסְפָ֥ה שׁוּב־אֵלָ֖יו עֽוֹד:

8:18 וַיֵּ֖צֵא־נֹ֑חַ וּבָנָ֛יו וְאִשְׁתּ֥וֹ וּנְשֵֽׁי־בָנָ֖יו אִתּֽוֹ: 8:19 מִן־הַתֵּבָֽה:

8:20 וַיִּ֥בֶן נֹ֛חַ מִזְבֵּ֖חַ לַֽיהוָ֑ה וַיִּקַּ֞ח מִכֹּ֣ל ׀ הַבְּהֵמָ֣ה הַטְּהוֹרָ֗ה וּמִכֹּל֙ הָע֣וֹף הַטָּהֹ֔ר וַיַּ֥עַל עֹלֹ֖ת בַּמִּזְבֵּֽחַ: 8:21 וַיָּ֣רַח יְהוָה֮ אֶת־רֵ֣יחַ הַנִּיחֹחַ֒ וַיֹּ֨אמֶר יְהוָ֜ה אֶל־לִבּ֗וֹ לֹֽא־אֹ֠סִף לְקַלֵּ֨ל ע֤וֹד אֶת־הָֽאֲדָמָה֙ בַּעֲב֣וּר הָֽאָדָ֔ם כִּ֠י יֵ֣צֶר לֵ֧ב הָאָדָ֛ם רַ֖ע מִנְּעֻרָ֑יו וְלֹֽא־אֹסִ֥ף ע֛וֹד לְהַכּ֥וֹת אֶת־כָּל־חַ֖י כַּאֲשֶׁ֥ר עָשִֽׂיתִי: 8:22 עֹ֖ד כָּל־יְמֵ֣י הָאָ֑רֶץ זֶ֡רַע וְ֠קָצִיר וְקֹ֨ר וָחֹ֜ם וְקַ֧יִץ וָחֹ֛רֶף וְי֥וֹם וָלַ֖יְלָה לֹ֥א יִשְׁבֹּֽתוּ:

In this chapter, J reveals the reason for preserving seven pairs of each pure animal: they were necessary in order for Noah to have something appropriate to sacrifice to the Lord upon leaving the ark. The Lord's promise not to annihilate humanity ever again immediately follows his acceptance of Noah's offering, but it is not articulated verbally to Noah—the Lord makes the promise silently to himself (whereas P deems it necessary to verbalize this as a covenant, and does so in the following chapter). Since J is focused on telling Noah's story, rather than meticulously chronicling events, his account here and in Chapters 6 and 7 includes just a handful of dates and figures.

GENESIS 8: CANON (J + P)

8:1 God remembered Noah, all the animals, and all the livestock that were with him in the ship; and God caused a wind to pass over the earth. The waters subsided. 8:2 The fountains of the deep and the sky's windows were closed, and the rain from the sky abated. 8:3 The waters gradually receded from the earth. At the end of one hundred fifty days the waters had abated. 8:4 The ship rested in the seventh month, on the seventeenth day of the month, on the mountains of Ararat. 8:5 The waters receded continually until the tenth month. In the tenth month, on the first day of the month, the tops of the mountains were visible.

8:6 It happened that after forty days, Noah opened the window of the ark which he had made, 8:7 and he sent out a raven. It went back and forth, until the waters dried up from the earth. 8:8 He sent out a dove, to see if the waters were abated from the face the earth, 8:9 but the dove found no place to rest her feet, and she returned to him, to the ark; for the waters were upon the surface of the entire earth. He put out his hand, and took her, and brought her to him into the ark. 8:10 He waited yet another seven days, and once again he sent the dove out of the ark. 8:11 The dove came back to him at evening, and, behold, in her mouth was a plucked olive leaf. So Noah knew that the waters were abated from the earth. 8:12 He waited yet another seven days, and sent out the dove; but she didn't return to him again.

8:13 It happened that on the six hundred and first year, on the first month, on the first day of the month, the waters were dried up from the earth. Noah removed the covering of the ark, and looked. He saw that the earth's surface was dried. 8:14 In the second month, on the twenty-seventh day of the month, the earth was dry.

8:15 God spoke to Noah, saying, 8:16 "Go out of the ark, you, and your wife, and your sons, and your sons' wives with you. 8:17 Bring out with you every living thing that is with you, all flesh, including birds, livestock, and every creeping thing that creeps upon the earth, that they may breed abundantly upon the earth, and be fruitful, and multiply upon the earth."

GENESIS 8: CANON (J + P) HEBREW

8:1 וַיִּזְכֹּ֤ר אֱלֹהִים֙ אֶת־נֹ֔חַ וְאֵ֤ת כָּל־הַֽחַיָּה֙ וְאֶת־כָּל־הַבְּהֵמָ֔ה אֲשֶׁ֥ר אִתּ֖וֹ בַּתֵּבָ֑ה וַיַּעֲבֵ֨ר אֱלֹהִ֥ים ר֙וּחַ֙ עַל־הָאָ֔רֶץ וַיָּשֹׁ֖כּוּ הַמָּֽיִם׃ 8:2 וַיִּסָּֽכְרוּ֙ מַעְיְנֹ֣ת תְּה֔וֹם וַֽאֲרֻבֹּ֖ת הַשָּׁמָ֑יִם וַיִּכָּלֵ֥א הַגֶּ֖שֶׁם מִן־הַשָּׁמָֽיִם׃ 8:3 וַיָּשֻׁ֧בוּ הַמַּ֛יִם מֵעַ֥ל הָאָ֖רֶץ הָל֣וֹךְ וָשׁ֑וֹב וַיַּחְסְר֣וּ הַמַּ֔יִם מִקְצֵ֕ה חֲמִשִּׁ֥ים וּמְאַ֖ת יֽוֹם׃ 8:4 וַתָּ֤נַח הַתֵּבָה֙ בַּחֹ֣דֶשׁ הַשְּׁבִיעִ֔י בְּשִׁבְעָה־עָשָׂ֥ר י֖וֹם לַחֹ֑דֶשׁ עַ֖ל הָרֵ֥י אֲרָרָֽט׃ 8:5 וְהַמַּ֗יִם הָיוּ֙ הָל֣וֹךְ וְחָס֔וֹר עַ֖ד הַחֹ֣דֶשׁ הָֽעֲשִׂירִ֑י בָּֽעֲשִׂירִי֙ בְּאֶחָ֣ד לַחֹ֔דֶשׁ נִרְא֖וּ רָאשֵׁ֥י הֶֽהָרִֽים׃ <mark>8:6 וַֽיְהִ֕י מִקֵּ֖ץ אַרְבָּעִ֣ים י֑וֹם וַיִּפְתַּ֣ח נֹ֔חַ אֶת־חַלּ֥וֹן הַתֵּבָ֖ה אֲשֶׁ֥ר עָשָֽׂה׃ 8:7 וַיְשַׁלַּ֖ח אֶת־הָֽעֹרֵ֑ב וַיֵּצֵ֤א יָצוֹא֙ וָשׁ֔וֹב עַד־יְבֹ֥שֶׁת הַמַּ֖יִם מֵעַ֥ל הָאָֽרֶץ׃ 8:8 וַיְשַׁלַּ֥ח אֶת־הַיּוֹנָ֖ה מֵאִתּ֑וֹ לִרְאוֹת֙ הֲקַ֣לּוּ הַמַּ֔יִם מֵעַ֖ל פְּנֵ֥י הָֽאֲדָמָֽה׃ 8:9 וְלֹֽא־מָצְאָה֩ הַיּוֹנָ֨ה מָנ֜וֹחַ לְכַף־רַגְלָ֗הּ וַתָּ֤שָׁב אֵלָיו֙ אֶל־הַתֵּבָ֔ה כִּי־מַ֖יִם עַל־פְּנֵ֣י כָל־הָאָ֑רֶץ וַיִּשְׁלַ֤ח יָדוֹ֙ וַיִּקָּחֶ֔הָ וַיָּבֵ֥א אֹתָ֛הּ אֵלָ֖יו אֶל־הַתֵּבָֽה׃ 8:10 וַיָּ֣חֶל ע֔וֹד שִׁבְעַ֥ת יָמִ֖ים אֲחֵרִ֑ים וַיֹּ֛סֶף שַׁלַּ֥ח אֶת־הַיּוֹנָ֖ה מִן־הַתֵּבָֽה׃ 8:11 וַתָּבֹ֨א אֵלָ֤יו הַיּוֹנָה֙ לְעֵ֣ת עֶ֔רֶב וְהִנֵּ֥ה עֲלֵה־זַ֖יִת טָרָ֣ף בְּפִ֑יהָ וַיֵּ֣דַע נֹ֔חַ כִּי־קַ֥לּוּ הַמַּ֖יִם מֵעַ֥ל הָאָֽרֶץ׃ 8:12 וַיִּיָּ֣חֶל ע֔וֹד שִׁבְעַ֥ת יָמִ֖ים אֲחֵרִ֑ים וַיְשַׁלַּח֙ אֶת־הַיּוֹנָ֔ה וְלֹֽא־יָסְפָ֥ה שׁוּב־אֵלָ֖יו עֽוֹד׃</mark> 8:13 וַֽ֠יְהִי בְּאַחַ֨ת וְשֵׁשׁ־מֵא֜וֹת שָׁנָ֗ה בָּֽרִאשׁוֹן֙ בְּאֶחָ֣ד לַחֹ֔דֶשׁ חָֽרְב֥וּ הַמַּ֖יִם מֵעַ֣ל הָאָ֑רֶץ וַיָּ֣סַר נֹ֗חַ אֶת־מִכְסֵ֤ה הַתֵּבָה֙ וַיַּ֔רְא וְהִנֵּ֥ה חָֽרְב֖וּ פְּנֵ֥י הָֽאֲדָמָֽה׃ 8:14 וּבַחֹ֙דֶשׁ֙ הַשֵּׁנִ֔י בְּשִׁבְעָ֧ה וְעֶשְׂרִ֛ים י֖וֹם לַחֹ֑דֶשׁ יָבְשָׁ֖ה הָאָֽרֶץ׃ ס

8:15 וַיְדַבֵּ֥ר אֱלֹהִ֖ים אֶל־נֹ֥חַ לֵאמֹֽר׃ 8:16 צֵ֖א מִן־הַתֵּבָ֑ה אַתָּ֕ה וְאִשְׁתְּךָ֛ וּבָנֶ֥יךָ וּנְשֵֽׁי־בָנֶ֖יךָ אִתָּֽךְ׃ 8:17 כָּל־הַחַיָּ֨ה אֲשֶֽׁר־אִתְּךָ֜ מִכָּל־בָּשָׂ֗ר בָּע֧וֹף וּבַבְּהֵמָ֛ה וּבְכָל־הָרֶ֛מֶשׂ הָרֹמֵ֥שׂ עַל־הָאָ֖רֶץ הוצא הַיְצֵ֣א אִתָּ֑ךְ וְשָֽׁרְצ֣וּ בָאָ֔רֶץ וּפָר֥וּ וְרָב֖וּ עַל־הָאָֽרֶץ׃

GENESIS 8: CANON (J + P) – CONTINUED

8:18 Noah went out, with his sons, his wife, and his sons' wives with him. 8:19 Every animal, every creeping thing, and every bird, whatever moves upon the earth, according to their families, went out of the ark.

8:20 Noah built an altar to Yahweh, and took of every clean animal, and of every clean bird, and offered burnt offerings on the altar. 8:21 Yahweh smelled the pleasant aroma. Yahweh said in his heart, "I will never again curse the ground because of human beings, because the ruminations of human beings' hearts is evil from their youth; neither will I ever again strike everything living, as I have done. 8:22 While the earth endures, seed time and harvest, and cold and heat, and summer and winter, and day and night shall not cease."

What P Adds

The chain of events in P is very orderly: 1) on the 17th day of the 2nd month, the flood begins with rain and underground water for 40 days; 2) the water level rises for 150 days until the 17th day of the 7th month, the peak height of the flood being 15 cubits above mountain level; 3) on the 17th day of the 7th month, the ark rests upon mount Ararat; 4) the water continues to ebb until the tops of the mountains are visible on the 1st day of the 10th month; 5) on the 1st day of the 1st month of the following year the ground is visible and drying; 6) on the 17th day of the 2nd month, exactly a year after the flood began, the land is dry and Noah's family leaves the ark. Once again, P's deluge of details makes us more inclined to accept his version of events as reliable. As is the norm in P, no event is overlooked, and no independent human action is displayed (for P, righteous human beings never act without divine permission). Thus, even after the dove that Noah releases does not return, signaling that the earth is beginning to dry out, Noah does not exit the ark until God explicitly commands him to do so.

The distinction between J and P's contributions to this chapter, as in previous chapters, is evidenced by their choice of names for God. P's meticulous chronicle, and his observation of the command-obedience paradigm, in which God's directives are immediately followed by their fulfillment, consistently coincides with the use of the name Elohim, whereas J's narrative about Noah coincides with the use of the name Yahweh in the final verses of the chapter. The fracture between J and P's version of events is also apparent in the syntactic awkwardness of verses 18 and 19. Verse 18 lacks an indirect object—that is, it tells us that Noah went out, but does not say from where. The missing indirect object—namely, the ark—appears instead at the end of verse 19. The awkwardness of this phrasing supports the conclusion that P inserted the list of animals that reside in the ark into the middle of J's account of Noah and his family leaving the ark.

GENESIS 8: CANON (J + P) HEBREW – CONTINUED

8:18 וַיֵּצֵא־נֹחַ וּבָנָיו וְאִשְׁתּוֹ וּנְשֵׁי־בָנָיו אִתּוֹ: 8:19 כָּל־הַחַיָּה כָּל־הָרֶמֶשׂ וְכָל־הָעוֹף כֹּל רוֹמֵשׂ עַל־הָאָרֶץ לְמִשְׁפְּחֹתֵיהֶם יָצְאוּ מִן־הַתֵּבָה:

8:20 וַיִּבֶן נֹחַ מִזְבֵּחַ לַיהוָה וַיִּקַּח מִכֹּל । הַבְּהֵמָה הַטְּהוֹרָה וּמִכֹּל הָעוֹף הַטָּהֹר וַיַּעַל עֹלֹת בַּמִּזְבֵּחַ: 8:21 וַיָּרַח יְהוָה אֶת־רֵיחַ הַנִּיחֹחַ וַיֹּאמֶר יְהוָה אֶל־לִבּוֹ לֹא־אֹסִף לְקַלֵּל עוֹד אֶת־הָאֲדָמָה בַּעֲבוּר הָאָדָם כִּי יֵצֶר לֵב הָאָדָם רַע מִנְּעֻרָיו וְלֹא־אֹסִף עוֹד לְהַכּוֹת אֶת־כָּל־חַי כַּאֲשֶׁר עָשִׂיתִי: 8:22 עֹד כָּל־יְמֵי הָאָרֶץ זֶרַע וְקָצִיר וְקֹר וָחֹם וְקַיִץ וָחֹרֶף וְיוֹם וָלַיְלָה לֹא יִשְׁבֹּתוּ:

THE CREATION STORY: GENESIS 9

God makes an explicit, vocalized promise to Noah to never again bring a flood upon his creatures, adding that He expects his creatures to follow his example and refrain from shedding one another's blood. Some time later, Noah becomes a famer, and the first thing he plants is a vineyard. Immediately thereafter Noah gets drunk on his own wine (this is the same Noah who had found favor in Yahweh's eyes just a few chapters earlier). His youngest son, Ham, walks in on him after he has passed out naked in his tent and engages in some sort of sexual misconduct with him, the nature of which is unclear; it might be anything from simply looking at his father's nakedness to sodomizing him. Ham then exits the tent and tells his brothers, Shem and Japheth, of their father's nakedness. Ham's brothers dutifully cover up their father, and he awakens. Noah realizes what Ham has done, and curses Ham's son, Canaan, to forever be a slave to his brothers.

GENESIS 9: THE J KERNEL

9:18 The sons of Noah who went out from the ship were Shem, Ham, and Japheth, and Canaan.

9:20 Noah started out as a farmer, and planted a vineyard. 9:21 He drank of the wine and got drunk. He lay naked within his tent. 9:22 Canaan saw the nakedness of his father, and told his two brothers outside. 9:23 Shem and Japheth took a garment, and laid it upon both their shoulders, walked backwards, and covered the nakedness of their father. Their faces were averted, and they didn't see their father's nakedness. 9:24 Noah awoke from his wine (-induced stupor), and knew what his youngest son had done to him. 9:25 He said, "Canaan is cursed. He will be a servant of servants (serving) his brothers." 9:26 He said, "Blessed be Yahweh, the God of Shem. Let Canaan be his servant. 9:27 May God make Japheth mighty. Let him dwell in the tents of Shem. Let Canaan be his servant."

GENESIS 9: THE J KERNEL (HEBREW)

9:18 וַיִּהְיוּ בְנֵי־נֹחַ הַיֹּצְאִים מִן־הַתֵּבָה שֵׁם וְחָם וָיָפֶת וְחָם הוּא אֲבִי כְנָעַן: 9:20 וַיָּחֶל נֹחַ אִישׁ הָאֲדָמָה וַיִּטַּע כָּרֶם: 9:21 וַיֵּשְׁתְּ מִן־הַיַּיִן וַיִּשְׁכָּר וַיִּתְגַּל בְּתוֹךְ אָהֳלֹה: 9:22 וַיַּרְא חָם אֲבִי כְנַעַן אֵת עֶרְוַת אָבִיו וַיַּגֵּד לִשְׁנֵי־אֶחָיו בַּחוּץ: 9:23 וַיִּקַּח שֵׁם וָיֶפֶת אֶת־הַשִּׂמְלָה וַיָּשִׂימוּ עַל־שְׁכֶם שְׁנֵיהֶם וַיֵּלְכוּ אֲחֹרַנִּית וַיְכַסּוּ אֵת עֶרְוַת אֲבִיהֶם וּפְנֵיהֶם אֲחֹרַנִּית וְעֶרְוַת אֲבִיהֶם לֹא רָאוּ: 9:24 וַיִּיקֶץ נֹחַ מִיֵּינוֹ וַיֵּדַע אֵת אֲשֶׁר־עָשָׂה־לוֹ בְּנוֹ הַקָּטָן: 9:25 וַיֹּאמֶר אָרוּר כְּנָעַן עֶבֶד עֲבָדִים יִהְיֶה לְאֶחָיו: 9:26 וַיֹּאמֶר בָּרוּךְ יְהֹוָה אֱלֹהֵי שֵׁם וִיהִי כְנַעַן עֶבֶד לָמוֹ: 9:27 יַפְתְּ אֱלֹהִים לְיֶפֶת וְיִשְׁכֹּן בְּאָהֳלֵי־שֵׁם וִיהִי כְנַעַן עֶבֶד לָמוֹ:

According to J, Noah has four sons, not three: Shem, Ham, Japheth, and Canaan. Although P holds that Noah has only three sons, he is not comfortable erasing Canaan entirely (according to the supplementary way of thinking, such erasure or deletion of material was rarely if ever employed), so instead he adds the clause "and Ham was the father of" to make it seem as if Canaan were Noah's grandson rather than his son. P adds these same words again in verse 22, thereby making Ham the assailant instead of Canaan. This, however, is problematic, since it is Canaan whom Noah curses—if Ham were the real perpetrator, why would Noah curse Ham's son rather than Ham himself?

Employing subtle language, J leaves Canaan's (or Ham's) sin to our imagination. To "see someone's nakedness," in Biblical parlance, can be taken at face value (in which case Noah's curse would seem to be rather extreme), but it could also imply sexual acts. J often adds sexual tension to his narratives to grab the reader's interest; compare Genesis 12:10–20, where it is unclear whether or not Pharaoh has sex with Sarah, but it is certainly suggested as a possibility.

GENESIS 9: CANON (J + P)

9:1 God blessed Noah and his sons, and said to them, "Be fruitful, and multiply, and replenish the earth. 9:2 Fear of you and dread of you will be upon every animal of the earth, and upon every bird of the sky. Everything with which the ground teems, and all the fish of the sea are delivered into your hand. 9:3 Every moving thing that lives will be food for you, as well as the plants of the field. I have given everything to you. 9:4 But flesh with its blood, its life-force, you shall not eat. 9:5 I will surely seek retribution for your life-blood. From every animal I will seek it. From every person, even from a man's brother, I will seek (retribution) for the life of a human being. 9:6 Whoever sheds a person's blood, his blood will be shed (in retribution) for the life of that person, for God made human beings in his own image. 9:7 Be fruitful and multiply. Increase abundantly upon the earth, and multiply upon it."

9:8 God spoke to Noah and to his sons with him, saying, 9:9 "As for me, behold, I establish my covenant with you, and with your offspring after you, 9:10 and with every living creature that is with you: the birds, the livestock, and every animal of the earth with you, all who have gone out of the ark, (with) every creature upon the earth. 9:11 I will establish my covenant with you: never again will all flesh be cut off by flood waters, neither will there ever be a flood again which would destroy the earth." 9:12 God said, "This is the token of the covenant which I make between me and you and every living creature that is with you, for all generations: 9:13 I set my rainbow among the clouds, and it will be for a sign of the covenant between me and the earth. 9:14 It will happen, when I cause clouds to come over the earth, that the rainbow will be apparent in the clouds,

GENESIS 9: CANON (J + P) HEBREW

9:1 וַיְבָ֣רֶךְ אֱלֹהִ֔ים אֶת־נֹ֖חַ וְאֶת־בָּנָ֑יו וַיֹּ֧אמֶר לָהֶ֛ם פְּר֥וּ וּרְב֖וּ וּמִלְא֥וּ אֶת־הָאָֽרֶץ: 9:2 וּמוֹרַאֲכֶ֤ם וְחִתְּכֶם֙ יִֽהְיֶ֔ה עַ֚ל כָּל־חַיַּ֣ת הָאָ֔רֶץ וְעַ֖ל כָּל־ע֣וֹף הַשָּׁמָ֑יִם בְּכֹל֩ אֲשֶׁ֨ר תִּרְמֹ֧שׂ הָֽאֲדָמָ֛ה וּֽבְכָל־דְּגֵ֥י הַיָּ֖ם בְּיֶדְכֶ֥ם נִתָּֽנוּ: 9:3 כָּל־רֶ֙מֶשׂ֙ אֲשֶׁ֣ר הוּא־חַ֔י לָכֶ֥ם יִהְיֶ֖ה לְאָכְלָ֑ה כְּיֶ֣רֶק עֵ֔שֶׂב נָתַ֥תִּי לָכֶ֖ם אֶת־כֹּֽל: 9:4 אַךְ־בָּשָׂ֕ר בְּנַפְשׁ֥וֹ דָמ֖וֹ לֹ֥א תֹאכֵֽלוּ: 9:5 וְאַ֨ךְ אֶת־דִּמְכֶ֤ם לְנַפְשֹֽׁתֵיכֶם֙ אֶדְרֹ֔שׁ מִיַּ֥ד כָּל־חַיָּ֖ה אֶדְרְשֶׁ֑נּוּ וּמִיַּ֣ד הָֽאָדָ֗ם מִיַּד֙ אִ֣ישׁ אָחִ֔יו אֶדְרֹ֖שׁ אֶת־נֶ֥פֶשׁ הָֽאָדָֽם: 9:6 שֹׁפֵךְ֙ דַּ֣ם הָֽאָדָ֔ם בָּֽאָדָ֖ם דָּמ֣וֹ יִשָּׁפֵ֑ךְ כִּ֚י בְּצֶ֣לֶם אֱלֹהִ֔ים עָשָׂ֖ה אֶת־הָאָדָֽם: 9:7 וְאַתֶּ֖ם פְּר֣וּ וּרְב֑וּ שִׁרְצ֥וּ בָאָ֖רֶץ וּרְבוּ־בָֽהּ: ס

9:8 וַיֹּ֤אמֶר אֱלֹהִים֙ אֶל־נֹ֔חַ וְאֶל־בָּנָ֥יו אִתּ֖וֹ לֵאמֹֽר: 9:9 וַאֲנִ֕י הִנְנִ֥י מֵקִ֛ים אֶת־בְּרִיתִ֖י אִתְּכֶ֑ם וְאֶֽת־זַרְעֲכֶ֖ם אַֽחֲרֵיכֶֽם: 9:10 וְאֵ֨ת כָּל־נֶ֤פֶשׁ הַֽחַיָּה֙ אֲשֶׁ֣ר אִתְּכֶ֔ם בָּע֧וֹף בַּבְּהֵמָ֛ה וּֽבְכָל־חַיַּ֥ת הָאָ֖רֶץ אִתְּכֶ֑ם מִכֹּל֙ יֹצְאֵ֣י הַתֵּבָ֔ה לְכֹ֖ל חַיַּ֥ת הָאָֽרֶץ: 9:11 וַהֲקִמֹתִ֤י אֶת־בְּרִיתִי֙ אִתְּכֶ֔ם וְלֹֽא־יִכָּרֵ֧ת כָּל־בָּשָׂ֛ר ע֖וֹד מִמֵּ֣י הַמַּבּ֑וּל וְלֹֽא־יִהְיֶ֥ה ע֛וֹד מַבּ֖וּל לְשַׁחֵ֥ת הָאָֽרֶץ: 9:12 וַיֹּ֣אמֶר אֱלֹהִ֗ים זֹ֤את אֽוֹת־הַבְּרִית֙ אֲשֶׁר־אֲנִ֣י נֹתֵ֗ן בֵּינִי֙ וּבֵ֣ינֵיכֶ֔ם וּבֵ֛ין כָּל־נֶ֥פֶשׁ חַיָּ֖ה אֲשֶׁ֣ר אִתְּכֶ֑ם לְדֹרֹ֖ת עוֹלָֽם: 9:13 אֶת־קַשְׁתִּ֕י נָתַ֖תִּי בֶּֽעָנָ֑ן וְהָֽיְתָה֙ לְא֣וֹת בְּרִ֔ית בֵּינִ֖י וּבֵ֥ין הָאָֽרֶץ: 9:14 וְהָיָ֕ה בְּעַֽנְנִ֥י עָנָ֖ן עַל־הָאָ֑רֶץ וְנִרְאֲתָ֥ה הַקֶּ֖שֶׁת בֶּעָנָֽן:

GENESIS 9: CANON (J + P) – CONTINUED

9:15 and I will remember my covenant, between me and you and every living creature and all flesh, and the waters will never again become a flood to destroy all flesh. 9:16 The rainbow will be in the clouds. I will look at it, so that I may remember the everlasting covenant between God and every living creature and all flesh that is on the earth." 9:17 God said to Noah, "This is the token of the covenant which I have established between me and all flesh that is on the earth."

9:18 The sons of Noah who went out from the ship were Shem, Ham, and Japheth. And Ham was the father of Canaan. 9:19 These three were the sons of Noah, and from these, the whole earth was populated.

9:20 Noah started out as a farmer, and planted a vineyard. 21 He drank of the wine and got drunk. He lay naked within his tent. 9:22 Ham, the father of Canaan, saw the nakedness of his father, and told his two brothers outside. 9:23 Shem and Japheth took a garment, and laid it upon both their shoulders, walked backwards, and covered the nakedness of their father. Their faces were averted, and they didn't see their father's nakedness. 9:24 Noah awoke from his wine (-induced stupor), and knew what his youngest son had done to him. 9:25 He said, "Canaan is cursed. He will be a servant of servants (serving) his brothers." 9:26 He said, "Blessed be Yahweh, the God of Shem. Let Canaan be his servant. 9:27 May God make Japheth mighty. Let him dwell in the tents of Shem. Let Canaan be his servant."

9:28 Noah lived three hundred fifty years after the flood. 9:29 Noah's entire lifespan was nine hundred fifty years; then he died.

What P Adds

P begins by elaborating upon J's nonverbal divine promise (see 8:21–22) to never again bring a flood to destroy all of God's creations. This is the first of four covenants between God and humans in the P source: the second is the Abrahamic covenant regarding circumcision in Genesis 17; the third, the covenant with Israel regarding the Sabbath in Exodus 31:16; and the fourth, the covenant with Phineas in Numbers 25, after he has saved Israel from God's wrath following the sin of Baal Peor. Note the prohibition against spilling blood given in verses 5–6, which is echoed in the Priestly laws of sacrifice in Leviticus 17 and elsewhere. According to P and H, blood is the essence or soul of all living things, and should therefore be treated reverently. Similarly, verse 7 echoes the Priestly command to be fruitful and multiply in Genesis 1:22 and 28.

GENESIS 9: CANON (J + P) HEBREW – CONTINUED

9:15 וְזָכַרְתִּ֣י אֶת־בְּרִיתִ֗י אֲשֶׁ֤ר בֵּינִי֙ וּבֵ֣ינֵיכֶ֔ם וּבֵ֛ין כָּל־נֶ֥פֶשׁ חַיָּ֖ה בְּכָל־בָּשָׂ֑ר וְלֹֽא־יִהְיֶ֨ה ע֤וֹד הַמַּ֨יִם֙ לְמַבּ֔וּל לְשַׁחֵ֖ת כָּל־בָּשָֽׂר: 9:16 וְהָיְתָ֥ה הַקֶּ֖שֶׁת בֶּֽעָנָ֑ן וּרְאִיתִ֗יהָ לִזְכֹּר֙ בְּרִ֣ית עוֹלָ֔ם בֵּ֣ין אֱלֹהִ֔ים וּבֵין֙ כָּל־נֶ֣פֶשׁ חַיָּ֔ה בְּכָל־בָּשָׂ֖ר אֲשֶׁ֥ר עַל־הָאָֽרֶץ: 9:17 וַיֹּ֥אמֶר אֱלֹהִ֖ים אֶל־נֹ֑חַ זֹ֤את אֽוֹת־הַבְּרִית֙ אֲשֶׁ֣ר הֲקִמֹ֔תִי בֵּינִ֕י וּבֵ֥ין כָּל־בָּשָׂ֖ר אֲשֶׁ֥ר עַל־הָאָֽרֶץ: פ

==9:18 וַיִּֽהְי֣וּ בְנֵי־נֹ֗חַ הַיֹּֽצְאִים֙ מִן־הַתֵּבָ֔ה שֵׁ֖ם וְחָ֣ם וָיָ֑פֶת וְחָ֕ם ה֖וּא אֲבִ֥י כְנָֽעַן: 9:19 שְׁלֹשָׁ֥ה אֵ֖לֶּה בְּנֵי־נֹ֑חַ וּמֵאֵ֖לֶּה נָֽפְצָ֥ה כָל־הָאָֽרֶץ: 9:20 וַיָּ֥חֶל נֹ֖חַ אִ֣ישׁ הָֽאֲדָמָ֑ה וַיִּטַּ֖ע כָּֽרֶם: 9:21 וַיֵּ֥שְׁתְּ מִן־הַיַּ֖יִן וַיִּשְׁכָּ֑ר וַיִּתְגַּ֖ל בְּת֥וֹךְ אָהֳלֹֽה: 9:22 וַיַּ֗רְא חָ֚ם אֲבִ֣י כְנַ֔עַן אֵ֖ת עֶרְוַ֣ת אָבִ֑יו וַיַּגֵּ֥ד לִשְׁנֵֽי־אֶחָ֖יו בַּחֽוּץ: 9:23 וַיִּקַּח֩ שֵׁ֨ם וָיֶ֜פֶת אֶת־הַשִּׂמְלָ֗ה וַיָּשִׂ֨ימוּ֙ עַל־שְׁכֶ֣ם שְׁנֵיהֶ֔ם וַיֵּֽלְכוּ֙ אֲחֹ֣רַנִּ֔ית וַיְכַסּ֕וּ אֵ֖ת עֶרְוַ֣ת אֲבִיהֶ֑ם וּפְנֵיהֶם֙ אֲחֹ֣רַנִּ֔ית וְעֶרְוַ֥ת אֲבִיהֶ֖ם לֹ֥א רָאֽוּ: 9:24 וַיִּ֥יקֶץ נֹ֖חַ מִיֵּינ֑וֹ וַיֵּ֕דַע אֵ֛ת אֲשֶׁר־עָ֥שָׂה־ל֖וֹ בְּנ֥וֹ הַקָּטָֽן: 9:25 וַיֹּ֖אמֶר אָר֣וּר כְּנָ֑עַן עֶ֥בֶד עֲבָדִ֖ים יִֽהְיֶ֥ה לְאֶחָֽיו: 9:26 וַיֹּ֕אמֶר בָּר֥וּךְ יְהֹוָ֖ה אֱלֹ֣הֵי שֵׁ֑ם וִיהִ֥י כְנַ֖עַן עֶ֥בֶד לָֽמוֹ: 9:27 יַ֤פְתְּ אֱלֹהִים֙ לְיֶ֔פֶת וְיִשְׁכֹּ֖ן בְּאָֽהֳלֵי־שֵׁ֑ם וִיהִ֥י כְנַ֖עַן עֶ֥בֶד לָֽמוֹ: 9:28 וַֽיְחִי־נֹ֖חַ==

אַחַ֣ר הַמַּבּ֑וּל שְׁלֹ֤שׁ מֵאוֹת֙ שָׁנָ֔ה וַחֲמִשִּׁ֖ים שָׁנָֽה: 9:29 וַיִּֽהְיוּ֙ כָּל־יְמֵי־נֹ֔חַ תְּשַׁ֤ע מֵאוֹת֙ שָׁנָ֔ה וַחֲמִשִּׁ֖ים שָׁנָ֑ה וַיָּמֹֽת: פ

THE CREATION STORY: GENESIS 10

This chapter chronicles the emergence of the seventy nations who are the descendants of Noah's children Shem, Ham, and Japheth. Most notable among them are Ham's grandson, Nimrod, who establishes the first empire in Babylon, and Shem's descendant, Joktan, who has thirteen children, more than any other figure in Genesis.

GENESIS 10: THE P KERNEL

10:1 These are the generations of Noah's sons, Shem, Ham, and Japheth. Children were born to them after the flood.

10:2 The sons of Japheth: Gomer, Magog, Madai, Javan, Tubal, Meshech, and Tiras. 10:3 The sons of Gomer: Ashkenaz, Riphath, and Togarmah. 10:4 The sons of Javan: Elishah, Tarshish, Kittim, and Dodanim. 10:6 The sons of Ham: Cush, Mizraim, Phut, and Canaan. 10:7 The sons of Cush: Seba, Havilah, Sabtah, Raamah, and Sabtecah. The sons of Raamah: Sheba and Dedan. 10:22 The sons of Shem: Elam, Asshur, Arpachshad, Lud, and Aram. 10:23 The sons of Aram: Uz, Hul, Gether, and Mash. 10:32 These are the families of the sons of Noah, according to their generations, and their nations. From these the nations were divided on earth after the flood.

After the story of Nimrod is trimmed away, the Priestly kernel of this chapter seems to be just another humdrum genealogical list. It makes more sense, however, when read together with the chapter that follows, in which P details the specific Semitic line that culminates in Abraham. P begins with this list of 37 descendants of Noah in order to build anticipation and distinguish the Abrahamic line from the rest of the nations of the world.

GENESIS 10: THE P KERNEL (HEBREW)

10:1 וְאֵ֙לֶּה֙ תּוֹלְדֹ֣ת בְּנֵי־נֹ֔חַ שֵׁ֖ם חָ֣ם וָיָ֑פֶת וַיִּוָּלְד֥וּ לָהֶ֛ם בָּנִ֖ים אַחַ֥ר הַמַּבּֽוּל׃

10:2 בְּנֵ֣י יֶ֔פֶת גֹּ֣מֶר וּמָג֑וֹג וּמָדַ֖י וְיָוָ֣ן וְתֻבָ֑ל וּמֶ֖שֶׁךְ וְתִירָֽס׃ 10:3 וּבְנֵ֖י גֹּ֑מֶר אַשְׁכֲּנַ֥ז וְרִיפַ֖ת וְתֹגַרְמָֽה׃ 10:4 וּבְנֵ֥י יָוָ֖ן אֱלִישָׁ֣ה וְתַרְשִׁ֑ישׁ כִּתִּ֖ים וְדֹדָנִֽים׃

10:6 וּבְנֵ֖י חָ֑ם כּ֥וּשׁ וּמִצְרַ֖יִם וּפ֥וּט וּכְנָֽעַן׃ 10:7 וּבְנֵ֣י כ֔וּשׁ סְבָא֙ וַחֲוִילָ֔ה וְסַבְתָּ֥ה וְרַעְמָ֖ה וְסַבְתְּכָ֑א וּבְנֵ֥י רַעְמָ֖ה שְׁבָ֥א וּדְדָֽן׃

10:22 בְּנֵ֣י שֵׁ֔ם עֵילָ֣ם וְאַשּׁ֑וּר וְאַרְפַּכְשַׁ֖ד וְל֥וּד וַאֲרָֽם׃ 10:23 וּבְנֵ֖י אֲרָ֑ם ע֥וּץ וְח֖וּל וְגֶ֥תֶר וָמַֽשׁ׃ 10:32 אֵ֣לֶּה מִשְׁפְּחֹ֧ת בְּנֵי־נֹ֛חַ לְתוֹלְדֹתָ֖ם בְּגוֹיֵהֶ֑ם וּמֵאֵ֜לֶּה נִפְרְד֧וּ הַגּוֹיִ֛ם בָּאָ֖רֶץ אַחַ֥ר הַמַּבּֽוּל׃ פ

GENESIS 10: CANON (P + B)

10:1 These are the generations of Noah's sons, Shem, Ham, and Japheth. Children were born to them after the flood.

10:2 The sons of Japheth: Gomer, Magog, Madai, Javan, Tubal, Meshech, and Tiras. 10:3 The sons of Gomer: Ashkenaz, Riphath, and Togarmah. 10:4 The sons of Javan: Elishah, Tarshish, Kittim, and Dodanim. 10:5 Of these were the islands of the nations divided in their lands, everyone after his language, after their families, in their nations.

10:6 The sons of Ham: Cush, Mizraim, Phut, and Canaan. 10:7 The sons of Cush: Seba, Havilah, Sabtah, Raamah, and Sabtecah. The sons of Raamah: Sheba and Dedan. 10:8 Cush became the father of Nimrod. He was the first hero on earth. 10:9 He was a mighty hunter before Yahweh. Therefore it is said, "Like Nimrod, a mighty hunter before Yahweh." 10:10 The beginning of his kingdom was Babel, Erech, Accad, and Calneh, in the land of Shinar. 10:11 From that land he went into Assyria, and built Nineveh, Rehoboth Ir, and Calah, 10:12 and Resen between Nineveh and Calah (the great city). 10:13 Mizraim became the father of Ludim, Anamim, Lehabim, Naphtuhim, 10:14 Pathrusim, Casluhim whom the Philistines descended from, and Caphtorim. 10:15 Canaan became the father of Sidon his firstborn, Heth, 10:16 the Jebusite, the Amorite, the Girgashite, 10:17 the Hivite, the Arkite, the Sinite, 10:18 the Arvadite, the Zemarite, and the Hamathite. Afterward the families of the Canaanites spread widely. 10:19 The border of the Canaanites was from Sidon, extending to Gerar, to Gaza; and extending toward Sodom, Gomorrah, Admah, and Zeboiim, to Lasha. 10:20 These are the sons of Ham, according to their families, their languages, their lands, and their nations.

10:21 Children were also born to Shem, the father of all the children of Eber, the elder brother of Japheth. 10:22 The sons of Shem: Elam, Asshur, Arpachshad, Lud, and Aram. 10:23 The sons of Aram: Uz, Hul, Gether, and Mash. 10:24 Arpachshad became the father of Shelah. Shelah became the father of Eber. 10:25 Two sons were born to Eber. The name of the one was Peleg, for in his days the earth was divided. His brother's name was Joktan. 10:26 Joktan became the father of Almodad, Sheleph, Hazarmaveth, Jerah, 10:27 Hadoram, Uzal, Diklah, 10:28 Obal, Abimael, Sheba, 10:29 Ophir, Havilah, and Jobab. All these were the sons of Joktan. 10:30 Their dwelling was from Mesha, extending toward Sephar, the mountain of the east. 10:31 These are the sons of Shem, according to their families, their languages, their lands, and their nations.

10:32 These are the families of the sons of Noah, according to their generations, and their nations. From these the nations were divided on earth after the flood.

GENESIS 10: CANON (P + B) HEBREW

10:1 וְאֵ֙לֶּה֙ תּוֹלְדֹ֣ת בְּנֵי־נֹ֔חַ שֵׁ֖ם חָ֣ם וָיָ֑פֶת וַיִּוָּלְד֥וּ לָהֶ֛ם בָּנִ֖ים אַחַ֥ר הַמַּבּֽוּל׃ 10:2 בְּנֵ֣י יֶ֔פֶת גֹּ֣מֶר וּמָג֔וֹג וּמָדַ֖י וְיָוָ֣ן וְתֻבָ֑ל וּמֶ֖שֶׁךְ וְתִירָֽס׃ 10:3 וּבְנֵ֖י גֹּ֑מֶר אַשְׁכֲּנַ֥ז וְרִיפַ֖ת וְתֹגַרְמָֽה׃ 10:4 וּבְנֵ֥י יָוָ֖ן אֱלִישָׁ֣ה וְתַרְשִׁ֑ישׁ כִּתִּ֖ים וְדֹדָנִֽים׃ 10:5 מֵ֠אֵלֶּה נִפְרְד֞וּ אִיֵּ֤י הַגּוֹיִם֙ בְּאַרְצֹתָ֔ם אִ֖ישׁ לִלְשֹׁנ֑וֹ לְמִשְׁפְּחֹתָ֖ם בְּגוֹיֵהֶֽם׃ 10:6 וּבְנֵ֖י חָ֑ם כּ֥וּשׁ וּמִצְרַ֖יִם וּפ֥וּט וּכְנָֽעַן׃ 10:7 וּבְנֵ֣י כ֔וּשׁ סְבָא֙ וַחֲוִילָ֔ה וְסַבְתָּ֥ה וְרַעְמָ֖ה וְסַבְתְּכָ֑א וּבְנֵ֥י רַעְמָ֖ה שְׁבָ֥א וּדְדָֽן׃ 10:8 וְכ֖וּשׁ יָלַ֣ד אֶת־נִמְרֹ֑ד ה֣וּא הֵחֵ֔ל לִֽהְי֥וֹת גִּבֹּ֖ר בָּאָֽרֶץ׃ 10:9 הֽוּא־הָיָ֥ה גִבֹּֽר־צַ֖יִד לִפְנֵ֣י יְהוָ֑ה עַל־כֵּן֙ יֵֽאָמַ֔ר כְּנִמְרֹ֛ד גִּבּ֥וֹר צַ֖יִד לִפְנֵ֥י יְהוָֽה׃ 10:10 וַתְּהִ֨י רֵאשִׁ֤ית מַמְלַכְתּוֹ֙ בָּבֶ֔ל וְאֶ֖רֶךְ וְאַכַּ֣ד וְכַלְנֵ֑ה בְּאֶ֖רֶץ שִׁנְעָֽר׃ 10:11 מִן־הָאָ֥רֶץ הַהִ֖וא יָצָ֣א אַשּׁ֑וּר וַיִּ֙בֶן֙ אֶת־נִ֣ינְוֵ֔ה וְאֶת־רְחֹבֹ֥ת עִ֖יר וְאֶת־כָּֽלַח׃ 10:12 וְֽאֶת־רֶ֔סֶן בֵּ֥ין נִֽינְוֵ֖ה וּבֵ֣ין כָּ֑לַח הִ֖וא הָעִ֥יר הַגְּדֹלָֽה׃ 10:13 וּמִצְרַ֡יִם יָלַ֞ד אֶת־לוּדִ֧ים וְאֶת־עֲנָמִ֛ים וְאֶת־לְהָבִ֖ים וְאֶת־נַפְתֻּחִֽים׃ 10:14 וְֽאֶת־פַּתְרֻסִ֞ים וְאֶת־כַּסְלֻחִ֗ים אֲשֶׁ֨ר יָצְא֥וּ מִשָּׁ֛ם פְּלִשְׁתִּ֖ים וְאֶת־כַּפְתֹּרִֽים׃ ס

10:15 וּכְנַ֗עַן יָלַ֛ד אֶת־צִידֹ֥ן בְּכֹר֖וֹ וְאֶת־חֵֽת׃ 10:16 וְאֶת־הַיְבוּסִי֙ וְאֶת־הָ֣אֱמֹרִ֔י וְאֵ֖ת הַגִּרְגָּשִֽׁי׃ 10:17 וְאֶת־הַחִוִּ֥י וְאֶת־הַֽעַרְקִ֖י וְאֶת־הַסִּינִֽי׃ 10:18 וְאֶת־הָֽאַרְוָדִ֥י וְאֶת־הַצְּמָרִ֖י וְאֶת־הַֽחֲמָתִ֑י וְאַחַ֣ר נָפֹ֔צוּ מִשְׁפְּח֖וֹת הַֽכְּנַעֲנִֽי׃ 10:19 וַֽיְהִ֞י גְּב֤וּל הַֽכְּנַעֲנִי֙ מִצִּידֹ֔ן בֹּאֲכָ֥ה גְרָ֖רָה עַד־עַזָּ֑ה בֹּאֲכָ֞ה סְדֹ֧מָה וַעֲמֹרָ֛ה וְאַדְמָ֥ה וּצְבֹיִ֖ם עַד־לָֽשַׁע׃ 10:20 אֵ֣לֶּה בְנֵי־חָ֔ם לְמִשְׁפְּחֹתָ֖ם לִלְשֹֽׁנֹתָ֑ם בְּאַרְצֹתָ֖ם בְּגוֹיֵהֶֽם׃ ס

10:21 וּלְשֵׁ֥ם יֻלַּ֖ד גַּם־ה֑וּא אֲבִי֙ כָּל־בְּנֵי־עֵ֔בֶר אֲחִ֖י יֶ֥פֶת הַגָּדֽוֹל׃ 10:22 בְּנֵ֥י שֵׁ֖ם עֵילָ֣ם וְאַשּׁ֑וּר וְאַרְפַּכְשַׁ֖ד וְל֥וּד וַֽאֲרָֽם׃ 10:23 וּבְנֵ֖י אֲרָ֑ם ע֥וּץ וְח֖וּל וְגֶ֥תֶר וָמַֽשׁ׃ 10:24 וְאַרְפַּכְשַׁ֖ד יָלַ֣ד אֶת־שָׁ֑לַח וְשֶׁ֖לַח יָלַ֥ד אֶת־עֵֽבֶר׃ 10:25 וּלְעֵ֥בֶר יֻלַּ֖ד שְׁנֵ֣י בָנִ֑ים שֵׁ֣ם הָֽאֶחָ֞ד פֶּ֗לֶג כִּ֤י בְיָמָיו֙ נִפְלְגָ֣ה הָאָ֔רֶץ וְשֵׁ֥ם אָחִ֖יו יָקְטָֽן׃ 10:26 וְיָקְטָ֣ן יָלַ֔ד אֶת־אַלְמוֹדָ֖ד וְאֶת־שָׁ֑לֶף וְאֶת־חֲצַרְמָ֖וֶת וְאֶת־יָֽרַח׃ 10:27 וְאֶת־הֲדוֹרָ֥ם וְאֶת־אוּזָ֖ל וְאֶת־דִּקְלָֽה׃ 10:28 וְאֶת־עוֹבָ֥ל וְאֶת־אֲבִֽימָאֵ֖ל וְאֶת־שְׁבָֽא׃ 10:29 וְאֶת־אוֹפִ֥ר וְאֶת־חֲוִילָ֖ה וְאֶת־יוֹבָ֑ב כָּל־אֵ֖לֶּה בְּנֵ֥י יָקְטָֽן׃ 10:30 וַֽיְהִ֥י מוֹשָׁבָ֖ם מִמֵּשָׁ֑א בֹּאֲכָ֥ה סְפָ֖רָה הַ֥ר הַקֶּֽדֶם׃ 10:31 אֵ֣לֶּה בְנֵי־שֵׁ֔ם לְמִשְׁפְּחֹתָ֖ם לִלְשֹׁנֹתָ֑ם בְּאַרְצֹתָ֖ם לְגוֹיֵהֶֽם׃ 10:32 אֵ֣לֶּה מִשְׁפְּחֹ֧ת בְּנֵי־נֹ֛חַ לְתוֹלְדֹתָ֖ם בְּגוֹיֵהֶ֑ם וּמֵאֵ֜לֶּה נִפְרְד֧וּ הַגּוֹיִ֛ם בָּאָ֖רֶץ אַחַ֥ר הַמַּבּֽוּל׃ פ

What B adds

B's most interesting addition to this chapter is the short hero myth concerning Nimrod in verses 8–11. This type of legend also appears at the beginning of Genesis 6 in the story of the sons of God, and is one of the defining features of late B texts. In this case, Nimrod's hero myth is clearly part of a secondary layer of genealogy, because it uses a different form of the Hebrew verb "to give birth" ("yalad") than P who prefers the forms "yivaled" and "holid" of the same verb (later on in 10:21, B will use the passive form "yulad" was born to, only found in his genealogies). It is also likely that the summarizing verses for each of Noah's sons (vss. 5, 20 and 31) were added by B, since they are helpful in summarizing his genealogies, but would seem redundant in the much shorter P text. One could reasonably posit that only the final verse, "These are the families of Noah's sons, according to their genealogies, in their nations; and from these the nations spread abroad on the earth after the flood" (vs. 32), which provides a satisfying conclusion to the whole list, is original to the P genealogy.

Another noteworthy addition to P's genealogy is the extensive list of Canaan's children. Unlike J, who curses Canaan, or P, who relegates him to a lower status (grandson instead of son) and later in the Bible commands that all Canaanites be utterly destroyed, B includes Canaan and his children among the nations descended from Noah. Including them helps to push the total number of nations toward seventy, a number that B wants to reach because it is the number of the nations, and of the gods, according to Canaanite myth (one god for each nation). Indeed, it seems that Joktan's thirteen children are included at the end of this list only because B needs them to round out the seventy nations. This move is a part of B's efforts to internationalize the Bible, recasting a primarily Israelite text as one relevant to other groups.

THE CREATION STORY: GENESIS 11

At first, all seventy nations live in one place, and together they try to build a gigantic tower with a pinnacle in heaven. The Lord feels threatened by their actions, and so sows confusion among the builders by causing them to speak different languages. Unable to communicate with one another, they abandon their project and disperse.

The rest of the chapter focuses on Shem's lineage, which ends after ten generations with Terah, and his children Abram, Nahor and Haran. They leave Ur of the Chaldeans, their homeland, ascend through the fertile crescent, and ultimately arrive in Syria, in a place also called Haran. Terah dies shortly thereafter.

GENESIS 11: THE J KERNEL

11:1 The whole earth (spoke) one language and was of one speech. 11:2 It happened, as they traveled east, that they found a plain in the land of Shinar, and they lived there. 11:3 They said one to another, "Come, let's make bricks, and burn them thoroughly." They had brick for building blocks, and they used tar for mortar. 11:4 They said, "Come, let's build ourselves a city, and a tower whose top reaches the sky, and let's make ourselves a name, lest we be scattered all over the surface of the whole earth."

11:5 Yahweh came down to see the city and the tower, which the children of men built. 11:6 Yahweh said, "Behold, they are one people, and they have all one language, and this is what they have begun to do. Now nothing will be withheld from them of what they intend to do. 11:7 Come, let's go down, and confuse their language, so that they will not understand one another's speech." 11:8 So Yahweh scattered them from there over of all the earth. They stopped building the city. 11:9 Therefore its name was called Babel, because it was there that Yahweh confused all of the earth's language. And from there, Yahweh scattered them over all of the earth.

GENESIS 11: THE J KERNEL

11:1 וַֽיְהִ֥י כָל־הָאָ֖רֶץ שָׂפָ֣ה אֶחָ֑ת וּדְבָרִ֖ים אֲחָדִֽים: 11:2 וַֽיְהִ֖י בְּנָסְעָ֣ם מִקֶּ֑דֶם וַֽיִּמְצְא֥וּ בִקְעָ֛ה בְּאֶ֥רֶץ שִׁנְעָ֖ר וַיֵּ֥שְׁבוּ שָֽׁם: 11:3 וַיֹּאמְר֞וּ אִ֣ישׁ אֶל־רֵעֵ֗הוּ הָ֚בָה נִלְבְּנָ֣ה לְבֵנִ֔ים וְנִשְׂרְפָ֖ה לִשְׂרֵפָ֑ה וַתְּהִ֨י לָהֶ֤ם הַלְּבֵנָה֙ לְאָ֔בֶן וְהַ֣חֵמָ֔ר הָיָ֥ה לָהֶ֖ם לַחֹֽמֶר: 11:4 וַיֹּאמְר֞וּ הָ֣בָה ׀ נִבְנֶה־לָּ֣נוּ עִ֗יר וּמִגְדָּל֙ וְרֹאשׁ֣וֹ בַשָּׁמַ֔יִם וְנַֽעֲשֶׂה־לָּ֖נוּ שֵׁ֑ם פֶּן־נָפ֖וּץ עַל־פְּנֵ֥י כָל־הָאָֽרֶץ: 11:5 וַיֵּ֣רֶד יְהוָ֔ה לִרְאֹ֥ת אֶת־הָעִ֖יר וְאֶת־הַמִּגְדָּ֑ל אֲשֶׁ֥ר בָּנ֖וּ בְּנֵ֥י הָאָדָֽם: 11:6 וַיֹּ֣אמֶר יְהוָ֗ה הֵ֣ן עַ֤ם אֶחָד֙ וְשָׂפָ֤ה אַחַת֙ לְכֻלָּ֔ם וְזֶ֖ה הַחִלָּ֣ם לַעֲשׂ֑וֹת וְעַתָּה֙ לֹֽא־יִבָּצֵ֣ר מֵהֶ֔ם כֹּ֛ל אֲשֶׁ֥ר יָזְמ֖וּ לַֽעֲשֽׂוֹת: 11:7 הָ֚בָה נֵֽרְדָ֔ה וְנָבְלָ֥ה שָׁ֖ם שְׂפָתָ֑ם אֲשֶׁר֙ לֹ֣א יִשְׁמְע֔וּ אִ֖ישׁ שְׂפַ֥ת רֵעֵֽהוּ: 11:8 וַיָּ֨פֶץ יְהוָ֥ה אֹתָ֛ם מִשָּׁ֖ם עַל־פְּנֵ֣י כָל־הָאָ֑רֶץ וַֽיַּחְדְּל֖וּ לִבְנֹ֥ת הָעִֽיר: 11:9 עַל־כֵּ֞ן קָרָ֤א שְׁמָהּ֙ בָּבֶ֔ל כִּי־שָׁ֛ם בָּלַ֥ל יְהוָ֖ה שְׂפַ֣ת כָּל־הָאָ֑רֶץ וּמִשָּׁם֙ הֱפִיצָ֣ם יְהוָ֔ה עַל־פְּנֵ֖י כָּל־הָאָֽרֶץ: פ

The most distinctive aspect of the story of the tower of Babel is the depiction of Yahweh. As in Genesis 3, Yahweh reacts to a perceived threat to his dominance by meting out a severe punishment to humanity. Though the humans' intentions sound innocent enough—"let's build ourselves a city, and a tower whose top reaches the sky, and let's make ourselves a name, lest we be scattered all over the surface of the whole earth"—it is construed by Yahweh as an act of war against him, leaving the reader to wonder how human beings could really pose a threat to the Lord. The only hint we have that the humans' initiative was anything but benign are the words "a tower whose top reaches the sky," which might suggest that the human beings intended to challenge the Lord's authority there. J leaves us with just enough information to justify Yahweh's actions, yet with room still to wonder at his motivations.

GENESIS 11: CANON (J + P)

11:1 The whole earth (spoke) one language and was of one speech. 11:2 It happened, as they traveled east, that they found a plain in the land of Shinar, and they lived there. 11:3 They said one to another, "Come, let's make bricks, and burn them thoroughly." They had brick for building blocks, and they used tar for mortar. 11:4 They said, "Come, let's build ourselves a city, and a tower whose top reaches the sky, and let's make ourselves a name, lest we be scattered all over the surface of the whole earth."

11:5 Yahweh came down to see the city and the tower, which the children of men built. 11:6 Yahweh said, "Behold, they are one people, and they have all one language, and this is what they have begun to do. Now nothing will be withheld from them of what they intend to do. 11:7 Come, let's go down, and confuse their language, so that they will not understand one another's speech." 11:8 So Yahweh scattered them from there over of all the earth. They stopped building the city. 11:9 Therefore its name was called Babel, because it was there that Yahweh confused all of the earth's language. And from there, Yahweh scattered them over all of the earth.

11:10 These are the generations of Shem. Shem was one hundred years old and fathered Arpachshad two years after the flood. 11:11 Shem lived five hundred years after he'd fathered Arpachshad, and sired sons and daughters.

11:12 Arpachshad lived thirty-five years and fathered Shelah. 11:13 Arpachshad lived four hundred three years after he'd fathered Shelah, and sired sons and daughters.

11:14 Shelah lived thirty years, and fathered Eber: 11:15 and Shelah lived four hundred three years after he'd fathered Eber, and sired sons and daughters.

GENESIS 11: CANON (J + P) HEBREW

11:1 וַיְהִי כָל־הָאָרֶץ שָׂפָה אֶחָת וּדְבָרִים אֲחָדִים: 11:2 וַיְהִי בְּנָסְעָם מִקֶּדֶם וַיִּמְצְאוּ בִקְעָה בְּאֶרֶץ שִׁנְעָר וַיֵּשְׁבוּ שָׁם: 11:3 וַיֹּאמְרוּ אִישׁ אֶל־רֵעֵהוּ הָבָה נִלְבְּנָה לְבֵנִים וְנִשְׂרְפָה לִשְׂרֵפָה וַתְּהִי לָהֶם הַלְּבֵנָה לְאָבֶן וְהַחֵמָר הָיָה לָהֶם לַחֹמֶר: 11:4 וַיֹּאמְרוּ הָבָה ׀ נִבְנֶה־לָּנוּ עִיר וּמִגְדָּל וְרֹאשׁוֹ בַשָּׁמַיִם וְנַעֲשֶׂה־לָּנוּ שֵׁם פֶּן־נָפוּץ עַל־פְּנֵי כָל־הָאָרֶץ: 11:5 וַיֵּרֶד יְהוָה לִרְאֹת אֶת־הָעִיר וְאֶת־הַמִּגְדָּל אֲשֶׁר בָּנוּ בְּנֵי הָאָדָם: 11:6 וַיֹּאמֶר יְהוָה הֵן עַם אֶחָד וְשָׂפָה אַחַת לְכֻלָּם וְזֶה הַחִלָּם לַעֲשׂוֹת וְעַתָּה לֹא־יִבָּצֵר מֵהֶם כֹּל אֲשֶׁר יָזְמוּ לַעֲשׂוֹת: 11:7 הָבָה נֵרְדָה וְנָבְלָה שָׁם שְׂפָתָם אֲשֶׁר לֹא יִשְׁמְעוּ אִישׁ שְׂפַת רֵעֵהוּ: 11:8 וַיָּפֶץ יְהוָה אֹתָם מִשָּׁם עַל־פְּנֵי כָל־הָאָרֶץ וַיַּחְדְּלוּ לִבְנֹת הָעִיר: 11:9 עַל־כֵּן קָרָא שְׁמָהּ בָּבֶל כִּי־שָׁם בָּלַל יְהוָה שְׂפַת כָּל־הָאָרֶץ וּמִשָּׁם הֱפִיצָם יְהוָה עַל־פְּנֵי כָּל־הָאָרֶץ: פ

11:10 אֵלֶּה תּוֹלְדֹת שֵׁם שֵׁם בֶּן־מְאַת שָׁנָה וַיּוֹלֶד אֶת־אַרְפַּכְשָׁד שְׁנָתַיִם אַחַר הַמַּבּוּל: 11:11 וַיְחִי־שֵׁם אַחֲרֵי הוֹלִידוֹ אֶת־אַרְפַּכְשָׁד חֲמֵשׁ מֵאוֹת שָׁנָה וַיּוֹלֶד בָּנִים וּבָנוֹת: ס

11:12 וְאַרְפַּכְשַׁד חַי חָמֵשׁ וּשְׁלֹשִׁים שָׁנָה וַיּוֹלֶד אֶת־שָׁלַח: 11:13 וַיְחִי אַרְפַּכְשַׁד אַחֲרֵי הוֹלִידוֹ אֶת־שֶׁלַח שָׁלֹשׁ שָׁנִים וְאַרְבַּע מֵאוֹת שָׁנָה וַיּוֹלֶד בָּנִים וּבָנוֹת:ס

11:14 וְשֶׁלַח חַי שְׁלֹשִׁים שָׁנָה וַיּוֹלֶד אֶת־עֵבֶר: 11:15 וַיְחִי־שֶׁלַח אַחֲרֵי הוֹלִידוֹ אֶת־עֵבֶר שָׁלֹשׁ שָׁנִים וְאַרְבַּע מֵאוֹת שָׁנָה וַיּוֹלֶד בָּנִים וּבָנוֹת: ס

GENESIS 11: CANON (J + P) – CONTINUED

11:16 Eber lived thirty-four years, and became the father of Peleg. 11:17 Eber lived four hundred thirty years after he'd fathered Peleg, and sired sons and daughters.

11:18 Peleg lived thirty years, and became the father of Reu. 11:19 Peleg lived two hundred nine years after he'd fathered Reu, and sired sons and daughters.

11:20 Reu lived thirty-two years, and became the father of Serug. 11:21 Reu lived two hundred seven years after he'd fathered Serug, and sired sons and daughters.

11:22 Serug lived thirty years, and became the father of Nahor. 11:23 Serug lived two hundred years after he'd fathered Nahor, and sired sons and daughters.

11:24 Nahor lived twenty-nine years, and became the father of Terah. 11:25 Nahor lived one hundred nineteen years after he'd fathered Terah, and sired sons and daughters.

11:26 Terah lived seventy years, and fathered Abram, Nahor, and Haran. 11:27 These are the generations of Terah. Terah fathered Abram, Nahor, and Haran. And Haran fathered Lot. 11:28 Haran died before his father Terah in the land of his birth, in Ur of the Chaldees. 11:29 Abram and Nahor took wives. The name of Abram's wife was Sarai, and the name of Nahor's wife was Milcah, the daughter of Haran, who was also the father of Iscah. 11:30 Sarai was barren. She had no child.

11:31 Terah took Abram his son, Lot the son of Haran, his son's son, and Sarai his daughter-in-law, his son Abram's wife. They left Ur of the Chaldees for the land of Canaan. They came to Haran and lived there. 11:32 The years of Terah's life were two hundred five years. Terah died in Haran.

What P Adds

According to P's chapter 10, by the time of the Babel narrative, the land has already been divided among the post-flood nations, and each is living in its own land (see 10:32). This division into nations and lands occurs before the tower of Babel, and directly contradicts J's account, since in 11:1 all the people dwell together. It is likely that P was uncomfortable of the theological implications of this account and therefore offered his own account of the division of the world in Chapter 10.

GENESIS 11: CANON (J + P) HEBREW – CONTINUED

11:16 וַיְחִי־עֵ֕בֶר אַרְבַּ֥ע וּשְׁלֹשִׁ֖ים שָׁנָ֑ה וַיּ֖וֹלֶד אֶת־פָּֽלֶג: 11:17 וַיְחִי־עֵ֗בֶר אַחֲרֵי֙ הוֹלִיד֣וֹ אֶת־פֶּ֔לֶג שְׁלֹשִׁ֣ים שָׁנָ֔ה וְאַרְבַּ֥ע מֵא֖וֹת שָׁנָ֑ה וַיּ֥וֹלֶד בָּנִ֖ים וּבָנֽוֹת: ס

11:18 וַיְחִי־פֶ֖לֶג שְׁלֹשִׁ֣ים שָׁנָ֑ה וַיּ֖וֹלֶד אֶת־רְעֽוּ: 11:19 וַיְחִי־פֶ֗לֶג אַחֲרֵי֙ הוֹלִיד֣וֹ אֶת־רְע֔וּ תֵּ֥שַׁע שָׁנִ֖ים וּמָאתַ֣יִם שָׁנָ֑ה וַיּ֥וֹלֶד בָּנִ֖ים וּבָנֽוֹת: ס

11:20 וַיְחִ֣י רְע֔וּ שְׁתַּ֥יִם וּשְׁלֹשִׁ֖ים שָׁנָ֑ה וַיּ֖וֹלֶד אֶת־שְׂרֽוּג: 11:21 וַיְחִ֣י רְע֗וּ אַחֲרֵי֙ הוֹלִיד֣וֹ אֶת־שְׂר֔וּג שֶׁ֥בַע שָׁנִ֖ים וּמָאתַ֣יִם שָׁנָ֑ה וַיּ֥וֹלֶד בָּנִ֖ים וּבָנֽוֹת: ס

11:22 וַיְחִ֣י שְׂר֔וּג שְׁלֹשִׁ֖ים שָׁנָ֑ה וַיּ֖וֹלֶד אֶת־נָחֽוֹר: 11:23 וַיְחִ֣י שְׂר֗וּג אַחֲרֵי֙ הוֹלִיד֣וֹ אֶת־נָח֔וֹר מָאתַ֣יִם שָׁנָ֑ה וַיּ֥וֹלֶד בָּנִ֖ים וּבָנֽוֹת: ס

11:24 וַיְחִ֣י נָח֔וֹר תֵּ֥שַׁע וְעֶשְׂרִ֖ים שָׁנָ֑ה וַיּ֖וֹלֶד אֶת־תָּֽרַח: 11:25 וַיְחִ֣י נָח֗וֹר אַחֲרֵי֙ הוֹלִיד֣וֹ אֶת־תֶּ֔רַח תְּשַֽׁע־עֶשְׂרֵ֥ה שָׁנָ֖ה וּמְאַ֣ת שָׁנָ֑ה וַיּ֥וֹלֶד בָּנִ֖ים וּבָנֽוֹת: ס

11:26 וַיְחִי־תֶ֖רַח שִׁבְעִ֣ים שָׁנָ֑ה וַיּ֙וֹלֶד֙ אֶת־אַבְרָ֔ם אֶת־נָח֖וֹר וְאֶת־הָרָֽן: 11:27 וְאֵ֙לֶּה֙ תּוֹלְדֹ֣ת תֶּ֔רַח תֶּ֚רַח הוֹלִ֣יד אֶת־אַבְרָ֔ם אֶת־נָח֖וֹר וְאֶת־הָרָ֑ן וְהָרָ֖ן הוֹלִ֥יד אֶת־לֽוֹט: 11:28 וַיָּ֣מָת הָרָ֔ן עַל־פְּנֵ֖י תֶּ֣רַח אָבִ֑יו בְּאֶ֥רֶץ מוֹלַדְתּ֖וֹ בְּא֥וּר כַּשְׂדִּֽים: 11:29 וַיִּקַּ֨ח אַבְרָ֧ם וְנָח֛וֹר לָהֶ֖ם נָשִׁ֑ים שֵׁ֤ם אֵֽשֶׁת־אַבְרָם֙ שָׂרָ֔י וְשֵׁ֤ם אֵֽשֶׁת־נָחוֹר֙ מִלְכָּ֔ה בַּת־הָרָ֥ן אֲבִֽי־מִלְכָּ֖ה וַֽאֲבִ֥י יִסְכָּֽה: 11:30 וַתְּהִ֥י שָׂרַ֖י עֲקָרָ֑ה אֵ֥ין לָ֖הּ וָלָֽד: 11:31 וַיִּקַּ֨ח תֶּ֜רַח אֶת־אַבְרָ֣ם בְּנ֗וֹ וְאֶת־ל֤וֹט בֶּן־הָרָן֙ בֶּן־בְּנ֔וֹ וְאֵת֙ שָׂרַ֣י כַּלָּת֔וֹ אֵ֖שֶׁת אַבְרָ֣ם בְּנ֑וֹ וַיֵּצְא֨וּ אִתָּ֜ם מֵא֣וּר כַּשְׂדִּ֗ים לָלֶ֙כֶת֙ אַ֣רְצָה כְּנַ֔עַן וַיָּבֹ֥אוּ עַד־חָרָ֖ן וַיֵּ֥שְׁבוּ שָֽׁם: 11:32 וַיִּהְי֣וּ יְמֵי־תֶ֔רַח חָמֵ֥שׁ שָׁנִ֖ים וּמָאתַ֣יִם שָׁנָ֑ה וַיָּ֥מָת תֶּ֖רַח בְּחָרָֽן: ס

Though J and P diverge sharply regarding the division of the world after the flood, it is still quite clear that P's writings were dependent upon J's. If P were independent of J, then he would not have had to mention Shem and his son Arpachshad again in these verses, having just mentioned them in 10:22. If he were writing with an awareness of J, however, then verses 10–11 would function as a resumptive repetition, getting the reader back on track, following the interruption caused by the Babel narrative.

At the end of his genealogy, P mentions that Terah's ultimate destination is Canaan (11:31), and since he doesn't quite make it there, the remainder of the journey is implicitly left to his sons. This is contrary to J, who has Abram leaving the anonymous land of his birth after being commanded to do so by the Lord (see Genesis 12). P's addition in verse 31, and the genealogy that precedes it, emphasize the continuity between Abram and the particular Semitic (a term derived from the name "Shem") line of which he is a part. J, on the other hand, is not invested in Abram being a part of the Semitic line, and so is content to begin Israelite history with Abram, without any mention of where he comes from.

APPENDIX: THE DOCUMENTARY HYPOTHESIS

The chief competitor to the Supplementary Hypothesis of Biblical construction is the Documentary Hypothesis, the first major theory of Biblical criticism to gain a significant following. Its most widely-accepted permutation was formulated by Julius Wellhausen in his late 19th century work, *Die Composition des Hexateuchs* (*The Composition of the Hexateuch*). Wellhausen posits that the five books of Moses actually comprise four independent, but largely parallel documents, which were fused together by a series of later editors or redactors. The two hypotheses thus agree upon multiple authorship, but differ significantly in the details of how, when and by whom the canonical text was written and compiled.

The most significant difference between the two theories is that the Supplementary Hypothesis posits that the narrative accreted over time, in contrast to the Documentary Hypothesis's assertion that the various documents were, for the most part, constructed independently and gradually edited together. I find the Supplementary Hypothesis much more persuasive than the Documentary Hypothesis, principally because it accords best with what we know about how other Biblical texts and later Jewish texts have developed.

One of the best examples of a Biblical text that clearly developed by accretion is the book of Jeremiah. The version that appears in the Masoretic Hebrew text (that is, the canonical text of the Hebrew Bible) contains nearly all of the same material as does the version found in the Hebrew precursor of the Septuagint, a Greek translation of the Hebrew Bible the composition of which began in the 3rd century BCE. However, the version found in the Masoretic text is sixteen percent longer than in the Septuagint, incorporating numerous additional glosses, verses, and even entire sections. Often, for example, instead of simply Jeremaiah or Baruch, the Masoretic text will mention Jeremiah the son of Helqiyah or Baruch the son of Neriah. Interestingly, Jeremiah is also the prophet who speaks most about authorship, including describing within the book of Jeremiah itself instances of textual accretion. Jeremiah recounts that on one occasion, after King Jehoiakim of Judah had burned one of his prophetic scrolls, he not only rewrote it, but added new prophecies to it (Jer. 36:32).

In contrast, there is no decisive textual evidence for the Documentary Hypothesis. None of the component documents posited by the Documentary Hypothesis have ever been found, nor are there other composite documents that proponents of this hypothesis can point to as having been constructed via a similar process to the one they posit for the construction of the Bible. Nevertheless, since the Documentary Hypothesis is generally more popular and better known than the Supplementary Hypothesis, I have decided to include in this appendix a brief description of how the Documentary Hypothesis conceives of each of the Biblical sources, as well as a breakdown of the Creation cycle according to the Documentary Hypothesis, without commentary, which can be viewed in parallel to the Supplementary Hypothesis versions offered throughout this book.

The Documentary Hypothesis posits a somewhat different list of Biblical sources from the ones posited by the Supplementary Hypothesis, and imagines each one as the author of his own independent document. These documents, in order of their composition, are:

1. J, the Yahwistic document, written in the Kingdom of Judah in the 10th century BCE (nearly three centuries earlier than J lived according to many proponents of the Supplementary Hypothesis). The Documentary Hypothesis usually identifies J, not E, as the earliest Biblical source, with the J document forming the base of most of the narrative of Genesis and Exodus, as well as parts of Numbers.

2. E, the Elohistic document, written in the Kingdom of Israel in the 9th century BCE. Only fragments of this document were incorporated into the Pentateuch, and they present a narrative parallel to J's better preserved account. The largest and best preserved concentration of E material is in Genesis 28–50, with Joseph, the father of the northern tribes, receiving the most attention.

3. D, the Deuteronomic document, written in the Kingdom of Judah sometime around the late 8th century or early 7th century BCE. D helped to introduce major religious reform, including the centralization of worship and sacrifice in Jerusalem after many of the other cities in Judah were destroyed in the Assyrian invasion during the reign of Hezekiah. Among the books of the Pentateuch, D is found almost exclusively in the book of Deuteronomy, but is also found as a later editorial layer in the subsequent Prophetical books. D recapitulates the desert account, with particular emphasis upon the Sinai narratives.

4. P, or the Priestly document, composed in the Babylonian exile in late 6th century BCE by priests from the house of Aaron. This document is largely concerned with cultic issues related to priests, such as sacrifices and tithes. It also includes the detailed account of the construction of the Tabernacle in the second half of Exodus, and the large body of sacrificial laws and Levitical regulations in the books of Leviticus and Numbers.

The chief difference between the Documentary and Supplementary Hypotheses is that the former claims that each of these documents existed independently, and were selectively edited together by a group of redactors. There is significant disagreement among modern proponents of the Documentary Hypothesis as to the number of redactors and the extent of redactional interference. Since I do not wish to enter this debate, I will simply provide the reader with one of the more widely accepted views about the identities of these redactors. This view states that the first redactor, called RJE, combined the J document and the E document into one (mostly) coherent story, choosing the J document as his base, and adding only fragments of the E document, plus some snippets of his own designed to smooth the transitions between J and E. The next redactor, RJEP, combined the JE document with the P document in a similar process. Finally, the JEP document was combined with the Deuteronomic tradition by a third redactor to form the canonical text. Occasionally, there is also material that Documentary scholars identify as expansions to a particular source, rather than redactional attempts at combining sources. When this is the case I will mark it as (RJ, RE, RP, or RD).

In the text that follows, the two documents that feature in the Creation cycle—namely, J and P—are presented separately, using the same color-coding system I used in the body of this work, in English and in Hebrew. (D and E do not feature at all in the Creation story cycle.) Since no source is preserved completely according to this hypothesis, there are breaks in the narrative, each of which is marked by a line of x's. Finally, I've included a short section featuring the redactors posited by the Documentary Hypothesis in these chapters.

THE J DOCUMENT

GENESIS 2: J

2:4 In the day that Yahweh God made the earth and the heavens, 2:5 no plant of the field was yet in the earth, and no herbs of the field had sprouted yet; for Yahweh God had not caused it to rain upon the earth. There was no one to till the ground, 2:6 but a mist arose from the earth, and watered the entire ground. 2:7 Yahweh God fashioned a man from the earth upon the ground, and breathed the breath of life into his nostrils; and man became a living thing. 2:8 Yahweh God planted a garden eastward, in Eden, and there he placed the man whom he had formed. 2:9 Yahweh God caused every tree that is pleasant to the sight and good for food to grow out of the ground; and the Tree of Life was in the midst of the garden, and the Tree of the Knowledge of Good and Evil.

2:10 A river flowed out of Eden to water the garden; and from there it branched, and became four tributaries. 2:11 The name of the first was Pishon, which flowed around the whole land of Havilah, where there was gold; 2:12 and the gold of that land was good. There was also aromatic resin and onyx stones there. 2:13 The name of the second river was Gihon, the same river that flowed around the whole land of Cush. 2:14 The name of the third river was Hiddekel, which flowed to the east of Assyria. The fourth river was the Euphrates. 2:15 Yahweh God took the man, and put him into the garden of Eden to tend to it and to preserve it. 2:16 Yahweh God commanded the man, thusly, "you may freely eat of every tree of the garden; 2:17 but of the Tree of the Knowledge of Good and Evil, you shall not eat of it; for on the day that you eat of it you will surely die."

2:18 Yahweh God said, "It is not good that the man is alone; I will make a suitable helper for him." 2:19 Yahweh God formed all animals of the field, and every bird of the sky, out of the ground, and brought them to the man to see what he would call them. Whatever the man called every living creature, that was its name. 2:20 The man gave names to all livestock, and to the birds of the sky, and to every animal of the field; but for the man no suitable helper was found. 2:21 Yahweh God caused a deep sleep to fall upon the man, and he slept; and he took one of his ribs, and closed up the flesh in its place. 2:22 He fashioned the rib, which He (Yahweh God) had taken from the man, into a woman, and brought her to the man. 2:23 The man said, "This is now a bone of my bones, and flesh of my flesh. She will be called 'woman,' because she was taken from man." 2:24 It is for this reason that man leaves his father and his mother, and cleaves to his wife, and they become one flesh. 2:25 They were both naked, the man and his wife, and were not ashamed.

GENESIS 3: J

3:1 Now the serpent was slyer than any wild animal which Yahweh God had made. He said to the woman, "Did God really say, 'You shall not eat of any tree of the garden?'"

Appendix: Documentary Hypothesis

GENESIS 2: J (HEBREW)

2:4 אֵלֶּה תוֹלְדוֹת הַשָּׁמַיִם וְהָאָרֶץ בְּהִבָּרְאָם בְּיוֹם עֲשׂוֹת יְהוָה אֱלֹהִים אֶרֶץ וְשָׁמָיִם: 2:5 וְכֹל ׀ שִׂיחַ הַשָּׂדֶה טֶרֶם יִהְיֶה בָאָרֶץ וְכָל־עֵשֶׂב הַשָּׂדֶה טֶרֶם יִצְמָח כִּי לֹא הִמְטִיר יְהוָה אֱלֹהִים עַל־הָאָרֶץ וְאָדָם אַיִן לַעֲבֹד אֶת־הָאֲדָמָה: 2:6 וְאֵד יַעֲלֶה מִן־הָאָרֶץ וְהִשְׁקָה אֶת־כָּל־פְּנֵי־הָאֲדָמָה: 2:7 וַיִּיצֶר יְהוָה אֱלֹהִים אֶת־הָאָדָם עָפָר מִן־הָאֲדָמָה וַיִּפַּח בְּאַפָּיו נִשְׁמַת חַיִּים וַיְהִי הָאָדָם לְנֶפֶשׁ חַיָּה: 2:8 וַיִּטַּע יְהוָה אֱלֹהִים גַּן־בְעֵדֶן מִקֶּדֶם וַיָּשֶׂם שָׁם אֶת־הָאָדָם אֲשֶׁר יָצָר: 2:9 וַיַּצְמַח יְהוָה אֱלֹהִים מִן־הָאֲדָמָה כָּל־עֵץ נֶחְמָד לְמַרְאֶה וְטוֹב לְמַאֲכָל וְעֵץ הַחַיִּים בְּתוֹךְ הַגָּן וְעֵץ הַדַּעַת טוֹב וָרָע:

2:10 וְנָהָר יֹצֵא מֵעֵדֶן לְהַשְׁקוֹת אֶת־הַגָּן וּמִשָּׁם יִפָּרֵד וְהָיָה לְאַרְבָּעָה רָאשִׁים: 2:11 שֵׁם הָאֶחָד פִּישׁוֹן הוּא הַסֹּבֵב אֵת כָּל־אֶרֶץ הַחֲוִילָה אֲשֶׁר־שָׁם הַזָּהָב: 2:12 וּזֲהַב הָאָרֶץ הַהִוא טוֹב שָׁם הַבְּדֹלַח וְאֶבֶן הַשֹּׁהַם: 2:13 וְשֵׁם־הַנָּהָר הַשֵּׁנִי גִּיחוֹן הוּא הַסּוֹבֵב אֵת כָּל־אֶרֶץ כּוּשׁ: 2:14 וְשֵׁם הַנָּהָר הַשְּׁלִישִׁי חִדֶּקֶל הוּא הַהֹלֵךְ קִדְמַת אַשּׁוּר וְהַנָּהָר הָרְבִיעִי הוּא פְרָת:

2:15 וַיִּקַּח יְהוָה אֱלֹהִים אֶת־הָאָדָם וַיַּנִּחֵהוּ בְגַן־עֵדֶן לְעָבְדָהּ וּלְשָׁמְרָהּ: 2:16 וַיְצַו יְהוָה אֱלֹהִים עַל־הָאָדָם לֵאמֹר מִכֹּל עֵץ־הַגָּן אָכֹל תֹּאכֵל: 2:17 וּמֵעֵץ הַדַּעַת טוֹב וָרָע לֹא תֹאכַל מִמֶּנּוּ כִּי בְּיוֹם אֲכָלְךָ מִמֶּנּוּ מוֹת תָּמוּת: 2:18 וַיֹּאמֶר יְהוָה אֱלֹהִים לֹא־טוֹב הֱיוֹת הָאָדָם לְבַדּוֹ אֶעֱשֶׂה־לּוֹ עֵזֶר כְּנֶגְדּוֹ: 2:19 וַיִּצֶר יְהוָה אֱלֹהִים מִן־הָאֲדָמָה כָּל־חַיַּת הַשָּׂדֶה וְאֵת כָּל־עוֹף הַשָּׁמַיִם וַיָּבֵא אֶל־הָאָדָם לִרְאוֹת מַה־יִּקְרָא־לוֹ וְכֹל אֲשֶׁר יִקְרָא־לוֹ הָאָדָם נֶפֶשׁ חַיָּה הוּא שְׁמוֹ: 2:20 וַיִּקְרָא הָאָדָם שֵׁמוֹת לְכָל־הַבְּהֵמָה וּלְעוֹף הַשָּׁמַיִם וּלְכֹל חַיַּת הַשָּׂדֶה וּלְאָדָם לֹא־מָצָא עֵזֶר כְּנֶגְדּוֹ: 2:21 וַיַּפֵּל יְהוָה אֱלֹהִים ׀ תַּרְדֵּמָה עַל־הָאָדָם וַיִּישָׁן וַיִּקַּח אַחַת מִצַּלְעֹתָיו וַיִּסְגֹּר בָּשָׂר תַּחְתֶּנָּה: 2:22 וַיִּבֶן יְהוָה אֱלֹהִים ׀ אֶת־הַצֵּלָע אֲשֶׁר־לָקַח מִן־הָאָדָם לְאִשָּׁה וַיְבִאֶהָ אֶל־הָאָדָם: 2:23 וַיֹּאמֶר הָאָדָם זֹאת הַפַּעַם עֶצֶם מֵעֲצָמַי וּבָשָׂר מִבְּשָׂרִי לְזֹאת יִקָּרֵא אִשָּׁה כִּי מֵאִישׁ לֻקֳחָה־זֹּאת: 2:24 עַל־כֵּן יַעֲזָב־אִישׁ אֶת־אָבִיו וְאֶת־אִמּוֹ וְדָבַק בְּאִשְׁתּוֹ וְהָיוּ לְבָשָׂר אֶחָד: 2:25 וַיִּהְיוּ שְׁנֵיהֶם עֲרוּמִּים הָאָדָם וְאִשְׁתּוֹ וְלֹא יִתְבֹּשָׁשׁוּ:

GENESIS 3: J (HEBREW)

3:1 וְהַנָּחָשׁ הָיָה עָרוּם מִכֹּל חַיַּת הַשָּׂדֶה אֲשֶׁר עָשָׂה יְהוָה אֱלֹהִים וַיֹּאמֶר אֶל־הָאִשָּׁה אַף כִּי־אָמַר אֱלֹהִים לֹא תֹאכְלוּ מִכֹּל עֵץ הַגָּן:

GENESIS 3: J – CONTINUED

3:2 The woman said to the serpent, "Of the fruit of the trees of the garden we may eat, 3 but of the fruit of the tree which is in the middle of the garden, God has said, 'You shall not eat of it, neither shall you touch it, lest you die.'" 3:4 The serpent said to the woman, "You won't die, 3:5 for God knows that on the day you eat it, your eyes will open, and you will be like God, and know good and evil." 3:6 When the woman saw that the tree's (fruit) was edible, and that it was delightful to the eyes, and that it was pleasantly stimulating, she took of its fruit, and ate it; and she gave some to her husband with her, and he ate. 3:7 The eyes of both of them were opened, and they knew that they were naked. They sewed fig leaves together, and made themselves aprons.

3:8 They heard the voice of Yahweh God walking in the garden in the middle of the day, and the man and his wife hid themselves from the presence of Yahweh God among the trees of the garden. 3:9 Yahweh God called to the man, and said to him, "Where are you?" 3:10 The man said, "I heard your voice in the garden, and I was afraid, because I was naked; and I hid myself." 3:11 God said, "Who told you that you were naked? Have you eaten from the tree that I commanded you not to eat from?" 3:12 The man said, "The woman whom you gave me to be with, she gave me of the tree, and I ate (from the fruit)." 3:13 Yahweh God said to the woman, "What is this you have done?" The woman said, "The serpent deceived me, and I ate (from the fruit)." 3:14 Yahweh God said to the serpent, "Because you have done this, you are cursed more than all livestock and wild animals. On your belly you shall crawl, and you shall eat dust all the days of your life. 3:15 I will cause there to be enmity between you and the woman, and between your offspring and her offspring. He will strike your head, and you will strike his heel."

3:16 To the woman he said, "I will increase your travails whilst you are in childbirth. Bearing children will be painful. You will covet your husband, and he will rule over you."

3:17 To Adam he said, "Because you listened to your wife and ate of the tree of which I commanded you, saying, 'You shall not eat of it,' the ground is cursed because of you. You will eat of it all the days of your life. 3:18 It will yield thorns and thistles to you; and you will eat the grass of the field. 3:19 You will eat bread by the sweat of your brow, until you return to the ground, for it is there you originated. For you are dust, and to dust you shall return."

3:20 The man called his wife Eve, because she was the mother of all living things. 3:21 Yahweh God made coats from (animal) skins for Adam and for his wife, and clothed them.

3:22 Yahweh God said, "Behold, the man has become like one of us, knowing good and evil. Now, lest he reach out, and take of the Tree of Life, and eat, and live forever…" 3:23 Therefore Yahweh God banished him from the garden of Eden, to till the ground from whence he originated. 3:24 He drove out the man; and he placed cherubim and a flaming sword which turned every way to guard the way to the Tree of Life.

GENESIS 3: J (HEBREW) – CONTINUED

3:2 וַתֹּאמֶר הָאִשָּׁה אֶל־הַנָּחָשׁ מִפְּרִי עֵץ־הַגָּן נֹאכֵל: 3:3 וּמִפְּרִי הָעֵץ אֲשֶׁר בְּתוֹךְ־הַגָּן אָמַר אֱלֹהִים לֹא תֹאכְלוּ מִמֶּנּוּ וְלֹא תִגְּעוּ בּוֹ פֶּן־תְּמֻתוּן: 3:4 וַיֹּאמֶר הַנָּחָשׁ אֶל־הָאִשָּׁה לֹא־מוֹת תְּמֻתוּן: 3:5 כִּי יֹדֵעַ אֱלֹהִים כִּי בְּיוֹם אֲכָלְכֶם מִמֶּנּוּ וְנִפְקְחוּ עֵינֵיכֶם וִהְיִיתֶם כֵּאלֹהִים יֹדְעֵי טוֹב וָרָע: 3:6 וַתֵּרֶא הָאִשָּׁה כִּי טוֹב הָעֵץ לְמַאֲכָל וְכִי תַאֲוָה־הוּא לָעֵינַיִם וְנֶחְמָד הָעֵץ לְהַשְׂכִּיל וַתִּקַּח מִפִּרְיוֹ וַתֹּאכַל וַתִּתֵּן גַּם־לְאִישָׁהּ עִמָּהּ וַיֹּאכַל: 3:7 וַתִּפָּקַחְנָה עֵינֵי שְׁנֵיהֶם וַיֵּדְעוּ כִּי עֵירֻמִּם הֵם וַיִּתְפְּרוּ עֲלֵה תְאֵנָה וַיַּעֲשׂוּ לָהֶם חֲגֹרֹת:

3:8 וַיִּשְׁמְעוּ אֶת־קוֹל יְהוָה אֱלֹהִים מִתְהַלֵּךְ בַּגָּן לְרוּחַ הַיּוֹם וַיִּתְחַבֵּא הָאָדָם וְאִשְׁתּוֹ מִפְּנֵי יְהוָה אֱלֹהִים בְּתוֹךְ עֵץ הַגָּן: 3:9 וַיִּקְרָא יְהוָה אֱלֹהִים אֶל־הָאָדָם וַיֹּאמֶר לוֹ אַיֶּכָּה: 3:10 וַיֹּאמֶר אֶת־קֹלְךָ שָׁמַעְתִּי בַּגָּן וָאִירָא כִּי־עֵירֹם אָנֹכִי וָאֵחָבֵא: 3:11 וַיֹּאמֶר מִי הִגִּיד לְךָ כִּי עֵירֹם אָתָּה הֲמִן־הָעֵץ אֲשֶׁר צִוִּיתִיךָ לְבִלְתִּי אֲכָל־מִמֶּנּוּ אָכָלְתָּ: 3:12 וַיֹּאמֶר הָאָדָם הָאִשָּׁה אֲשֶׁר נָתַתָּה עִמָּדִי הִוא נָתְנָה־לִּי מִן־הָעֵץ וָאֹכֵל: 3:13 וַיֹּאמֶר יְהוָה אֱלֹהִים לָאִשָּׁה מַה־זֹּאת עָשִׂית וַתֹּאמֶר הָאִשָּׁה הַנָּחָשׁ הִשִּׁיאַנִי וָאֹכֵל: 3:14 וַיֹּאמֶר יְהוָֹה אֱלֹהִים ׀ אֶל־הַנָּחָשׁ כִּי עָשִׂיתָ זֹּאת אָרוּר אַתָּה מִכָּל־הַבְּהֵמָה וּמִכֹּל חַיַּת הַשָּׂדֶה עַל־גְּחֹנְךָ תֵלֵךְ וְעָפָר תֹּאכַל כָּל־יְמֵי חַיֶּיךָ: 3:15 וְאֵיבָה ׀ אָשִׁית בֵּינְךָ וּבֵין הָאִשָּׁה וּבֵין זַרְעֲךָ וּבֵין זַרְעָהּ הוּא יְשׁוּפְךָ רֹאשׁ וְאַתָּה תְּשׁוּפֶנּוּ עָקֵב: ס

3:16 אֶל־הָאִשָּׁה אָמַר הַרְבָּה אַרְבֶּה עִצְּבוֹנֵךְ וְהֵרֹנֵךְ בְּעֶצֶב תֵּלְדִי בָנִים וְאֶל־אִישֵׁךְ תְּשׁוּקָתֵךְ וְהוּא יִמְשָׁל־בָּךְ: ס

3:17 וּלְאָדָם אָמַר כִּי־שָׁמַעְתָּ לְקוֹל אִשְׁתֶּךָ וַתֹּאכַל מִן־הָעֵץ אֲשֶׁר צִוִּיתִיךָ לֵאמֹר לֹא תֹאכַל מִמֶּנּוּ אֲרוּרָה הָאֲדָמָה בַּעֲבוּרֶךָ בְּעִצָּבוֹן תֹּאכֲלֶנָּה כֹּל יְמֵי חַיֶּיךָ: 3:18 וְקוֹץ וְדַרְדַּר תַּצְמִיחַ לָךְ וְאָכַלְתָּ אֶת־עֵשֶׂב הַשָּׂדֶה: 3:19 בְּזֵעַת אַפֶּיךָ תֹּאכַל לֶחֶם עַד שׁוּבְךָ אֶל־הָאֲדָמָה כִּי מִמֶּנָּה לֻקָּחְתָּ כִּי־עָפָר אַתָּה וְאֶל־עָפָר תָּשׁוּב: 3:20 וַיִּקְרָא הָאָדָם שֵׁם אִשְׁתּוֹ חַוָּה כִּי הִוא הָיְתָה אֵם כָּל־חָי: 3:21 וַיַּעַשׂ יְהוָה אֱלֹהִים לְאָדָם וּלְאִשְׁתּוֹ כָּתְנוֹת עוֹר וַיַּלְבִּשֵׁם: פ

3:22 וַיֹּאמֶר ׀ יְהוָה אֱלֹהִים הֵן הָאָדָם הָיָה כְּאַחַד מִמֶּנּוּ לָדַעַת טוֹב וָרָע וְעַתָּה ׀ פֶּן־יִשְׁלַח יָדוֹ וְלָקַח גַּם מֵעֵץ הַחַיִּים וְאָכַל וָחַי לְעֹלָם: 3:23 וַיְשַׁלְּחֵהוּ יְהוָה אֱלֹהִים מִגַּן־עֵדֶן לַעֲבֹד אֶת־הָאֲדָמָה אֲשֶׁר לֻקַּח מִשָּׁם: 3:24 וַיְגָרֶשׁ אֶת־הָאָדָם וַיַּשְׁכֵּן מִקֶּדֶם לְגַן־עֵדֶן אֶת־הַכְּרֻבִים וְאֵת לַהַט הַחֶרֶב הַמִּתְהַפֶּכֶת לִשְׁמֹר אֶת־דֶּרֶךְ עֵץ הַחַיִּים: ס

GENESIS 4: J

4:1 The man knew his wife Eve. She conceived, and gave birth to Cain, and said, "I have created a man with Yahweh." 4:2 Again she gave birth, to Cain's brother, Abel. Abel was a keeper of sheep, but Cain was a tiller of soil. 4:3 After a time, Cain brought an offering to Yahweh from the fruit of the field. 4:4 Abel also brought of the firstborn of his flock and of their fat. Yahweh held Abel and his offering in high regard, 4:5 but didn't regard Cain and his offering. Cain was very angry, and his face fell. 4:6 Yahweh said to Cain, "Why are you angry and why has your face fallen? 4:7 If you behave uprightly (then all the better). If you don't behave uprightly, sin crouches at the door. It desires you, but you can rule over it." 4:8 Cain said to Abel, his brother, ("Let's go into the field.") It happened that when they were in the field, Cain rose up against Abel, his brother, and killed him.

4:9 Yahweh said to Cain, "Where is Abel, your brother?" He said, "I don't know. Am I my brother's keeper?" 4:10 Yahweh said, "What have you done? The voice of your brother's blood cries to me from the ground. 4:11 Now you are cursed because of the ground, which has opened its mouth to receive your brother's blood from your hand. 4:12 From this point forward, when you till the ground, it won't yield its fruit to you. You shall be a peripatetic wanderer upon the earth." 4:13 Cain said to Yahweh, "My punishment is greater than I can bear. 4:14 Behold, you have driven me out today from (settling upon) the face of the earth. I will be hidden from your face, and I will be a fugitive and a wanderer upon the earth. It will happen that whoever finds me will kill me." 4:15 Yahweh said to him, "Therefore whoever slays Cain, vengeance will be taken on him sevenfold." Yahweh appointed a sign for Cain, lest any finding him should strike him. 4:16 Cain went out from Yahweh's presence, and lived in the land of Nod, east of Eden. 4:17 Cain knew his wife. She conceived, and gave birth to Enoch. He built a city, and named the city, after his son, Enoch. 4:18 To Enoch was born Irad. Irad fathered Mehujael. Mehujael fathered Methushael. Methushael fathered Lamech. 4:19 Lamech took two wives: the name of the one was Adah, and the name of the other Zillah.

4:20 Adah gave birth to Jabal, who was the progenitor of those who dwell in tents and tend livestock. 4:21 His brother's name was Jubal, the progenitor of all who play the harp and pipe. 4:22 Zillah also gave birth to Tubal Cain, the forger of every cutting implement of brass and iron. Tubal Cain's sister was Naamah. 4:23 Lamech said to his wives, "Adah and Zillah, hear my voice. Wives of Lamech, listen to my words, for I have slain a man for wounding me, a young man for bruising me. 4:24 If Cain will be avenged seven times, surely Lamech (shall be avenged) seventy-seven times."

4:25 Adam knew his wife again. She gave birth to a son, and named him Seth, "for God has granted me another child instead of Abel, whom Cain killed." 4:26 Seth as well was granted progeny, and he named him Enosh. Then men began to call on Yahweh's name.

xxxxxxxxxxxxxxxxxxxxxxxxxxxxxxxxxxxxxxxxxxxxxxxxxxxxxxxxxxxxxxxxxxxxxxxxx

GENESIS 4: J (HEBREW)

4:1 וְהָאָדָם יָדַע אֶת־חַוָּה אִשְׁתּוֹ וַתַּהַר וַתֵּלֶד אֶת־קַיִן וַתֹּאמֶר קָנִיתִי אִישׁ אֶת־יְהוָה: 4:2 וַתֹּסֶף לָלֶדֶת אֶת־אָחִיו אֶת־הָבֶל וַיְהִי־הֶבֶל רֹעֵה צֹאן וְקַיִן הָיָה עֹבֵד אֲדָמָה: 4:3 וַיְהִי מִקֵּץ יָמִים וַיָּבֵא קַיִן מִפְּרִי הָאֲדָמָה מִנְחָה לַיהוָה: 4:4 וְהֶבֶל הֵבִיא גַם־הוּא מִבְּכֹרוֹת צֹאנוֹ וּמֵחֶלְבֵהֶן וַיִּשַׁע יְהוָה אֶל־הֶבֶל וְאֶל־מִנְחָתוֹ: 4:5 וְאֶל־קַיִן וְאֶל־מִנְחָתוֹ לֹא שָׁעָה וַיִּחַר לְקַיִן מְאֹד וַיִּפְּלוּ פָּנָיו: 4:6 וַיֹּאמֶר יְהוָה אֶל־קָיִן לָמָּה חָרָה לָךְ וְלָמָּה נָפְלוּ פָנֶיךָ: 4:7 הֲלוֹא אִם־תֵּיטִיב שְׂאֵת וְאִם לֹא תֵיטִיב לַפֶּתַח חַטָּאת רֹבֵץ וְאֵלֶיךָ תְּשׁוּקָתוֹ וְאַתָּה תִּמְשָׁל־בּוֹ: 4:8 וַיֹּאמֶר קַיִן אֶל־הֶבֶל אָחִיו וַיְהִי בִּהְיוֹתָם בַּשָּׂדֶה וַיָּקָם קַיִן אֶל־הֶבֶל אָחִיו וַיַּהַרְגֵהוּ:

4:9 וַיֹּאמֶר יְהוָה אֶל־קַיִן אֵי הֶבֶל אָחִיךָ וַיֹּאמֶר לֹא יָדַעְתִּי הֲשֹׁמֵר אָחִי אָנֹכִי: 4:10 וַיֹּאמֶר מֶה עָשִׂיתָ קוֹל דְּמֵי אָחִיךָ צֹעֲקִים אֵלַי מִן־הָאֲדָמָה: 4:11 וְעַתָּה אָרוּר אָתָּה מִן־הָאֲדָמָה אֲשֶׁר פָּצְתָה אֶת־פִּיהָ לָקַחַת אֶת־דְּמֵי אָחִיךָ מִיָּדֶךָ: 4:12 כִּי תַעֲבֹד אֶת־הָאֲדָמָה לֹא־תֹסֵף תֵּת־כֹּחָהּ לָךְ נָע וָנָד תִּהְיֶה בָאָרֶץ: 4:13 וַיֹּאמֶר קַיִן אֶל־יְהוָה גָּדוֹל עֲוֹנִי מִנְּשֹׂא: 4:14 הֵן גֵּרַשְׁתָּ אֹתִי הַיּוֹם מֵעַל פְּנֵי הָאֲדָמָה וּמִפָּנֶיךָ אֶסָּתֵר וְהָיִיתִי נָע וָנָד בָּאָרֶץ וְהָיָה כָל־מֹצְאִי יַהַרְגֵנִי: 4:15 וַיֹּאמֶר לוֹ יְהוָה לָכֵן כָּל־הֹרֵג קַיִן שִׁבְעָתַיִם יֻקָּם וַיָּשֶׂם יְהוָה לְקַיִן אוֹת לְבִלְתִּי הַכּוֹת־אֹתוֹ כָּל־מֹצְאוֹ:

4:16 וַיֵּצֵא קַיִן מִלִּפְנֵי יְהוָה וַיֵּשֶׁב בְּאֶרֶץ־נוֹד קִדְמַת־עֵדֶן: 4:17 וַיֵּדַע קַיִן אֶת־אִשְׁתּוֹ וַתַּהַר וַתֵּלֶד אֶת־חֲנוֹךְ וַיְהִי בֹּנֶה עִיר וַיִּקְרָא שֵׁם הָעִיר כְּשֵׁם בְּנוֹ חֲנוֹךְ: 4:18 וַיִּוָּלֵד לַחֲנוֹךְ אֶת־עִירָד וְעִירָד יָלַד אֶת־מְחוּיָאֵל וּמְחִיָּיאֵל יָלַד אֶת־מְתוּשָׁאֵל וּמְתוּשָׁאֵל יָלַד אֶת־לָמֶךְ: 4:19 וַיִּקַּח־לוֹ לֶמֶךְ שְׁתֵּי נָשִׁים שֵׁם הָאַחַת עָדָה וְשֵׁם הַשֵּׁנִית צִלָּה:

4:20 וַתֵּלֶד עָדָה אֶת־יָבָל הוּא הָיָה אֲבִי יֹשֵׁב אֹהֶל וּמִקְנֶה: 4:21 וְשֵׁם אָחִיו יוּבָל הוּא הָיָה אֲבִי כָּל־תֹּפֵשׂ כִּנּוֹר וְעוּגָב: 4:22 וְצִלָּה גַם־הִוא יָלְדָה אֶת־תּוּבַל קַיִן לֹטֵשׁ כָּל־חֹרֵשׁ נְחֹשֶׁת וּבַרְזֶל וַאֲחוֹת תּוּבַל־קַיִן נַעֲמָה: 4:23 וַיֹּאמֶר לֶמֶךְ לְנָשָׁיו עָדָה וְצִלָּה שְׁמַעַן קוֹלִי נְשֵׁי לֶמֶךְ הַאְזֵנָּה אִמְרָתִי כִּי אִישׁ הָרַגְתִּי לְפִצְעִי וְיֶלֶד לְחַבֻּרָתִי: 4:24 כִּי שִׁבְעָתַיִם יֻקַּם־קָיִן וְלֶמֶךְ שִׁבְעִים וְשִׁבְעָה: 4:25 וַיֵּדַע אָדָם עוֹד אֶת־אִשְׁתּוֹ וַתֵּלֶד בֵּן וַתִּקְרָא אֶת־שְׁמוֹ שֵׁת כִּי שָׁת־לִי אֱלֹהִים זֶרַע אַחֵר תַּחַת הֶבֶל כִּי הֲרָגוֹ קָיִן: 4:26 וּלְשֵׁת גַּם־הוּא יֻלַּד־בֵּן וַיִּקְרָא אֶת־שְׁמוֹ אֱנוֹשׁ אָז הוּחַל לִקְרֹא בְּשֵׁם יְהוָה: פ

xxxxxxxxxxxxxxxxxxxxxxxxxxxxxxxxxxxxxxxxxxxxxxxxxxxxxxxxxxxx

GENESIS 5: J

5:29 and he named him Noah, saying, "He will comfort us in our work and in the toil of our hands, for Yahweh has cursed the earth."

xxxxxxxxxxxxxxxxxxxxxxxxxxxxxxxxxxxxxxxxxxxxxxxxxxxxxxxxxxxxxxxxxxxxxxxxxxxxxxxx

GENESIS 6: J

6:1 It happened, that when people began to multiply upon the face of the earth, daughters were born to them. 6:2 God's sons saw that the daughters of the humans were beautiful, and they took wives for themselves from anywhere they chose. 6:3 Yahweh said, "My Spirit will not strive with man forever, for he is flesh; and thus his days will be one hundred twenty years." 6:4 The Nephilim were in the earth in those days, and also after that, when God's sons copulated with men's daughters, who bore them children. Those were the mighty heroes of old, men of renown.

6:5 Yahweh saw that the wickedness of the human being was great upon the earth, and all the thoughts emanating from his heart were only evil all the time. 6:6 Yahweh regretted that he had made human beings upon the earth, and it grieved his heart. 6:7 Yahweh said, "I will destroy the humans whom I have created from the face of the earth; men, along with animals, creeping things, and the birds of the sky; for I regret having made them." 6:8 But Noah found favor in Yahweh's eyes.

GENESIS 7: J

7:1 Yahweh said to Noah, "Come with all of your household into the ark, for I have seen that you are righteous before me in this generation. 7:2 You shall take seven pairs of every clean animal with you, the male and its female mate. Of the animals that are not clean, take two (each), of the male and its female mate. 7:3 Also of the birds of the sky, seven and seven, male and female, to keep seed alive on the surface of all the earth.

7:4 In seven days, I will cause it to rain on the earth for forty days and forty nights. Every living thing that I have made, I will destroy from the face of the earth." 7:5 Noah did everything that Yahweh commanded him.

7:7 Noah went into the ship with his sons, his wife, and his sons' wives, anticipating the waters of the flood. 7:8 Clean animals, animals that are not clean, birds, and everything that creeps on the ground 7:10 Seven days later, the waters of the flood swept over the earth. 7:12 It rained on the earth for forty days and forty nights. 7:16 And Yahweh shut him in. 7:17 The waters increased, and lifted up the ark, and it rose above the earth.

xxxxxxxxxxxxxxxxxxxxxxxxxxxxxxxxxxxxxxxxxxxxxxxxxxxxxxxxxxxxxxxxxxxxxxxxxxxxxxxx

GENESIS 5: J (HEBREW)

5:29 וַיִּקְרָ֧א אֶת־שְׁמ֛וֹ נֹ֖חַ לֵאמֹ֑ר זֶ֞֠ה יְנַחֲמֵ֤נוּ מִֽמַּעֲשֵׂ֙נוּ֙ וּמֵעִצְּב֣וֹן יָדֵ֔ינוּ מִן־הָ֣אֲדָמָ֔ה אֲשֶׁ֥ר אֵֽרְרָ֖הּ יְהוָֽה׃

xxxxxxxxxxxxxxxxxxxxxxxxxxxxxxxxxxxxxxxxxxxxxxxxxxxxxxxxx

GENESIS 6: J (HEBREW)

6:1 וַֽיְהִי֙ כִּֽי־הֵחֵ֣ל הָֽאָדָ֔ם לָרֹ֖ב עַל־פְּנֵ֣י הָֽאֲדָמָ֑ה וּבָנ֖וֹת יֻלְּד֥וּ לָהֶֽם׃ 6:2 וַיִּרְא֤וּ בְנֵי־הָֽאֱלֹהִים֙ אֶת־בְּנ֣וֹת הָֽאָדָ֔ם כִּ֥י טֹבֹ֖ת הֵ֑נָּה וַיִּקְח֤וּ לָהֶם֙ נָשִׁ֔ים מִכֹּ֖ל אֲשֶׁ֥ר בָּחָֽרוּ׃ 6:3 וַיֹּ֣אמֶר יְהוָ֗ה לֹֽא־יָד֨וֹן רוּחִ֤י בָֽאָדָם֙ לְעֹלָ֔ם בְּשַׁגַּ֖ם ה֣וּא בָשָׂ֑ר וְהָי֣וּ יָמָ֔יו מֵאָ֥ה וְעֶשְׂרִ֖ים שָׁנָֽה׃ 6:4 הַנְּפִלִ֞ים הָי֣וּ בָאָרֶץ֮ בַּיָּמִ֣ים הָהֵם֒ וְגַ֣ם אַֽחֲרֵי־כֵ֗ן אֲשֶׁ֨ר יָבֹ֜אוּ בְּנֵ֤י הָֽאֱלֹהִים֙ אֶל־בְּנ֣וֹת הָֽאָדָ֔ם וְיָלְד֖וּ לָהֶ֑ם הֵ֧מָּה הַגִּבֹּרִ֛ים אֲשֶׁ֥ר מֵעוֹלָ֖ם אַנְשֵׁ֥י הַשֵּֽׁם׃ פ

6:5 וַיַּ֣רְא יְהוָ֔ה כִּ֥י רַבָּ֛ה רָעַ֥ת הָאָדָ֖ם בָּאָ֑רֶץ וְכָל־יֵ֙צֶר֙ מַחְשְׁבֹ֣ת לִבּ֔וֹ רַ֥ק רַ֖ע כָּל־הַיּֽוֹם׃ 6:6 וַיִּנָּ֣חֶם יְהוָ֔ה כִּֽי־עָשָׂ֥ה אֶת־הָֽאָדָ֖ם בָּאָ֑רֶץ וַיִּתְעַצֵּ֖ב אֶל־לִבּֽוֹ׃ 6:7 וַיֹּ֣אמֶר יְהוָ֗ה אֶמְחֶ֨ה אֶת־הָאָדָ֤ם אֲשֶׁר־בָּרָ֙אתִי֙ מֵעַל֙ פְּנֵ֣י הָֽאֲדָמָ֔ה מֵֽאָדָם֙ עַד־בְּהֵמָ֔ה עַד־רֶ֖מֶשׂ וְעַד־ע֣וֹף הַשָּׁמָ֑יִם כִּ֥י נִחַ֖מְתִּי כִּ֥י עֲשִׂיתִֽם׃ 6:8 וְנֹ֕חַ מָ֥צָא חֵ֖ן בְּעֵינֵ֥י יְהוָֽה׃ פ

GENESIS 7: J (HEBREW)

7:1 וַיֹּ֤אמֶר יְהוָה֙ לְנֹ֔חַ בֹּֽא־אַתָּ֥ה וְכָל־בֵּֽיתְךָ֖ אֶל־הַתֵּבָ֑ה כִּֽי־אֹתְךָ֥ רָאִ֛יתִי צַדִּ֥יק לְפָנַ֖י בַּדּ֥וֹר הַזֶּֽה׃ 7:2 מִכֹּ֣ל ׀ הַבְּהֵמָ֣ה הַטְּהוֹרָ֗ה תִּֽקַּח־לְךָ֛ שִׁבְעָ֥ה שִׁבְעָ֖ה אִ֣ישׁ וְאִשְׁתּ֑וֹ וּמִן־הַ֠בְּהֵמָה אֲ֣שֶׁר לֹ֥א טְהֹרָ֛ה הִ֖וא שְׁנַ֥יִם אִ֥ישׁ וְאִשְׁתּֽוֹ׃ 7:3 גַּ֣ם מֵע֧וֹף הַשָּׁמַ֛יִם שִׁבְעָ֥ה שִׁבְעָ֖ה זָכָ֣ר וּנְקֵבָ֑ה לְחַיּ֥וֹת זֶ֖רַע עַל־פְּנֵ֥י כָל־הָאָֽרֶץ׃ 7:4 כִּי֩ לְיָמִ֨ים ע֜וֹד שִׁבְעָ֗ה אָֽנֹכִי֙ מַמְטִ֣יר עַל־הָאָ֔רֶץ אַרְבָּעִ֣ים י֔וֹם וְאַרְבָּעִ֖ים לָ֑יְלָה וּמָחִ֗יתִי אֶֽת־כָּל־הַיְקוּם֙ אֲשֶׁ֣ר עָשִׂ֔יתִי מֵעַ֖ל פְּנֵ֥י הָֽאֲדָמָֽה׃ 7:5 וַיַּ֖עַשׂ נֹ֑חַ כְּכֹ֥ל אֲשֶׁר־צִוָּ֖הוּ יְהוָֽה׃ 7:7 וַיָּ֣בֹא נֹ֔חַ וּ֠בָנָיו וְאִשְׁתּ֧וֹ וּנְשֵֽׁי־בָנָ֛יו אִתּ֖וֹ אֶל־הַתֵּבָ֑ה מִפְּנֵ֖י מֵ֥י הַמַּבּֽוּל׃ 7:8 מִן־הַבְּהֵמָה֙ הַטְּהוֹרָ֔ה וּמִן־הַ֙בְּהֵמָ֔ה אֲשֶׁ֥ר אֵינֶ֖נָּה טְהֹרָ֑ה וּמִ֨ן־הָע֔וֹף וְכֹ֥ל אֲשֶׁר־רֹמֵ֖שׂ עַל־הָֽאֲדָמָֽה׃ 7:10 וַֽיְהִ֖י לְשִׁבְעַ֣ת הַיָּמִ֑ים וּמֵ֣י הַמַּבּ֔וּל הָי֖וּ עַל־הָאָֽרֶץ׃ 7:12 וַֽיְהִ֥י הַגֶּ֖שֶׁם עַל־הָאָ֑רֶץ אַרְבָּעִ֣ים י֔וֹם וְאַרְבָּעִ֖ים לָֽיְלָה׃ 7:16 וַיִּסְגֹּ֥ר יְהוָ֖ה בַּעֲדֽוֹ׃ 7:17 וַיִּרְבּ֣וּ הַמַּ֔יִם וַיִּשְׂאוּ֙ אֶת־הַתֵּבָ֔ה וַתָּ֖רָם מֵעַ֥ל הָאָֽרֶץ׃

xxxxxxxxxxxxxxxxxxxxxxxxxxxxxxxxxxxxxxxxxxxxxxxxxxxxxxxxxxx

GENESIS 7: J – CONTINUED

7:22 All in whose nostrils was the animating breath of life, all who were on dry land, died. 7:23 He blotted out every living thing that was on the face of the earth, including people, livestock, creeping things, and birds of the sky.

xxxxxxxxxxxxxxxxxxxxxxxxxxxxxxxxxxxxxxxxxxxxxxxxxxxxxxxxxxxxxxxxxxxxxxxxxxxxxxxxxxxx

GENESIS 8: J

8:2 The rain from the sky abated. 8:3 The waters gradually receded from the earth. 8:6 It happened that after forty days, Noah opened the window of the ark which he had made, 8:7 and he sent out a raven. It went back and forth, until the waters dried up from the earth. 8:8 He sent out a dove, to see if the waters were abated from the face the earth, 8:9 but the dove found no place to rest her feet, and she returned to him, to the ark; for the waters were upon the surface of the entire earth. He put out his hand, and took her, and brought her to him into the ark. 8:10 He waited yet another seven days, and once again he sent the dove out of the ark. 8:11 The dove came back to him at evening, and, behold, in her mouth was a plucked olive leaf. So Noah knew that the waters were abated from the earth. 8:12 He waited yet another seven days, and sent out the dove; but she didn't return to him again. 8:13 Noah removed the covering of the ark, and looked. He saw that the earth's surface was dried.

xxxxxxxxxxxxxxxxxxxxxxxxxxxxxxxxxxxxxxxxxxxxxxxxxxxxxxxxxxxxxxxxxxxxxxxxxxxxxxxxxxxx

8:20 Noah built an altar to Yahweh, and took of every clean animal, and of every clean bird, and offered burnt offerings on the altar. 8:21 Yahweh smelled the pleasant aroma. Yahweh said in his heart, "I will never again curse the ground because of human beings, because the ruminations of human beings' hearts is evil from their youth; neither will I ever again strike everything living, as I have done. 8:22 While the earth endures, seed time and harvest, and cold and heat, and summer and winter, and day and night shall not cease."

GENESIS 9: J

9:18 The sons of Noah who went out from the ship were Shem, Ham, and Japheth. And Ham was the father of Canaan. 9:19 These three were the sons of Noah, and from these, the whole earth was populated. 9:20 Noah started out as a farmer, and planted a vineyard. 9:21 He drank of the wine and got drunk. He lay naked within his tent. 9:22 Ham, the father of Canaan, saw the nakedness of his father, and told his two brothers outside. 9:23 Shem and Japheth took a garment, and laid it upon both their shoulders, walked backwards, and covered the nakedness of their father. Their faces were averted, and they didn't see their father's nakedness. 9:24 Noah awoke from his wine (-induced stupor), and knew what his youngest son had done to him.

Appendix: Documentary Hypothesis

GENESIS 7: J (HEBREW) – CONTINUED

7:22 כֹּל אֲשֶׁר נִשְׁמַת־רוּחַ חַיִּים בְּאַפָּיו מִכֹּל אֲשֶׁר בֶּחָרָבָה מֵתוּ: 7:23 וַיִּמַח אֶת־כָּל־הַיְקוּם ׀ אֲשֶׁר ׀ עַל־פְּנֵי הָאֲדָמָה מֵאָדָם עַד־בְּהֵמָה עַד־רֶמֶשׂ וְעַד־עוֹף הַשָּׁמַיִם וַיִּמָּחוּ מִן־הָאָרֶץ וַיִּשָּׁאֶר אַךְ־נֹחַ וַאֲשֶׁר אִתּוֹ בַּתֵּבָה:

xxxxxxxxxxxxxxxxxxxxxxxxxxxxxxxxxxxxxxxxxxxxxxxxxxxxxxxxxxxxxxx

GENESIS 8: J (HEBREW)

8:2 וַיִּכָּלֵא הַגֶּשֶׁם מִן־הַשָּׁמָיִם: 8:3 וַיָּשֻׁבוּ הַמַּיִם מֵעַל הָאָרֶץ הָלוֹךְ וָשׁוֹב 8:6 וַיְהִי מִקֵּץ אַרְבָּעִים יוֹם וַיִּפְתַּח נֹחַ אֶת־חַלּוֹן הַתֵּבָה אֲשֶׁר עָשָׂה: 8:7 וַיְשַׁלַּח אֶת־הָעֹרֵב וַיֵּצֵא יָצוֹא וָשׁוֹב עַד־יְבֹשֶׁת הַמַּיִם מֵעַל הָאָרֶץ: 8:8 וַיְשַׁלַּח אֶת־הַיּוֹנָה מֵאִתּוֹ לִרְאוֹת הֲקַלּוּ הַמַּיִם מֵעַל פְּנֵי הָאֲדָמָה: 8:9 וְלֹא־מָצְאָה הַיּוֹנָה מָנוֹחַ לְכַף־רַגְלָהּ וַתָּשָׁב אֵלָיו אֶל־הַתֵּבָה כִּי־מַיִם עַל־פְּנֵי כָל־הָאָרֶץ וַיִּשְׁלַח יָדוֹ וַיִּקָּחֶהָ וַיָּבֵא אֹתָהּ אֵלָיו אֶל־הַתֵּבָה: 8:10 וַיָּחֶל עוֹד שִׁבְעַת יָמִים אֲחֵרִים וַיֹּסֶף שַׁלַּח אֶת־הַיּוֹנָה מִן־הַתֵּבָה: 8:11 וַתָּבֹא אֵלָיו הַיּוֹנָה לְעֵת עֶרֶב וְהִנֵּה עֲלֵה־זַיִת טָרָף בְּפִיהָ וַיֵּדַע נֹחַ כִּי־קַלּוּ הַמַּיִם מֵעַל הָאָרֶץ: 8:12 וַיִּיָּחֶל עוֹד שִׁבְעַת יָמִים אֲחֵרִים וַיְשַׁלַּח אֶת־הַיּוֹנָה וְלֹא־יָסְפָה שׁוּב־אֵלָיו עוֹד: 8:13 וַיָּסַר נֹחַ אֶת־מִכְסֵה הַתֵּבָה וַיַּרְא וְהִנֵּה חָרְבוּ פְּנֵי הָאֲדָמָה:

xxxxxxxxxxxxxxxxxxxxxxxxxxxxxxxxxxxxxxxxxxxxxxxxxxxxxxxxxxxxxxx

8:20 וַיִּבֶן נֹחַ מִזְבֵּחַ לַיהוָה וַיִּקַּח מִכֹּל ׀ הַבְּהֵמָה הַטְּהוֹרָה וּמִכֹּל הָעוֹף הַטָּהֹר וַיַּעַל עֹלֹת בַּמִּזְבֵּחַ: 8:21 וַיָּרַח יְהוָה אֶת־רֵיחַ הַנִּיחֹחַ וַיֹּאמֶר יְהוָה אֶל־לִבּוֹ לֹא־אֹסִף לְקַלֵּל עוֹד אֶת־הָאֲדָמָה בַּעֲבוּר הָאָדָם כִּי יֵצֶר לֵב הָאָדָם רַע מִנְּעֻרָיו וְלֹא־אֹסִף עוֹד לְהַכּוֹת אֶת־כָּל־חַי כַּאֲשֶׁר עָשִׂיתִי: 8:22 עֹד כָּל־יְמֵי הָאָרֶץ זֶרַע וְקָצִיר וְקֹר וָחֹם וְקַיִץ וָחֹרֶף וְיוֹם וָלַיְלָה לֹא יִשְׁבֹּתוּ:

GENESIS 9: J (HEBREW)

9:18 וַיִּהְיוּ בְנֵי־נֹחַ הַיֹּצְאִים מִן־הַתֵּבָה שֵׁם וְחָם וָיָפֶת 9:19 שְׁלֹשָׁה אֵלֶּה בְּנֵי־נֹחַ וּמֵאֵלֶּה נָפְצָה כָל־הָאָרֶץ: 9:20 וַיָּחֶל נֹחַ אִישׁ הָאֲדָמָה וַיִּטַּע כָּרֶם: 9:21 וַיֵּשְׁתְּ מִן־הַיַּיִן וַיִּשְׁכָּר וַיִּתְגַּל בְּתוֹךְ אָהֳלֹה: 9:22 וַיַּרְא חָם אֲבִי כְנַעַן אֵת עֶרְוַת אָבִיו וַיַּגֵּד לִשְׁנֵי־אֶחָיו בַּחוּץ: 9:23 וַיִּקַּח שֵׁם וָיֶפֶת אֶת־הַשִּׂמְלָה וַיָּשִׂימוּ עַל־שְׁכֶם שְׁנֵיהֶם וַיֵּלְכוּ אֲחֹרַנִּית וַיְכַסּוּ אֵת עֶרְוַת אֲבִיהֶם וּפְנֵיהֶם אֲחֹרַנִּית וְעֶרְוַת אֲבִיהֶם לֹא רָאוּ: 9:24 וַיִּיקֶץ נֹחַ מִיֵּינוֹ וַיֵּדַע אֵת אֲשֶׁר־עָשָׂה־לוֹ בְּנוֹ הַקָּטָן:

GENESIS 9: J – CONTINUED

9:25 He said, "Canaan is cursed. He will be a servant of servants (serving) his brothers." 9:26 He said, "Blessed be Yahweh, the God of Shem. Let Canaan be his servant. 9:27 May God make Japheth mighty. Let him dwell in the tents of Shem. Let Canaan be his servant."

xxxxxxxxxxxxxxxxxxxxxxxxxxxxxxxxxxxxxxxxxxxxxxxxxxxxxxxxxxxxxxxxxxxxxxxxxxxxxxxxxxxx

GENESIS 10: J

10:8 Cush became the father of Nimrod. He was the first hero on earth. 10:9 He was a mighty hunter before Yahweh. Therefore it is said, "Like Nimrod, a mighty hunter before Yahweh." 10:10 The beginning of his kingdom was Babel, Erech, Accad, and Calneh, in the land of Shinar. 10:11 From that land he went into Assyria, and built Nineveh, Rehoboth Ir, and Calah, 10:12 and Resen between Nineveh and Calah (the great city). 10:13 Mizraim became the father of Ludim, Anamim, Lehabim, Naphtuhim, 10:14 Pathrusim, Casluhim (whom the Philistines descended from), and Caphtorim.

10:15 Canaan became the father of Sidon (his firstborn), Heth, 10:18 Afterward the families of the Canaanites spread widely. 10:19 The border of the Canaanites was from Sidon, extending to Gerar, to Gaza; and extending toward Sodom, Gomorrah, Admah, and Zeboiim, to Lasha.

10:21 Children were also born to Shem, the father of all the children of Eber, the elder brother of Japheth.

xxxxxxxxxxxxxxxxxxxxxxxxxxxxxxxxxxxxxxxxxxxxxxxxxxxxxxxxxxxxxxxxxxxxxxxxxxxxxxxxxxxx

10:24 Arpachshad became the father of Shelah. Shelah became the father of Eber. 10:25 Two sons were born to Eber. The name of the one was Peleg, for in his days the earth was divided. His brother's name was Joktan. 10:26 Joktan became the father of Almodad, Sheleph, Hazarmaveth, Jerah, 10:27 Hadoram, Uzal, Diklah, 10:28 Obal, Abimael, Sheba, 10:29 Ophir, Havilah, and Jobab. All these were the sons of Joktan.

10:30 Their dwelling was from Mesha, extending toward Sephar, the mountain of the east.

GENESIS 11: J

11:1 The whole earth (spoke) one language and was of one speech. 11:2 It happened, as they traveled east, that they found a plain in the land of Shinar, and they lived there. 11:3 They said one to another, "Come, let's make bricks, and burn them thoroughly." They had brick for building blocks, and they used tar for mortar. 11:4 They said, "Come, let's build ourselves a city, and a tower whose top reaches the sky, and let's make ourselves a name, lest we be scattered all over the surface of the whole earth."

GENESIS 9: J (HEBREW) – CONTINUED

9:25 וַיֹּאמֶר אָרוּר כְּנָעַן עֶבֶד עֲבָדִים יִהְיֶה לְאֶחָיו: 9:26 וַיֹּאמֶר בָּרוּךְ יְהֹוָה אֱלֹהֵי שֵׁם וִיהִי כְנַעַן עֶבֶד לָמוֹ:

9:27 יַפְתְּ אֱלֹהִים לְיֶפֶת וְיִשְׁכֹּן בְּאָהֳלֵי־שֵׁם וִיהִי כְנַעַן עֶבֶד לָמוֹ:

xxxxxxxxxxxxxxxxxxxxxxxxxxxxxxxxxxxxxxxxxxxxxxxxxxxxxxxxxxxx

GENESIS 10: J (HEBREW)

10:8 וְכוּשׁ יָלַד אֶת־נִמְרֹד הוּא הֵחֵל לִהְיוֹת גִּבֹּר בָּאָרֶץ: 10:9 הוּא־הָיָה גִבֹּר־צַיִד לִפְנֵי יְהֹוָה עַל־כֵּן יֵאָמַר כְּנִמְרֹד גִּבּוֹר צַיִד לִפְנֵי יְהֹוָה: 10:10 וַתְּהִי רֵאשִׁית מַמְלַכְתּוֹ בָּבֶל וְאֶרֶךְ וְאַכַּד וְכַלְנֵה בְּאֶרֶץ שִׁנְעָר: 10:11 מִן־הָאָרֶץ הַהִוא יָצָא אַשּׁוּר וַיִּבֶן אֶת־נִינְוֵה וְאֶת־רְחֹבֹת עִיר וְאֶת־כָּלַח: 10:12 וְאֶת־רֶסֶן בֵּין נִינְוֵה וּבֵין כָּלַח הִוא הָעִיר הַגְּדֹלָה: 10:13 וּמִצְרַיִם יָלַד אֶת־לוּדִים וְאֶת־עֲנָמִים וְאֶת־לְהָבִים וְאֶת־נַפְתֻּחִים: 10:14 וְאֶת־פַּתְרֻסִים וְאֶת־כַּסְלֻחִים אֲשֶׁר יָצְאוּ מִשָּׁם פְּלִשְׁתִּים וְאֶת־כַּפְתֹּרִים: 10:15 וּכְנַעַן יָלַד אֶת־צִידֹן בְּכֹרוֹ וְאֶת־חֵת: 10:18 וְאַחַר נָפֹצוּ מִשְׁפְּחוֹת הַכְּנַעֲנִי: 10:19 וַיְהִי גְּבוּל הַכְּנַעֲנִי מִצִּידֹן בֹּאֲכָה גְרָרָה עַד־עַזָּה בֹּאֲכָה סְדֹמָה וַעֲמֹרָה וְאַדְמָה וּצְבֹיִם עַד־לָשַׁע:ס

10:21 וּלְשֵׁם יֻלַּד גַּם־הוּא אֲבִי כָּל־בְּנֵי־עֵבֶר אֲחִי יֶפֶת הַגָּדוֹל:

xxxxxxxxxxxxxxxxxxxxxxxxxxxxxxxxxxxxxxxxxxxxxxxxxxxxxxxxxxxx

10:24 וְאַרְפַּכְשַׁד יָלַד אֶת־שָׁלַח וְשֶׁלַח יָלַד אֶת־עֵבֶר: 10:25 וּלְעֵבֶר יֻלַּד שְׁנֵי בָנִים שֵׁם הָאֶחָד פֶּלֶג כִּי בְיָמָיו נִפְלְגָה הָאָרֶץ וְשֵׁם אָחִיו יָקְטָן: 10:26 וְיָקְטָן יָלַד אֶת־אַלְמוֹדָד וְאֶת־שָׁלֶף וְאֶת־חֲצַרְמָוֶת וְאֶת־יָרַח: 10:27 וְאֶת־הֲדוֹרָם וְאֶת־אוּזָל וְאֶת־דִּקְלָה: 10:28 וְאֶת־עוֹבָל וְאֶת־אֲבִימָאֵל וְאֶת־שְׁבָא: 10:29 וְאֶת־אוֹפִר וְאֶת־חֲוִילָה וְאֶת־יוֹבָב כָּל־אֵלֶּה בְּנֵי יָקְטָן: 10:30 וַיְהִי מוֹשָׁבָם מִמֵּשָׁא בֹּאֲכָה סְפָרָה הַר הַקֶּדֶם:

GENESIS 11: J (HEBREW)

11:1 וַיְהִי כָל־הָאָרֶץ שָׂפָה אֶחָת וּדְבָרִים אֲחָדִים: 11:2 וַיְהִי בְּנָסְעָם מִקֶּדֶם וַיִּמְצְאוּ בִקְעָה בְּאֶרֶץ שִׁנְעָר וַיֵּשְׁבוּ שָׁם:

11:3 וַיֹּאמְרוּ אִישׁ אֶל־רֵעֵהוּ הָבָה נִלְבְּנָה לְבֵנִים וְנִשְׂרְפָה לִשְׂרֵפָה וַתְּהִי לָהֶם הַלְּבֵנָה לְאָבֶן וְהַחֵמָר הָיָה לָהֶם לַחֹמֶר:

11:4 וַיֹּאמְרוּ הָבָה | נִבְנֶה־לָּנוּ עִיר וּמִגְדָּל וְרֹאשׁוֹ בַשָּׁמַיִם וְנַעֲשֶׂה־לָּנוּ שֵׁם פֶּן־נָפוּץ עַל־פְּנֵי כָל־הָאָרֶץ:

GENESIS 11: J – CONTINUED

11:5 Yahweh came down to see the city and the tower, which the children of men built. 11:6 Yahweh said, "Behold, they are one people, and they have all one language, and this is what they have begun to do. Now nothing will be withheld from them of what they intend to do. 11:7 Come, let's go down, and confuse their language, so that they will not understand one another's speech." 11:8 So Yahweh scattered them from there over of all the earth. They stopped building the city. 11:9 Therefore its name was called Babel, because it was there that Yahweh confused all of the earth's language. And from there, Yahweh scattered them over all of the earth.

xxxxxxxxxxxxxxxxxxxxxxxxxxxxxxxxxxxxxxxxxxxxxxxxxxxxxxxxxxxxxxxxxxxxxxxxxxxxxxxxx

11:28 Haran died before his father Terah in the land of his birth, in Ur of the Chaldees. 11:29 Abram and Nahor took wives. The name of Abram's wife was Sarai, and the name of Nahor's wife was Milcah, the daughter of Haran, who was also the father of Iscah. 11:30 Sarai was barren. She had no child.

GENESIS 11: J (HEBREW) – CONTINUED

11:5 וַיֵּרֶד יְהוָה לִרְאֹת אֶת־הָעִיר וְאֶת־הַמִּגְדָּל אֲשֶׁר בָּנוּ בְּנֵי הָאָדָם: 11:6 וַיֹּאמֶר יְהוָה הֵן עַם אֶחָד וְשָׂפָה אַחַת לְכֻלָּם וְזֶה הַחִלָּם לַעֲשׂוֹת וְעַתָּה לֹא־יִבָּצֵר מֵהֶם כֹּל אֲשֶׁר יָזְמוּ לַעֲשׂוֹת: 11:7 הָבָה נֵרְדָה וְנָבְלָה שָׁם שְׂפָתָם אֲשֶׁר לֹא יִשְׁמְעוּ אִישׁ שְׂפַת רֵעֵהוּ: 11:8 וַיָּפֶץ יְהוָה אֹתָם מִשָּׁם עַל־פְּנֵי כָל־הָאָרֶץ וַיַּחְדְּלוּ לִבְנֹת הָעִיר: 11:9 עַל־כֵּן קָרָא שְׁמָהּ בָּבֶל כִּי־שָׁם בָּלַל יְהוָה שְׂפַת כָּל־הָאָרֶץ וּמִשָּׁם הֱפִיצָם יְהוָה עַל־פְּנֵי כָּל־הָאָרֶץ: פ

xxxxxxxxxxxxxxxxxxxxxxxxxxxxxxxxxxxxxxxxxxxxxxxxxxxxxxxxxxxxxxxxxxxx

11:28 וַיָּמָת הָרָן עַל־פְּנֵי תֶּרַח אָבִיו בְּאֶרֶץ מוֹלַדְתּוֹ בְּאוּר כַּשְׂדִּים: 11:29 וַיִּקַּח אַבְרָם וְנָחוֹר לָהֶם נָשִׁים שֵׁם אֵשֶׁת־אַבְרָם שָׂרָי וְשֵׁם אֵשֶׁת־נָחוֹר מִלְכָּה בַּת־הָרָן אֲבִי־מִלְכָּה וַאֲבִי יִסְכָּה: 11:30 וַתְּהִי שָׂרַי עֲקָרָה אֵין לָהּ וָלָד:

THE P DOCUMENT

GENESIS 1: P

1:1 In the beginning when God created the heavens and the earth, 1:2 the earth was a formless void, and darkness covered the face of the deep, while a wind from God swept over the face of the waters. 1:3 Then God said, "Let there be light;" and there was light. 1:4 And God saw that the light was good; and God separated the light from the darkness. 1:5 God called the light Day, and the darkness he called Night. And there was evening and there was morning, the first day.

1:6 And God said, "Let there be a plane in the midst of the waters, and let it distinguish between water and water." 1:7 So God made the plane and separated the waters that were under the plane from the waters that were above the plane. And it was so. 1:8 God called the plane Sky. And there was evening and there was morning, the second day.

1:9 And God said, "Let the waters under the sky be gathered together into one place, and let the dry land appear." And it was so. 1:10 God called the dry land Earth, and the waters that were gathered together he called Seas. And God saw that it was good. 1:11 Then God said, "Let the earth sprout vegetation: plants with seed, and fruit trees of every kind on earth that bear fruit with the seed in it." And it was so. 1:12 The earth brought forth vegetation: plants yielding seed of every kind, and trees of every kind bearing fruit with the seed in it. And God saw that it was good. 1:13 And there was evening and there was morning, the third day.

1:14 And God said, "Let there be lights upon the surface of the sky to separate the day from the night; and let them be signs for seasons and for days and years, 1:15 and let them be luminaries upon the surface of the sky to light up the earth." And it was so. 1:16 God made the two great luminaries—the greater luminary to rule the day and the lesser luminary to rule the night—and the stars. 1:17 God placed them upon the surface of the sky to give light upon the earth, 1:18 to rule over the day and over the night, and to separate light from darkness. And God saw that it was good. 1:19 And there was evening and there was morning, the fourth day.

1:20 And God said, "Let the waters bring forth swarms of living creatures, and let birds fly above the earth across the sky's surface." 1:21 So God created the great sea monsters and every living creature that moves, of all types, that swarm in the waters and every winged bird of every kind. And God saw that it was good. 1:22 God blessed them, saying, "Be fruitful and multiply and fill the waters in the seas, and let birds multiply upon the earth." 1:23 And there was evening and there was morning, the fifth day.

1:24 And God said, "Let the earth bring forth living creatures of all types: cattle and creeping things and wild animals of the earth of all types." And it was so. 1:25 God made wild animals of the earth of all types, and the cattle of all types, and everything that creeps upon the ground of all types. And God saw that it was good.

Appendix: Documentary Hypothesis

GENESIS 1: P (HEBREW)

1:1 בְּרֵאשִׁית בָּרָא אֱלֹהִים אֵת הַשָּׁמַיִם וְאֵת הָאָרֶץ: 1:2 וְהָאָרֶץ הָיְתָה תֹהוּ וָבֹהוּ וְחֹשֶׁךְ עַל־פְּנֵי תְהוֹם וְרוּחַ אֱלֹהִים מְרַחֶפֶת עַל־פְּנֵי הַמָּיִם: 1:3 וַיֹּאמֶר אֱלֹהִים יְהִי אוֹר וַיְהִי־אוֹר: 1:4 וַיַּרְא אֱלֹהִים אֶת־הָאוֹר כִּי־טוֹב וַיַּבְדֵּל אֱלֹהִים בֵּין הָאוֹר וּבֵין הַחֹשֶׁךְ: 1:5 וַיִּקְרָא אֱלֹהִים ׀ לָאוֹר יוֹם וְלַחֹשֶׁךְ קָרָא לָיְלָה וַיְהִי־עֶרֶב וַיְהִי־בֹקֶר יוֹם אֶחָד: פ

1:6 וַיֹּאמֶר אֱלֹהִים יְהִי רָקִיעַ בְּתוֹךְ הַמָּיִם וִיהִי מַבְדִּיל בֵּין מַיִם לָמָיִם: 1:7 וַיַּעַשׂ אֱלֹהִים אֶת־הָרָקִיעַ וַיַּבְדֵּל בֵּין הַמַּיִם אֲשֶׁר מִתַּחַת לָרָקִיעַ וּבֵין הַמַּיִם אֲשֶׁר מֵעַל לָרָקִיעַ וַיְהִי־כֵן: 1:8 וַיִּקְרָא אֱלֹהִים לָרָקִיעַ שָׁמָיִם וַיְהִי־עֶרֶב וַיְהִי־בֹקֶר יוֹם שֵׁנִי: פ

1:9 וַיֹּאמֶר אֱלֹהִים יִקָּווּ הַמַּיִם מִתַּחַת הַשָּׁמַיִם אֶל־מָקוֹם אֶחָד וְתֵרָאֶה הַיַּבָּשָׁה וַיְהִי־כֵן: 1:10 וַיִּקְרָא אֱלֹהִים ׀ לַיַּבָּשָׁה אֶרֶץ וּלְמִקְוֵה הַמַּיִם קָרָא יַמִּים וַיַּרְא אֱלֹהִים כִּי־טוֹב: 1:11 וַיֹּאמֶר אֱלֹהִים תַּדְשֵׁא הָאָרֶץ דֶּשֶׁא עֵשֶׂב מַזְרִיעַ זֶרַע עֵץ פְּרִי עֹשֶׂה פְּרִי לְמִינוֹ אֲשֶׁר זַרְעוֹ־בוֹ עַל־הָאָרֶץ וַיְהִי־כֵן: 1:12 וַתּוֹצֵא הָאָרֶץ דֶּשֶׁא עֵשֶׂב מַזְרִיעַ זֶרַע לְמִינֵהוּ וְעֵץ עֹשֶׂה־פְּרִי אֲשֶׁר זַרְעוֹ־בוֹ לְמִינֵהוּ וַיַּרְא אֱלֹהִים כִּי־טוֹב: 1:13 וַיְהִי־עֶרֶב וַיְהִי־בֹקֶר יוֹם שְׁלִישִׁי: פ

1:14 וַיֹּאמֶר אֱלֹהִים יְהִי מְאֹרֹת בִּרְקִיעַ הַשָּׁמַיִם לְהַבְדִּיל בֵּין הַיּוֹם וּבֵין הַלָּיְלָה וְהָיוּ לְאֹתֹת וּלְמוֹעֲדִים וּלְיָמִים וְשָׁנִים: 1:15 וְהָיוּ לִמְאוֹרֹת בִּרְקִיעַ הַשָּׁמַיִם לְהָאִיר עַל־הָאָרֶץ וַיְהִי־כֵן: 1:16 וַיַּעַשׂ אֱלֹהִים אֶת־שְׁנֵי הַמְּאֹרֹת הַגְּדֹלִים אֶת־הַמָּאוֹר הַגָּדֹל לְמֶמְשֶׁלֶת הַיּוֹם וְאֶת־הַמָּאוֹר הַקָּטֹן לְמֶמְשֶׁלֶת הַלַּיְלָה וְאֵת הַכּוֹכָבִים: 1:17 וַיִּתֵּן אֹתָם אֱלֹהִים בִּרְקִיעַ הַשָּׁמָיִם לְהָאִיר עַל־הָאָרֶץ: 1:18 וְלִמְשֹׁל בַּיּוֹם וּבַלַּיְלָה וּלֲהַבְדִּיל בֵּין הָאוֹר וּבֵין הַחֹשֶׁךְ וַיַּרְא אֱלֹהִים כִּי־טוֹב: 1:19 וַיְהִי־עֶרֶב וַיְהִי־בֹקֶר יוֹם רְבִיעִי: פ

1:20 וַיֹּאמֶר אֱלֹהִים יִשְׁרְצוּ הַמַּיִם שֶׁרֶץ נֶפֶשׁ חַיָּה וְעוֹף יְעוֹפֵף עַל־הָאָרֶץ עַל־פְּנֵי רְקִיעַ הַשָּׁמָיִם: 1:21 וַיִּבְרָא אֱלֹהִים אֶת־הַתַּנִּינִם הַגְּדֹלִים וְאֵת כָּל־נֶפֶשׁ הַחַיָּה ׀ הָרֹמֶשֶׂת אֲשֶׁר שָׁרְצוּ הַמַּיִם לְמִינֵהֶם וְאֵת כָּל־עוֹף כָּנָף לְמִינֵהוּ וַיַּרְא אֱלֹהִים כִּי־טוֹב: 1:22 וַיְבָרֶךְ אֹתָם אֱלֹהִים לֵאמֹר פְּרוּ וּרְבוּ וּמִלְאוּ אֶת־הַמַּיִם בַּיַּמִּים וְהָעוֹף יִרֶב בָּאָרֶץ: 1:23 וַיְהִי־עֶרֶב וַיְהִי־בֹקֶר יוֹם חֲמִישִׁי: פ

1:24 וַיֹּאמֶר אֱלֹהִים תּוֹצֵא הָאָרֶץ נֶפֶשׁ חַיָּה לְמִינָהּ בְּהֵמָה וָרֶמֶשׂ וְחַיְתוֹ־אֶרֶץ לְמִינָהּ וַיְהִי־כֵן: 1:25 וַיַּעַשׂ אֱלֹהִים אֶת־חַיַּת הָאָרֶץ לְמִינָהּ וְאֶת־הַבְּהֵמָה לְמִינָהּ וְאֵת כָּל־רֶמֶשׂ הָאֲדָמָה לְמִינֵהוּ וַיַּרְא אֱלֹהִים כִּי־טוֹב:

GENESIS 1: P – CONTINUED

1:26 Then God said, "Let us make humankind in our image, according to our likeness; and let them have dominion over the fish of the sea, and over the birds of the air, and over the cattle, and over all the wild animals of the earth, and over every creeping thing that creeps upon the earth." 1:27 So God created humankind in his image; he created them in the image of God; he created them male and female. 1:28 God blessed them, and God said to them, "Be fruitful and multiply, and fill the earth and subdue it; and have dominion over the fish of the sea and over the birds of the air and over every living thing that moves upon the earth." 1:29 God said, "See, I have given you every plant with seeds that is upon the face of all the earth, and every tree with seed in its fruit, as food for you. 1:30 And to every beast of the earth, and to every bird of the air, and to everything that creeps on the earth, everything that has the breath of life, I have given every sprouting plant as food." And it was so. 1:31 God saw everything that he had made, and indeed, it was very good. And there was evening and there was morning, the sixth day.

GENESIS 2: P

2:1 The heavens and the earth were finished, and all their vast array. 2:2 On the seventh day God finished his work which he had made; and he rested on the seventh day from all his work which he had made. 2:3 God blessed the seventh day, and made it holy, because he rested in it from all his work which he had created and made.

GENESIS 5: P

5:1 This is an account of Adam's generations. In the day that God created man, he made him in God's likeness. 5:2 He created them male and female, and blessed them, and called them "humans" on the day when they were created.

5:3 Adam lived one hundred and thirty years, and fathered a son in his own likeness, and in his own image, and named him Seth. 5:4 The days of Adam after he'd fathered Seth were eight hundred years, and he sired sons and daughters. 5:5 All the years that Adam lived amounted to nine hundred and thirty years; then he died.

5:6 Seth lived one hundred and five years, and fathered Enosh. 5:7 Seth lived eight hundred and seven years after he'd fathered Enosh, and sired sons and daughters. 5:8 All the years of Seth's (life) were nine hundred and twelve years; then he died.

5:9 Enosh lived ninety years, and fathered Kenan. 5:10 Enosh lived eight hundred and fifteen years after he'd fathered Kenan, and sired sons and daughters. 5:11 All the years of Enosh's (life) were nine hundred and five years; then he died.

Appendix: Documentary Hypothesis

GENESIS 1: P (HEBREW) – CONTINUED

1:26 וַיֹּ֣אמֶר אֱלֹהִ֗ים נַֽעֲשֶׂ֥ה אָדָ֛ם בְּצַלְמֵ֖נוּ כִּדְמוּתֵ֑נוּ וְיִרְדּוּ֩ בִדְגַ֨ת הַיָּ֜ם וּבְע֣וֹף הַשָּׁמַ֗יִם וּבַבְּהֵמָה֙ וּבְכָל־הָאָ֔רֶץ וּבְכָל־הָרֶ֖מֶשׂ הָֽרֹמֵ֥שׂ עַל־הָאָֽרֶץ׃ 1:27 וַיִּבְרָ֨א אֱלֹהִ֤ים ׀ אֶת־הָֽאָדָם֙ בְּצַלְמ֔וֹ בְּצֶ֥לֶם אֱלֹהִ֖ים בָּרָ֣א אֹת֑וֹ זָכָ֥ר וּנְקֵבָ֖ה בָּרָ֥א אֹתָֽם׃ 1:28 וַיְבָ֣רֶךְ אֹתָם֮ אֱלֹהִים֒ וַיֹּ֨אמֶר לָהֶ֜ם אֱלֹהִ֗ים פְּר֥וּ וּרְב֛וּ וּמִלְא֥וּ אֶת־הָאָ֖רֶץ וְכִבְשֻׁ֑הָ וּרְד֞וּ בִּדְגַ֤ת הַיָּם֙ וּבְע֣וֹף הַשָּׁמַ֔יִם וּבְכָל־חַיָּ֖ה הָֽרֹמֶ֥שֶׂת עַל־הָאָֽרֶץ׃ 1:29 וַיֹּ֣אמֶר אֱלֹהִ֗ים הִנֵּה֩ נָתַ֨תִּי לָכֶ֜ם אֶת־כָּל־עֵ֣שֶׂב ׀ זֹרֵ֣עַ זֶ֗רַע אֲשֶׁר֙ עַל־פְּנֵ֣י כָל־הָאָ֔רֶץ וְאֶת־כָּל־הָעֵ֛ץ אֲשֶׁר־בּ֥וֹ פְרִי־עֵ֖ץ זֹרֵ֣עַ זָ֑רַע לָכֶ֥ם יִֽהְיֶ֖ה לְאָכְלָֽה׃ 1:30 וּֽלְכָל־חַיַּ֣ת הָ֠אָרֶץ וּלְכָל־ע֨וֹף הַשָּׁמַ֜יִם וּלְכֹ֣ל ׀ רוֹמֵ֣שׂ עַל־הָאָ֗רֶץ אֲשֶׁר־בּוֹ֙ נֶ֣פֶשׁ חַיָּ֔ה אֶת־כָּל־יֶ֥רֶק עֵ֖שֶׂב לְאָכְלָ֑ה וַֽיְהִי־כֵֽן׃ 1:31 וַיַּ֤רְא אֱלֹהִים֙ אֶת־כָּל־אֲשֶׁ֣ר עָשָׂ֔ה וְהִנֵּה־ט֖וֹב מְאֹ֑ד וַֽיְהִי־עֶ֥רֶב וַֽיְהִי־בֹ֖קֶר י֥וֹם הַשִּׁשִּֽׁי׃ פ

GENESIS 2: P (HEBREW)

2:1 וַיְכֻלּ֛וּ הַשָּׁמַ֥יִם וְהָאָ֖רֶץ וְכָל־צְבָאָֽם׃ 2:2 וַיְכַ֤ל אֱלֹהִים֙ בַּיּ֣וֹם הַשְּׁבִיעִ֔י מְלַאכְתּ֖וֹ אֲשֶׁ֣ר עָשָׂ֑ה וַיִּשְׁבֹּת֙ בַּיּ֣וֹם הַשְּׁבִיעִ֔י מִכָּל־מְלַאכְתּ֖וֹ אֲשֶׁ֥ר עָשָֽׂה׃ 2:3 וַיְבָ֤רֶךְ אֱלֹהִים֙ אֶת־י֣וֹם הַשְּׁבִיעִ֔י וַיְקַדֵּ֖שׁ אֹת֑וֹ כִּ֣י ב֤וֹ שָׁבַת֙ מִכָּל־מְלַאכְתּ֔וֹ אֲשֶׁר־בָּרָ֥א אֱלֹהִ֖ים לַעֲשֽׂוֹת׃ פ

GENESIS 5: P (HEBREW)

5:1 זֶ֣ה סֵ֔פֶר תּוֹלְדֹ֖ת אָדָ֑ם בְּי֗וֹם בְּרֹ֤א אֱלֹהִים֙ אָדָ֔ם בִּדְמ֥וּת אֱלֹהִ֖ים עָשָׂ֥ה אֹתֽוֹ׃ 5:2 זָכָ֥ר וּנְקֵבָ֖ה בְּרָאָ֑ם וַיְבָ֣רֶךְ אֹתָ֗ם וַיִּקְרָ֤א אֶת־שְׁמָם֙ אָדָ֔ם בְּי֖וֹם הִבָּֽרְאָֽם׃ 5:3 וַֽיְחִ֣י אָדָ֗ם שְׁלֹשִׁ֤ים וּמְאַת֙ שָׁנָ֔ה וַיּ֥וֹלֶד בִּדְמוּת֖וֹ כְּצַלְמ֑וֹ וַיִּקְרָ֥א אֶת־שְׁמ֖וֹ שֵֽׁת׃ 5:4 וַיִּֽהְי֣וּ יְמֵי־אָדָ֗ם אַֽחֲרֵי֙ הוֹלִיד֣וֹ אֶת־שֵׁ֔ת שְׁמֹנֶ֥ה מֵאֹ֖ת שָׁנָ֑ה וַיּ֥וֹלֶד בָּנִ֖ים וּבָנֽוֹת׃ 5:5 וַיִּֽהְי֞וּ כָּל־יְמֵ֤י אָדָם֙ אֲשֶׁר־חַ֔י תְּשַׁ֤ע מֵאוֹת֙ שָׁנָ֔ה וּשְׁלֹשִׁ֖ים שָׁנָ֑ה וַיָּמֹֽת׃ ס

5:6 וַֽיְחִי־שֵׁ֕ת חָמֵ֥שׁ שָׁנִ֖ים וּמְאַ֣ת שָׁנָ֑ה וַיּ֖וֹלֶד אֶת־אֱנֽוֹשׁ׃ 5:7 וַֽיְחִי־שֵׁ֗ת אַֽחֲרֵי֙ הוֹלִיד֣וֹ אֶת־אֱנ֔וֹשׁ שֶׁ֣בַע שָׁנִ֔ים וּשְׁמֹנֶ֥ה מֵא֖וֹת שָׁנָ֑ה וַיּ֥וֹלֶד בָּנִ֖ים וּבָנֽוֹת׃ 5:8 וַיִּֽהְיוּ֙ כָּל־יְמֵי־שֵׁ֔ת שְׁתֵּ֤ים עֶשְׂרֵה֙ שָׁנָ֔ה וּתְשַׁ֥ע מֵא֖וֹת שָׁנָ֑ה וַיָּמֹֽת׃ ס

5:9 וַֽיְחִ֣י אֱנ֔וֹשׁ תִּשְׁעִ֖ים שָׁנָ֑ה וַיּ֖וֹלֶד אֶת־קֵינָֽן׃ 5:10 וַֽיְחִ֣י אֱנ֗וֹשׁ אַֽחֲרֵי֙ הוֹלִיד֣וֹ אֶת־קֵינָ֔ן חֲמֵ֤שׁ עֶשְׂרֵה֙ שָׁנָ֔ה וּשְׁמֹנֶ֥ה מֵא֖וֹת שָׁנָ֑ה וַיּ֥וֹלֶד בָּנִ֖ים וּבָנֽוֹת׃ 5:11 וַיִּֽהְיוּ֙ כָּל־יְמֵ֣י אֱנ֔וֹשׁ חָמֵ֣שׁ שָׁנִ֔ים וּתְשַׁ֥ע מֵא֖וֹת שָׁנָ֑ה וַיָּמֹֽת׃ ס

GENESIS 5: P – CONTINUED

5:12 Kenan lived seventy years, and fathered Mahalalel. 5:13 Kenan lived eight hundred and forty years after he'd fathered Mahalalel, and sired sons and daughters, 5:14 and all the years of Kenan's (life) were nine hundred and ten years; then he died.

5:15 Mahalalel lived sixty-five years, and fathered Jared. 5:16 Mahalalel lived eight hundred and thirty years after he'd fathered Jared, and sired sons and daughters. 5:17 All the years of Mahalalel's (life) were eight hundred and ninety-five years; then he died.

5:18 Jared lived one hundred and sixty-two years, and fathered Enoch. 5:19 Jared lived eight hundred years after he'd fathered Enoch, and sired sons and daughters. 5:20 All the years of Jared's (life) were nine hundred and sixty-two years; then he died.

5:21 Enoch lived sixty-five years, and fathered Methuselah. 5:22 Enoch walked with God for three hundred years after he'd fathered Methuselah, and sired sons and daughters. 5:23 All the years of Enoch's (life) were three hundred and sixty-five years. 5:24 Enoch walked with God, and he disappeared, for God took him.

5:25 Methuselah lived one hundred and eighty-seven years, and fathered Lamech. 5:26 Methuselah lived seven hundred and eighty-two years after he'd fathered Lamech, and sired sons and daughters. 5:27 All the years of Methuselah's (life) were nine hundred and sixty-nine years; then he died.

5:28 Lamech lived one hundred and eighty-two years, and fathered a son,
xxxxxxxxxxxxxxxxxxxxxxxxxxxxxxxxxxxxxxxxxxxxxxxxxxxxxxxxxxxxxxxxxxxxxxxxxxxxxxxxxxxxxx
5:30 Lamech lived five hundred and ninety-five years after he'd fathered Noah, and sired sons and daughters. 5:31 All the years of Lamech's (life) were seven hundred seventy-seven years; then he died.

5:32 Noah was five hundred years old, and Noah fathered Shem, Ham, and Japheth.

GENESIS 6: P

6:9 These are the generations of Noah. Noah was a righteous man, blameless among the people of his time. Noah walked with God. 6:10 Noah fathered three sons: Shem, Ham, and Japheth. 6:11 The earth was corrupt before God, and the earth was filled with violence. 6:12 God saw the earth, that it was corrupt, for all flesh on earth had become corrupt.

6:13 God said to Noah, "The end of all flesh has come for I (have decreed it), since the earth is filled with violence because of them. Behold, I will destroy them with the earth.

GENESIS 5: P (HEBREW) – CONTINUED

5:12 וַיְחִי קֵינָן שִׁבְעִים שָׁנָה וַיּוֹלֶד אֶת־מַהֲלַלְאֵל: 5:13 וַיְחִי קֵינָן אַחֲרֵי הוֹלִידוֹ אֶת־מַהֲלַלְאֵל אַרְבָּעִים שָׁנָה וּשְׁמֹנֶה מֵאוֹת שָׁנָה וַיּוֹלֶד בָּנִים וּבָנוֹת: 5:14 וַיִּהְיוּ כָּל־יְמֵי קֵינָן עֶשֶׂר שָׁנִים וּתְשַׁע מֵאוֹת שָׁנָה וַיָּמֹת: ס

5:15 וַיְחִי מַהֲלַלְאֵל חָמֵשׁ שָׁנִים וְשִׁשִּׁים שָׁנָה וַיּוֹלֶד אֶת־יָרֶד: 5:16 וַיְחִי מַהֲלַלְאֵל אַחֲרֵי הוֹלִידוֹ אֶת־יֶרֶד שְׁלֹשִׁים שָׁנָה וּשְׁמֹנֶה מֵאוֹת שָׁנָה וַיּוֹלֶד בָּנִים וּבָנוֹת: 5:17 וַיִּהְיוּ כָּל־יְמֵי מַהֲלַלְאֵל חָמֵשׁ וְתִשְׁעִים שָׁנָה וּשְׁמֹנֶה מֵאוֹת שָׁנָה וַיָּמֹת: ס

5:18 וַיְחִי־יֶרֶד שְׁתַּיִם וְשִׁשִּׁים שָׁנָה וּמְאַת שָׁנָה וַיּוֹלֶד אֶת־חֲנוֹךְ: 5:19 וַיְחִי־יֶרֶד אַחֲרֵי הוֹלִידוֹ אֶת־חֲנוֹךְ שְׁמֹנֶה מֵאוֹת שָׁנָה וַיּוֹלֶד בָּנִים וּבָנוֹת: 5:20 וַיִּהְיוּ כָּל־יְמֵי־יֶרֶד שְׁתַּיִם וְשִׁשִּׁים שָׁנָה וּתְשַׁע מֵאוֹת שָׁנָה וַיָּמֹת: פ

5:21 וַיְחִי חֲנוֹךְ חָמֵשׁ וְשִׁשִּׁים שָׁנָה וַיּוֹלֶד אֶת־מְתוּשָׁלַח: 5:22 וַיִּתְהַלֵּךְ חֲנוֹךְ אֶת־הָאֱלֹהִים אַחֲרֵי הוֹלִידוֹ אֶת־מְתוּשֶׁלַח שְׁלֹשׁ מֵאוֹת שָׁנָה וַיּוֹלֶד בָּנִים וּבָנוֹת: 5:23 וַיְהִי כָּל־יְמֵי חֲנוֹךְ חָמֵשׁ וְשִׁשִּׁים שָׁנָה וּשְׁלֹשׁ מֵאוֹת שָׁנָה: 5:24 וַיִּתְהַלֵּךְ חֲנוֹךְ אֶת־הָאֱלֹהִים וְאֵינֶנּוּ כִּי־לָקַח אֹתוֹ אֱלֹהִים: פ

5:25 וַיְחִי מְתוּשֶׁלַח שֶׁבַע וּשְׁמֹנִים שָׁנָה וּמְאַת שָׁנָה וַיּוֹלֶד אֶת־לָמֶךְ: 5:26 וַיְחִי מְתוּשֶׁלַח אַחֲרֵי הוֹלִידוֹ אֶת־לֶמֶךְ שְׁתַּיִם וּשְׁמוֹנִים שָׁנָה וּשְׁבַע מֵאוֹת שָׁנָה וַיּוֹלֶד בָּנִים וּבָנוֹת: 5:27 וַיִּהְיוּ כָּל־יְמֵי מְתוּשֶׁלַח תֵּשַׁע וְשִׁשִּׁים שָׁנָה וּתְשַׁע מֵאוֹת שָׁנָה וַיָּמֹת: פ

5:28 וַיְחִי־לֶמֶךְ שְׁתַּיִם וּשְׁמֹנִים שָׁנָה וּמְאַת שָׁנָה וַיּוֹלֶד בֵּן:

xxxxxxxxxxxxxxxxxxxxxxxxxxxxxxxxxxxxxxxxxxxxxxxxxxxxxxxxxx

5:30 וַיְחִי־לֶמֶךְ אַחֲרֵי הוֹלִידוֹ אֶת־נֹחַ חָמֵשׁ וְתִשְׁעִים שָׁנָה וַחֲמֵשׁ מֵאֹת שָׁנָה וַיּוֹלֶד בָּנִים וּבָנוֹת: 5:31 וַיְהִי כָּל־יְמֵי־לֶמֶךְ שֶׁבַע וְשִׁבְעִים שָׁנָה וּשְׁבַע מֵאוֹת שָׁנָה וַיָּמֹת: ס

5:32 וַיְהִי־נֹחַ בֶּן־חֲמֵשׁ מֵאוֹת שָׁנָה וַיּוֹלֶד נֹחַ אֶת־שֵׁם אֶת־חָם וְאֶת־יָפֶת:

GENESIS 6: P (HEBREW)

6:9 אֵלֶּה תּוֹלְדֹת נֹחַ נֹחַ אִישׁ צַדִּיק תָּמִים הָיָה בְּדֹרֹתָיו אֶת־הָאֱלֹהִים הִתְהַלֶּךְ־נֹחַ: 6:10 וַיּוֹלֶד נֹחַ שְׁלֹשָׁה בָנִים אֶת־שֵׁם אֶת־חָם וְאֶת־יָפֶת: 6:11 וַתִּשָּׁחֵת הָאָרֶץ לִפְנֵי הָאֱלֹהִים וַתִּמָּלֵא הָאָרֶץ חָמָס: 6:12 וַיַּרְא אֱלֹהִים אֶת־הָאָרֶץ וְהִנֵּה נִשְׁחָתָה כִּי־הִשְׁחִית כָּל־בָּשָׂר אֶת־דַּרְכּוֹ עַל־הָאָרֶץ: 6:13 וַיֹּאמֶר אֱלֹהִים לְנֹחַ קֵץ כָּל־בָּשָׂר בָּא לְפָנַי כִּי־מָלְאָה הָאָרֶץ חָמָס מִפְּנֵיהֶם וְהִנְנִי מַשְׁחִיתָם אֶת־הָאָרֶץ:

GENESIS 6: P – CONTINUED

6:14 Make an ark of gopher wood. You shall partition the ark, and shall seal it inside and outside with pitch. 6:15 This is how you shall make it. The length of the ark will be three hundred cubits, its breadth fifty cubits, and its height thirty cubits. 6:16 You shall construct a window for the ark, which you shall place a cubit above. You shall set the door of the ship in its side. You shall make it with lower, second, and third decks.

6:17 I will then bring a flood of waters upon this earth, to destroy all breathing creatures from under the sky. Everything that is upon the earth will die. 6:18 But I will establish my covenant with you. You shall come into the ship, you, your sons, your wife, and your sons' wives with you. 6:19 Of every living thing of all flesh, you shall bring two of every sort into the ship, to keep them alive with you. They shall be male and female. 6:20 Of species of birds, of species of livestock, of every species of creepers upon the ground, two of every sort shall come with you, to keep them alive. 6:21 Take with you of all food that is eaten, and gather it to yourself; and it will sustain both you and them." 6:22 Thus Noah did. As God had commanded him, so he did.

GENESIS 7: P

7:6 Noah was six hundred years old when the flood of waters swept over the earth. 7:11 In the six hundredth year of Noah's life, in the second month, on the seventeenth day of the month, on the same day all the fountains of the great deep burst forth, and the sky's apertures were opened. 7:13 On the same day Noah, and Shem, Ham, and Japheth, the sons of Noah, and Noah's wife, and his sons' three wives, entered into the ark with them; 7:14 they, and every animal according to its species, all the livestock according to their species, every creeping thing that creeps on the earth according to its species, and every bird according to its species, every bird of every sort. 7:15 They went to Noah into the ark, by pairs, all flesh with the breath of life in them. 7:16 Those who went in, male and female of all flesh, went in as God had commanded him; 7:17 The flood lasted for forty days on the earth. 7:18 The waters swelled, and increased greatly on the earth; and the ark floated on the surface of the waters. 7:19 The waters swelled exceedingly on the earth. All the high mountains that were under the whole sky were covered. 7:20 The waters rose fifteen cubits upward, and the mountains were covered. 7:21 All flesh that moved upon the earth died, including birds, livestock, animals, every creeping thing that creeps upon the earth, and every person. 7:24 The waters increased upon the earth for one hundred fifty days.

GENESIS 8: P

8:1 God remembered Noah, all the animals, and all the livestock that were with him in the ship; and God caused a wind to pass over the earth. The waters subsided.

GENESIS 6: P (HEBREW) – CONTINUED

6:14 עֲשֵׂה לְךָ תֵּבַת עֲצֵי־גֹפֶר קִנִּים תַּעֲשֶׂה אֶת־הַתֵּבָה וְכָפַרְתָּ אֹתָהּ מִבַּיִת וּמִחוּץ בַּכֹּפֶר: 6:15 וְזֶה אֲשֶׁר תַּעֲשֶׂה אֹתָהּ שְׁלֹשׁ מֵאוֹת אַמָּה אֹרֶךְ הַתֵּבָה חֲמִשִּׁים אַמָּה רָחְבָּהּ וּשְׁלֹשִׁים אַמָּה קוֹמָתָהּ: 6:16 צֹהַר ׀ תַּעֲשֶׂה לַתֵּבָה וְאֶל־אַמָּה תְּכַלֶּנָּה מִלְמַעְלָה וּפֶתַח הַתֵּבָה בְּצִדָּהּ תָּשִׂים תַּחְתִּיִּם שְׁנִיִּם וּשְׁלִשִׁים תַּעֲשֶׂהָ:

6:17 וַאֲנִי הִנְנִי מֵבִיא אֶת־הַמַּבּוּל מַיִם עַל־הָאָרֶץ לְשַׁחֵת כָּל־בָּשָׂר אֲשֶׁר־בּוֹ רוּחַ חַיִּים מִתַּחַת הַשָּׁמָיִם כֹּל אֲשֶׁר־בָּאָרֶץ יִגְוָע: 6:18 וַהֲקִמֹתִי אֶת־בְּרִיתִי אִתָּךְ וּבָאתָ אֶל־הַתֵּבָה אַתָּה וּבָנֶיךָ וְאִשְׁתְּךָ וּנְשֵׁי־בָנֶיךָ אִתָּךְ: 6:19 וּמִכָּל־הָחַי מִכָּל־בָּשָׂר שְׁנַיִם מִכֹּל תָּבִיא אֶל־הַתֵּבָה לְהַחֲיֹת אִתָּךְ זָכָר וּנְקֵבָה יִהְיוּ: 6:20 מֵהָעוֹף לְמִינֵהוּ וּמִן־הַבְּהֵמָה לְמִינָהּ מִכֹּל רֶמֶשׂ הָאֲדָמָה לְמִינֵהוּ שְׁנַיִם מִכֹּל יָבֹאוּ אֵלֶיךָ לְהַחֲיוֹת: 6:21 וְאַתָּה קַח־לְךָ מִכָּל־מַאֲכָל אֲשֶׁר יֵאָכֵל וְאָסַפְתָּ אֵלֶיךָ וְהָיָה לְךָ וְלָהֶם לְאָכְלָה: 6:22 וַיַּעַשׂ נֹחַ כְּכֹל אֲשֶׁר צִוָּה אֹתוֹ אֱלֹהִים כֵּן עָשָׂה: ס

GENESIS 7: P (HEBREW)

7:6 וְנֹחַ בֶּן־שֵׁשׁ מֵאוֹת שָׁנָה וְהַמַּבּוּל הָיָה מַיִם עַל־הָאָרֶץ: 7:11 בִּשְׁנַת שֵׁשׁ־מֵאוֹת שָׁנָה לְחַיֵּי־נֹחַ בַּחֹדֶשׁ הַשֵּׁנִי בְּשִׁבְעָה־עָשָׂר יוֹם לַחֹדֶשׁ בַּיּוֹם הַזֶּה נִבְקְעוּ כָּל־מַעְיְנֹת תְּהוֹם רַבָּה וַאֲרֻבֹּת הַשָּׁמַיִם נִפְתָּחוּ: 7:13 בְּעֶצֶם הַיּוֹם הַזֶּה בָּא נֹחַ וְשֵׁם־וְחָם וָיֶפֶת בְּנֵי־נֹחַ וְאֵשֶׁת נֹחַ וּשְׁלֹשֶׁת נְשֵׁי־בָנָיו אִתָּם אֶל־הַתֵּבָה: 7:14 הֵמָּה וְכָל־הַחַיָּה לְמִינָהּ וְכָל־הַבְּהֵמָה לְמִינָהּ וְכָל־הָרֶמֶשׂ הָרֹמֵשׂ עַל־הָאָרֶץ לְמִינֵהוּ וְכָל־הָעוֹף לְמִינֵהוּ כֹּל צִפּוֹר כָּל־כָּנָף: 7:15 וַיָּבֹאוּ אֶל־נֹחַ אֶל־הַתֵּבָה שְׁנַיִם שְׁנַיִם מִכָּל־הַבָּשָׂר אֲשֶׁר־בּוֹ רוּחַ חַיִּים: 7:16 וְהַבָּאִים זָכָר וּנְקֵבָה מִכָּל־בָּשָׂר בָּאוּ כַּאֲשֶׁר צִוָּה אֹתוֹ אֱלֹהִים: 7:17 וַיְהִי הַמַּבּוּל אַרְבָּעִים יוֹם עַל־הָאָרֶץ 7:18 וַיִּגְבְּרוּ הַמַּיִם וַיִּרְבּוּ מְאֹד עַל־הָאָרֶץ וַתֵּלֶךְ הַתֵּבָה עַל־פְּנֵי הַמָּיִם: 7:19 וְהַמַּיִם גָּבְרוּ מְאֹד מְאֹד עַל־הָאָרֶץ וַיְכֻסּוּ כָּל־הֶהָרִים הַגְּבֹהִים אֲשֶׁר־תַּחַת כָּל־הַשָּׁמָיִם: 7:20 חֲמֵשׁ עֶשְׂרֵה אַמָּה מִלְמַעְלָה גָּבְרוּ הַמָּיִם וַיְכֻסּוּ הֶהָרִים: 7:21 וַיִּגְוַע כָּל־בָּשָׂר ׀ הָרֹמֵשׂ עַל־הָאָרֶץ בָּעוֹף וּבַבְּהֵמָה וּבַחַיָּה וּבְכָל־הַשֶּׁרֶץ הַשֹּׁרֵץ עַל־הָאָרֶץ וְכֹל הָאָדָם: 7:24 וַיִּגְבְּרוּ הַמַּיִם עַל־הָאָרֶץ חֲמִשִּׁים וּמְאַת יוֹם:

GENESIS 8: P (HEBREW)

8:1 וַיִּזְכֹּר אֱלֹהִים אֶת־נֹחַ וְאֵת כָּל־הַחַיָּה וְאֶת־כָּל־הַבְּהֵמָה אֲשֶׁר אִתּוֹ בַּתֵּבָה וַיַּעֲבֵר אֱלֹהִים רוּחַ עַל־הָאָרֶץ וַיָּשֹׁכּוּ הַמָּיִם:

GENESIS 8: P – CONTINUED

8:2 The fountains of the deep and the sky's windows were closed. 8:3 The waters gradually receded from the earth. At the end of one hundred fifty days the waters had abated. 8:4 The ship rested in the seventh month, on the seventeenth day of the month, on the mountains of Ararat. 8:5 The waters receded continually until the tenth month. In the tenth month, on the first day of the month, the tops of the mountains were visible.

8:13 It happened that on the six hundred and first year, on the first month, on the first day of the month, the waters were dried up from the earth. 8:14 In the second month, on the twenty-seventh day of the month, the earth was dry.

8:15 God spoke to Noah, saying, 8:16 "Go out of the ark, you, and your wife, and your sons, and your sons' wives with you. 8:17 Bring out with you every living thing that is with you, all flesh, including birds, livestock, and every creeping thing that creeps upon the earth, that they may breed abundantly upon the earth, and be fruitful, and multiply upon the earth."

8:18 Noah went out, with his sons, his wife, and his sons' wives with him. 8:19 Every animal, every creeping thing, and every bird, whatever moves upon the earth, according to their families, went out of the ark.

GENESIS 9: P

9:1 God blessed Noah and his sons, and said to them, "Be fruitful, and multiply, and replenish the earth. 9:2 Fear of you and dread of you will be upon every animal of the earth, and upon every bird of the sky. Everything with which the ground teems, and all the fish of the sea are delivered into your hand. 9:3 Every moving thing that lives will be food for you, as well as the plants of the field. I have given everything to you.

9:4 But flesh with its blood, its life-force, you shall not eat. 9:5 I will surely seek retribution for your life-blood. From every animal I will seek it. From every person, even from a man's brother, I will seek (retribution) for the life of a human being. 9:6 Whoever sheds a person's blood, his blood will be shed [in retribution] for the life of that person, for God made human beings in his own image. 9:7 Be fruitful and multiply. Increase abundantly upon the earth, and multiply upon it."

9:8 God spoke to Noah and to his sons with him, saying, 9:9 "As for me, behold, I establish my covenant with you, and with your offspring after you, 9:10 and with every living creature that is with you: the birds, the livestock, and every animal of the earth with you, all who have gone out of the ark, (with) every creature upon the earth. 9:11 I will establish my covenant with you: never again will all flesh be cut off by flood waters, neither will there ever be a flood again which would destroy the earth."

GENESIS 8: P (HEBREW) – CONTINUED

8:2 וַיִּסָּכְרוּ֙ מַעְיְנֹ֣ת תְּה֔וֹם וַֽאֲרֻבֹּ֖ת הַשָּׁמָ֑יִם 8:3 וַיָּשֻׁ֧בוּ הַמַּ֛יִם מֵעַ֥ל הָאָ֖רֶץ הָל֣וֹךְ וָשׁ֑וֹב וַיַּחְסְר֣וּ הַמַּ֔יִם מִקְצֵ֕ה חֲמִשִּׁ֥ים וּמְאַ֖ת יֽוֹם׃ 8:4 וַתָּ֤נַח הַתֵּבָה֙ בַּחֹ֣דֶשׁ הַשְּׁבִיעִ֔י בְּשִׁבְעָה־עָשָׂ֥ר י֖וֹם לַחֹ֑דֶשׁ עַ֖ל הָרֵ֥י אֲרָרָֽט׃ 8:5 וְהַמַּ֗יִם הָיוּ֙ הָל֣וֹךְ וְחָס֔וֹר עַ֖ד הַחֹ֣דֶשׁ הָֽעֲשִׂירִ֑י בָּֽעֲשִׂירִי֙ בְּאֶחָ֣ד לַחֹ֔דֶשׁ נִרְא֖וּ רָאשֵׁ֥י הֶֽהָרִֽים׃

8:13 וַֽ֠יְהִי בְּאַחַ֨ת וְשֵׁשׁ־מֵא֜וֹת שָׁנָ֗ה בָּֽרִאשׁוֹן֙ בְּאֶחָ֣ד לַחֹ֔דֶשׁ חָֽרְב֥וּ הַמַּ֖יִם מֵעַ֣ל הָאָ֑רֶץ 8:14 וּבַחֹ֙דֶשׁ֙ הַשֵּׁנִ֔י בְּשִׁבְעָ֧ה וְעֶשְׂרִ֛ים י֖וֹם לַחֹ֑דֶשׁ יָבְשָׁ֖ה הָאָֽרֶץ׃ ס

8:15 וַיְדַבֵּ֥ר אֱלֹהִ֖ים אֶל־נֹ֥חַ לֵאמֹֽר׃ 8:16 צֵ֖א מִן־הַתֵּבָ֑ה אַתָּ֕ה וְאִשְׁתְּךָ֛ וּבָנֶ֥יךָ וּנְשֵֽׁי־בָנֶ֖יךָ אִתָּֽךְ׃ 8:17 כָּל־הַֽחַיָּ֣ה אֲשֶֽׁר־אִתְּךָ֡ מִכָּל־בָּשָׂ֡ר בָּע֧וֹף וּבַבְּהֵמָ֛ה וּבְכָל־הָרֶ֛מֶשׂ הָרֹמֵ֥שׂ עַל־הָאָ֖רֶץ הוצא הַיְצֵ֣א אִתָּ֑ךְ וְשָֽׁרְצ֣וּ בָאָ֔רֶץ וּפָר֥וּ וְרָב֖וּ עַל־הָאָֽרֶץ׃ 8:18 וַיֵּ֖צֵא־נֹ֑חַ וּבָנָ֛יו וְאִשְׁתּ֥וֹ וּנְשֵֽׁי־בָנָ֖יו אִתּֽוֹ׃ 8:19 כָּל־הַֽחַיָּ֗ה כָּל־הָרֶ֙מֶשׂ֙ וְכָל־הָע֔וֹף כֹּ֖ל רוֹמֵ֣שׂ עַל־הָאָ֑רֶץ לְמִשְׁפְּחֹ֣תֵיהֶ֔ם יָֽצְא֖וּ מִן־הַתֵּבָֽה׃

GENESIS 9: P (HEBREW)

9:1 וַיְבָ֣רֶךְ אֱלֹהִ֔ים אֶת־נֹ֖חַ וְאֶת־בָּנָ֑יו וַיֹּ֧אמֶר לָהֶ֛ם פְּר֥וּ וּרְב֖וּ וּמִלְא֥וּ אֶת־הָאָֽרֶץ׃ 9:2 וּמוֹרַֽאֲכֶ֤ם וְחִתְּכֶם֙ יִֽהְיֶ֔ה עַ֚ל כָּל־חַיַּ֣ת הָאָ֔רֶץ וְעַ֖ל כָּל־ע֣וֹף הַשָּׁמָ֑יִם בְּכֹל֩ אֲשֶׁ֨ר תִּרְמֹ֧שׂ הָֽאֲדָמָ֛ה וּֽבְכָל־דְּגֵ֥י הַיָּ֖ם בְּיֶדְכֶ֥ם נִתָּֽנוּ׃ 9:3 כָּל־רֶ֙מֶשׂ֙ אֲשֶׁ֣ר הוּא־חַ֔י לָכֶ֥ם יִֽהְיֶ֖ה לְאָכְלָ֑ה כְּיֶ֣רֶק עֵ֔שֶׂב נָתַ֥תִּי לָכֶ֖ם אֶת־כֹּֽל׃ 9:4 אַךְ־בָּשָׂ֕ר בְּנַפְשׁ֥וֹ דָמ֖וֹ לֹ֥א תֹאכֵֽלוּ׃ 9:5 וְאַ֨ךְ אֶת־דִּמְכֶ֤ם לְנַפְשֹֽׁתֵיכֶם֙ אֶדְרֹ֔שׁ מִיַּ֥ד כָּל־חַיָּ֖ה אֶדְרְשֶׁ֑נּוּ וּמִיַּ֣ד הָֽאָדָ֗ם מִיַּד֙ אִ֣ישׁ אָחִ֔יו אֶדְרֹ֖שׁ אֶת־נֶ֥פֶשׁ הָֽאָדָֽם׃ 9:6 שֹׁפֵךְ֙ דַּ֣ם הָֽאָדָ֔ם בָּֽאָדָ֖ם דָּמ֣וֹ יִשָּׁפֵ֑ךְ כִּ֚י בְּצֶ֣לֶם אֱלֹהִ֔ים עָשָׂ֖ה אֶת־הָֽאָדָֽם׃ 9:7 וְאַתֶּ֖ם פְּר֣וּ וּרְב֑וּ שִׁרְצ֥וּ בָאָ֖רֶץ וּרְבוּ־בָֽהּ׃ ס

9:8 וַיֹּ֤אמֶר אֱלֹהִים֙ אֶל־נֹ֔חַ וְאֶל־בָּנָ֥יו אִתּ֖וֹ לֵאמֹֽר׃ 9:9 וַֽאֲנִ֗י הִנְנִ֥י מֵקִ֛ים אֶת־בְּרִיתִ֖י אִתְּכֶ֑ם וְאֶֽת־זַרְעֲכֶ֖ם אַֽחֲרֵיכֶֽם׃ 9:10 וְאֵ֨ת כָּל־נֶ֤פֶשׁ הַֽחַיָּה֙ אֲשֶׁ֣ר אִתְּכֶ֔ם בָּע֥וֹף בַּבְּהֵמָ֖ה וּֽבְכָל־חַיַּ֣ת הָאָ֑רֶץ אִתְּכֶ֑ם מִכֹּל֙ יֹצְאֵ֣י הַתֵּבָ֔ה לְכֹ֖ל חַיַּ֥ת הָאָֽרֶץ׃ 9:11 וַהֲקִמֹתִ֤י אֶת־בְּרִיתִי֙ אִתְּכֶ֔ם וְלֹֽא־יִכָּרֵ֧ת כָּל־בָּשָׂ֛ר ע֖וֹד מִמֵּ֣י הַמַּבּ֑וּל וְלֹֽא־יִֽהְיֶ֥ה ע֛וֹד מַבּ֖וּל לְשַׁחֵ֥ת הָאָֽרֶץ׃

GENESIS 9: P – CONTINUED

9:12 God said, "This is the token of the covenant which I make between me and you and every living creature that is with you, for all generations: 9:13 I set my rainbow among the clouds, and it will be for a sign of the covenant between me and the earth. 9:14 It will happen, when I cause clouds to come over the earth, that the rainbow will be apparent in the clouds, 9:15 and I will remember my covenant, between me and you and every living creature and all flesh, and the waters will never again become a flood to destroy all flesh. 9:16 The rainbow will be in the clouds. I will look at it, so that I may remember the everlasting covenant between God and every living creature and all flesh that is on the earth." 9:17 God said to Noah, "This is the token of the covenant which I have established between me and all flesh that is on the earth." 9:28 Noah lived three hundred fifty years after the flood. 9:29 Noah's entire lifespan was nine hundred fifty years; then he died.

GENESIS 10: P

10:1 These are the generations of Noah's sons, Shem, Ham, and Japheth. Children were born to them after the flood. 10:2 The sons of Japheth: Gomer, Magog, Madai, Javan, Tubal, Meshech, and Tiras. 10:3 The sons of Gomer: Ashkenaz, Riphath, and Togarmah. 10:4 The sons of Javan: Elishah, Tarshish, Kittim, and Dodanim. 10:5 Of these were the islands of the nations divided in their lands, everyone after his language, after their families, in their nations.

10:6 The sons of Ham: Cush, Mizraim, Phut, and Canaan. 10:7 The sons of Cush: Seba, Havilah, Sabtah, Raamah, and Sabtecah. The sons of Raamah: Sheba and Dedan. 10:20 These are the sons of Ham, according to their families, their languages, their lands, and their nations.

10:22 The sons of Shem: Elam, Asshur, Arpachshad, Lud, and Aram. 10:23 The sons of Aram: Uz, Hul, Gether, and Mash. 10:31 These are the sons of Shem, according to their families, their languages, their lands, and their nations. 10:32 These are the families of the sons of Noah, according to their generations, and their nations. From these the nations were divided on earth after the flood.

GENESIS 11: P

11:10 These are the generations of Shem. Shem was one hundred years old and fathered Arpachshad two years after the flood. 11:11 Shem lived five hundred years after he'd fathered Arpachshad, and sired sons and daughters.

11:12 Arpachshad lived thirty-five years and fathered Shelah. 11:13 Arpachshad lived four hundred three years after he'd fathered Shelah, and sired sons and daughters.

GENESIS 9: P (HEBREW) – CONTINUED

9:12 וַיֹּאמֶר אֱלֹהִים זֹאת אוֹת־הַבְּרִית אֲשֶׁר־אֲנִי נֹתֵן בֵּינִי וּבֵינֵיכֶם וּבֵין כָּל־נֶפֶשׁ חַיָּה אֲשֶׁר אִתְּכֶם לְדֹרֹת עוֹלָם: 9:13 אֶת־קַשְׁתִּי נָתַתִּי בֶּעָנָן וְהָיְתָה לְאוֹת בְּרִית בֵּינִי וּבֵין הָאָרֶץ: 9:14 וְהָיָה בְּעַנְנִי עָנָן עַל־הָאָרֶץ וְנִרְאֲתָה הַקֶּשֶׁת בֶּעָנָן: 9:15 וְזָכַרְתִּי אֶת־בְּרִיתִי אֲשֶׁר בֵּינִי וּבֵינֵיכֶם וּבֵין כָּל־נֶפֶשׁ חַיָּה בְּכָל־בָּשָׂר וְלֹא־יִהְיֶה עוֹד הַמַּיִם לְמַבּוּל לְשַׁחֵת כָּל־בָּשָׂר: 9:16 וְהָיְתָה הַקֶּשֶׁת בֶּעָנָן וּרְאִיתִיהָ לִזְכֹּר בְּרִית עוֹלָם בֵּין אֱלֹהִים וּבֵין כָּל־נֶפֶשׁ חַיָּה בְּכָל־בָּשָׂר אֲשֶׁר עַל־הָאָרֶץ: 9:17 וַיֹּאמֶר אֱלֹהִים אֶל־נֹחַ זֹאת אוֹת־הַבְּרִית אֲשֶׁר הֲקִמֹתִי בֵּינִי וּבֵין כָּל־בָּשָׂר אֲשֶׁר עַל־הָאָרֶץ: 9:28 וַיְחִי־נֹחַ אַחַר הַמַּבּוּל שְׁלֹשׁ מֵאוֹת שָׁנָה וַחֲמִשִּׁים שָׁנָה: 9:29 וַיִּהְיוּ כָּל־יְמֵי־נֹחַ תְּשַׁע מֵאוֹת שָׁנָה וַחֲמִשִּׁים שָׁנָה וַיָּמֹת: פ

GENESIS 10: P (HEBREW)

10:1 וְאֵלֶּה תּוֹלְדֹת בְּנֵי־נֹחַ שֵׁם חָם וָיָפֶת וַיִּוָּלְדוּ לָהֶם בָּנִים אַחַר הַמַּבּוּל: 10:2 בְּנֵי יֶפֶת גֹּמֶר וּמָגוֹג וּמָדַי וְיָוָן וְתֻבָל וּמֶשֶׁךְ וְתִירָס: 10:3 וּבְנֵי גֹּמֶר אַשְׁכְּנַז וְרִיפַת וְתֹגַרְמָה: 10:4 וּבְנֵי יָוָן אֱלִישָׁה וְתַרְשִׁישׁ כִּתִּים וְדֹדָנִים: 10:5 מֵאֵלֶּה נִפְרְדוּ אִיֵּי הַגּוֹיִם בְּאַרְצֹתָם אִישׁ לִלְשֹׁנוֹ לְמִשְׁפְּחֹתָם בְּגוֹיֵהֶם:

10:6 וּבְנֵי חָם כּוּשׁ וּמִצְרַיִם וּפוּט וּכְנָעַן: 10:7 וּבְנֵי כוּשׁ סְבָא וַחֲוִילָה וְסַבְתָּה וְרַעְמָה וְסַבְתְּכָא וּבְנֵי רַעְמָה שְׁבָא וּדְדָן: 10:20 אֵלֶּה בְנֵי־חָם לְמִשְׁפְּחֹתָם לִלְשֹׁנֹתָם בְּאַרְצֹתָם בְּגוֹיֵהֶם: ס

10:22 בְּנֵי שֵׁם עֵילָם וְאַשּׁוּר וְאַרְפַּכְשַׁד וְלוּד וַאֲרָם: 10:23 וּבְנֵי אֲרָם עוּץ וְחוּל וְגֶתֶר וָמַשׁ: 10:31 אֵלֶּה בְנֵי־שֵׁם לְמִשְׁפְּחֹתָם לִלְשֹׁנֹתָם בְּאַרְצֹתָם לְגוֹיֵהֶם: 10:32 אֵלֶּה מִשְׁפְּחֹת בְּנֵי־נֹחַ לְתוֹלְדֹתָם בְּגוֹיֵהֶם וּמֵאֵלֶּה נִפְרְדוּ הַגּוֹיִם בָּאָרֶץ אַחַר הַמַּבּוּל: פ

GENESIS 11: P (HEBREW)

11:10 אֵלֶּה תּוֹלְדֹת שֵׁם שֵׁם בֶּן־מְאַת שָׁנָה וַיּוֹלֶד אֶת־אַרְפַּכְשָׁד שְׁנָתַיִם אַחַר הַמַּבּוּל: 11:11 וַיְחִי־שֵׁם אַחֲרֵי הוֹלִידוֹ אֶת־אַרְפַּכְשָׁד חֲמֵשׁ מֵאוֹת שָׁנָה וַיּוֹלֶד בָּנִים וּבָנוֹת: ס

11:12 וְאַרְפַּכְשַׁד חַי חָמֵשׁ וּשְׁלֹשִׁים שָׁנָה וַיּוֹלֶד אֶת־שָׁלַח: 11:13 וַיְחִי אַרְפַּכְשַׁד אַחֲרֵי הוֹלִידוֹ אֶת־שֶׁלַח שָׁלֹשׁ שָׁנִים וְאַרְבַּע מֵאוֹת שָׁנָה וַיּוֹלֶד בָּנִים וּבָנוֹת:ס

GENESIS 11: P – CONTINUED

11:14 Shelah lived thirty years, and fathered Eber: 11:15 and Shelah lived four hundred three years after he'd fathered Eber, and sired sons and daughters.

11:16 Eber lived thirty-four years, and became the father of Peleg. 11:17 Eber lived four hundred thirty years after he'd fathered Peleg, and sired sons and daughters.

11:18 Peleg lived thirty years, and became the father of Reu. 11:19 Peleg lived two hundred nine years after he'd fathered Reu, and sired sons and daughters.

11:20 Reu lived thirty-two years, and became the father of Serug. 11:21 Reu lived two hundred seven years after he'd fathered Serug, and sired sons and daughters.

11:22 Serug lived thirty years, and became the father of Nahor. 11:23 Serug lived two hundred years after he'd fathered Nahor, and sired sons and daughters.

11:24 Nahor lived twenty-nine years, and became the father of Terah. 11:25 Nahor lived one hundred nineteen years after he'd fathered Terah, and sired sons and daughters.

11:26 Terah lived seventy years, and fathered Abram, Nahor, and Haran.

11:27 These are the generations of Terah. Terah fathered Abram, Nahor, and Haran. And Haran fathered Lot. 11:31 Terah took Abram his son, Lot the son of Haran, his son's son, and Sarai his daughter-in-law, his son Abram's wife. They left Ur of the Chaldees for the land of Canaan. They came to Haran and lived there.

11:32 The years of Terah's (life) were two hundred five years. Terah died in Haran.

GENESIS 11: P (HEBREW) – CONTINUED

11:14 וְשֶׁ֣לַח חַ֔י שְׁלֹשִׁ֖ים שָׁנָ֑ה וַיּ֖וֹלֶד אֶת־עֵֽבֶר: 11:15 וַֽיְחִי־שֶׁ֗לַח אַֽחֲרֵי֙ הוֹלִיד֣וֹ אֶת־עֵ֔בֶר שָׁלֹ֣שׁ שָׁנִ֔ים וְאַרְבַּ֥ע מֵא֖וֹת שָׁנָ֑ה וַיּ֥וֹלֶד בָּנִ֖ים וּבָנֽוֹת: ס

11:16 וַֽיְחִי־עֵ֕בֶר אַרְבַּ֥ע וּשְׁלֹשִׁ֖ים שָׁנָ֑ה וַיּ֖וֹלֶד אֶת־פָּֽלֶג: 11:17 וַֽיְחִי־עֵ֗בֶר אַֽחֲרֵי֙ הוֹלִיד֣וֹ אֶת־פֶּ֔לֶג שְׁלֹשִׁ֣ים שָׁנָ֔ה וְאַרְבַּ֥ע מֵא֖וֹת שָׁנָ֑ה וַיּ֥וֹלֶד בָּנִ֖ים וּבָנֽוֹת: ס

11:18 וַֽיְחִי־פֶ֖לֶג שְׁלֹשִׁ֣ים שָׁנָ֑ה וַיּ֖וֹלֶד אֶת־רְעֽוּ: 11:19 וַֽיְחִי־פֶ֗לֶג אַֽחֲרֵי֙ הוֹלִיד֣וֹ אֶת־רְע֔וּ תֵּ֥שַׁע שָׁנִ֖ים וּמָאתַ֣יִם שָׁנָ֑ה וַיּ֥וֹלֶד בָּנִ֖ים וּבָנֽוֹת: ס

11:20 וַיְחִ֣י רְע֔וּ שְׁתַּ֥יִם וּשְׁלֹשִׁ֖ים שָׁנָ֑ה וַיּ֖וֹלֶד אֶת־שְׂרֽוּג: 11:21 וַיְחִ֣י רְע֗וּ אַֽחֲרֵי֙ הוֹלִיד֣וֹ אֶת־שְׂר֔וּג שֶׁ֥בַע שָׁנִ֖ים וּמָאתַ֣יִם שָׁנָ֑ה וַיּ֥וֹלֶד בָּנִ֖ים וּבָנֽוֹת: ס

11:22 וַיְחִ֥י שְׂר֖וּג שְׁלֹשִׁ֣ים שָׁנָ֑ה וַיּ֖וֹלֶד אֶת־נָחֽוֹר: 11:23 וַיְחִ֣י שְׂר֗וּג אַֽחֲרֵי֙ הוֹלִיד֣וֹ אֶת־נָח֔וֹר מָאתַ֖יִם שָׁנָ֑ה וַיּ֥וֹלֶד בָּנִ֖ים וּבָנֽוֹת: ס

11:24 וַיְחִ֣י נָח֔וֹר תֵּ֥שַׁע וְעֶשְׂרִ֖ים שָׁנָ֑ה וַיּ֖וֹלֶד אֶת־תָּֽרַח: 11:25 וַיְחִ֣י נָח֗וֹר אַֽחֲרֵי֙ הוֹלִיד֣וֹ אֶת־תֶּ֔רַח תְּשַֽׁע־עֶשְׂרֵ֥ה שָׁנָ֖ה וּמְאַ֣ת שָׁנָ֑ה וַיּ֥וֹלֶד בָּנִ֖ים וּבָנֽוֹת: ס

11:26 וַֽיְחִי־תֶ֖רַח שִׁבְעִ֣ים שָׁנָ֑ה וַיּ֨וֹלֶד֙ אֶת־אַבְרָ֔ם אֶת־נָח֖וֹר וְאֶת־הָרָֽן: 11:27 וְאֵ֙לֶּה֙ תּוֹלְדֹ֣ת תֶּ֔רַח תֶּ֚רַח הוֹלִ֣יד אֶת־אַבְרָ֔ם אֶת־נָח֖וֹר וְאֶת־הָרָ֑ן וְהָרָ֖ן הוֹלִ֥יד אֶת־לֽוֹט: 11:31 וַיִּקַּ֨ח תֶּ֜רַח אֶת־אַבְרָ֣ם בְּנ֗וֹ וְאֶת־ל֤וֹט בֶּן־הָרָן֙ בֶּן־בְּנ֔וֹ וְאֵת֙ שָׂרַ֣י כַּלָּת֔וֹ אֵ֖שֶׁת אַבְרָ֣ם בְּנ֑וֹ וַיֵּצְא֨וּ אִתָּ֜ם מֵא֣וּר כַּשְׂדִּ֗ים לָלֶ֙כֶת֙ אַ֣רְצָה כְּנַ֔עַן וַיָּבֹ֥אוּ עַד־חָרָ֖ן וַיֵּ֥שְׁבוּ שָֽׁם: 11:32 וַיִּֽהְי֣וּ יְמֵי־תֶ֔רַח חָמֵ֥שׁ שָׁנִ֖ים וּמָאתַ֣יִם שָׁנָ֑ה וַיָּ֥מָת תֶּ֖רַח בְּחָרָֽן: ס

THE REDACTORS

GENESIS 1 - 2 – J + RJEP + P

1:24 And God said, "Let the earth bring forth living creatures of all types: cattle and creeping things and wild animals of the earth of all types." And it was so. 1:25 God made wild animals of the earth of all types, and the cattle of all types, and everything that creeps upon the ground of all types. And God saw that it was good.

1:26 Then God said, "Let us make humankind in our image, according to our likeness; and let them have dominion over the fish of the sea, and over the birds of the air, and over the cattle, and over all the wild animals of the earth, and over every creeping thing that creeps upon the earth." 1:27 So God created humankind in his image; he created them in the image of God; he created them male and female. 1:28 God blessed them, and God said to them, "Be fruitful and multiply, and fill the earth and subdue it; and have dominion over the fish of the sea and over the birds of the air and over every living thing that moves upon the earth." 1:29 God said, "See, I have given you every plant with seeds that is upon the face of all the earth, and every tree with seed in its fruit, as food for you. 1:30 And to every beast of the earth, and to every bird of the air, and to everything that creeps on the earth, everything that has the breath of life, I have given every sprouting plant as food." And it was so. 1:31 God saw everything that he had made, and indeed, it was very good. And there was evening and there was morning, the sixth day.

2:1 The heavens and the earth were finished, and all their vast array. 2:2 On the seventh day God finished his work which he had made; and he rested on the seventh day from all his work which he had made. 2:3 God blessed the seventh day, and made it holy, because he rested in it from all his work which he had created and made.

2:4 This is the history of the heavens and of the earth when they were created:

in the day that Yahweh God made the earth and the heavens, 2:5 no plant of the field was yet in the earth, and no herbs of the field had sprouted yet; for Yahweh God had not caused it to rain upon the earth. There was no one to till the ground, 2:6 but a mist arose from the earth, and watered the entire ground. 2:7 Yahweh God fashioned a man from the earth upon the ground, and breathed the breath of life into his nostrils; and man became a living thing.

2:8 Yahweh God planted a garden eastward, in Eden, and there he placed the man whom he had formed. 2:9 Yahweh God caused every tree that is pleasant to the sight and good for food to grow out of the ground; and the Tree of Life was in the midst of the garden, and the Tree of the Knowledge of Good and Evil.

GENESIS 1 - 2 – J + RJEP + P

1:26 וַיֹּאמֶר אֱלֹהִים נַעֲשֶׂה אָדָם בְּצַלְמֵנוּ כִּדְמוּתֵנוּ וְיִרְדּוּ בִדְגַת הַיָּם וּבְעוֹף הַשָּׁמַיִם וּבַבְּהֵמָה וּבְכָל־הָאָרֶץ וּבְכָל־הָרֶמֶשׂ הָרֹמֵשׂ עַל־הָאָרֶץ: 1:27 וַיִּבְרָא אֱלֹהִים ׀ אֶת־הָאָדָם בְּצַלְמוֹ בְּצֶלֶם אֱלֹהִים בָּרָא אֹתוֹ זָכָר וּנְקֵבָה בָּרָא אֹתָם:

1:28 וַיְבָרֶךְ אֹתָם אֱלֹהִים וַיֹּאמֶר לָהֶם אֱלֹהִים פְּרוּ וּרְבוּ וּמִלְאוּ אֶת־הָאָרֶץ וְכִבְשֻׁהָ וּרְדוּ בִּדְגַת הַיָּם וּבְעוֹף הַשָּׁמַיִם וּבְכָל־חַיָּה הָרֹמֶשֶׂת עַל־הָאָרֶץ: 1:29 וַיֹּאמֶר אֱלֹהִים הִנֵּה נָתַתִּי לָכֶם אֶת־כָּל־עֵשֶׂב ׀ זֹרֵעַ זֶרַע אֲשֶׁר עַל־פְּנֵי כָל־הָאָרֶץ וְאֶת־כָּל־הָעֵץ אֲשֶׁר־בּוֹ פְרִי־עֵץ זֹרֵעַ זָרַע לָכֶם יִהְיֶה לְאָכְלָה: 1:30 וּלְכָל־חַיַּת הָאָרֶץ וּלְכָל־עוֹף הַשָּׁמַיִם וּלְכֹל ׀ רוֹמֵשׂ עַל־הָאָרֶץ אֲשֶׁר־בּוֹ נֶפֶשׁ חַיָּה אֶת־כָּל־יֶרֶק עֵשֶׂב לְאָכְלָה וַיְהִי־כֵן: 1:31 וַיַּרְא אֱלֹהִים אֶת־כָּל־אֲשֶׁר עָשָׂה וְהִנֵּה־טוֹב מְאֹד וַיְהִי־עֶרֶב וַיְהִי־בֹקֶר יוֹם הַשִּׁשִּׁי: פ

2:1 וַיְכֻלּוּ הַשָּׁמַיִם וְהָאָרֶץ וְכָל־צְבָאָם: 2:2 וַיְכַל אֱלֹהִים בַּיּוֹם הַשְּׁבִיעִי מְלַאכְתּוֹ אֲשֶׁר עָשָׂה וַיִּשְׁבֹּת בַּיּוֹם הַשְּׁבִיעִי מִכָּל־מְלַאכְתּוֹ אֲשֶׁר עָשָׂה: 2:3 וַיְבָרֶךְ אֱלֹהִים אֶת־יוֹם הַשְּׁבִיעִי וַיְקַדֵּשׁ אֹתוֹ כִּי בוֹ שָׁבַת מִכָּל־מְלַאכְתּוֹ אֲשֶׁר־בָּרָא אֱלֹהִים לַעֲשׂוֹת: פ

2:4 אֵלֶּה תוֹלְדוֹת הַשָּׁמַיִם וְהָאָרֶץ בְּהִבָּרְאָם

<mark>בְּיוֹם עֲשׂוֹת יְהוָה אֱלֹהִים אֶרֶץ וְשָׁמָיִם: 2:5 וְכֹל ׀ שִׂיחַ הַשָּׂדֶה טֶרֶם יִהְיֶה בָאָרֶץ וְכָל־עֵשֶׂב הַשָּׂדֶה טֶרֶם יִצְמָח כִּי לֹא הִמְטִיר יְהוָה אֱלֹהִים עַל־הָאָרֶץ וְאָדָם אַיִן לַעֲבֹד אֶת־הָאֲדָמָה: 2:6 וְאֵד יַעֲלֶה מִן־הָאָרֶץ וְהִשְׁקָה אֶת־כָּל־פְּנֵי־הָאֲדָמָה: 2:7 וַיִּיצֶר יְהוָה אֱלֹהִים אֶת־הָאָדָם עָפָר מִן־הָאֲדָמָה וַיִּפַּח בְּאַפָּיו נִשְׁמַת חַיִּים וַיְהִי הָאָדָם לְנֶפֶשׁ חַיָּה:

2:8 וַיִּטַּע יְהוָה אֱלֹהִים גַּן־בְעֵדֶן מִקֶּדֶם וַיָּשֶׂם שָׁם אֶת־הָאָדָם אֲשֶׁר יָצָר: 2:9 וַיַּצְמַח יְהוָה אֱלֹהִים מִן־הָאֲדָמָה כָּל־עֵץ נֶחְמָד לְמַרְאֶה וְטוֹב לְמַאֲכָל וְעֵץ הַחַיִּים בְּתוֹךְ הַגָּן וְעֵץ הַדַּעַת טוֹב וָרָע:</mark>

GENESIS 7 – J + RJEP + P

<mark>7:1 Yahweh said to Noah, "Come with all of your household into the ark, for I have seen that you are righteous before me in this generation. 7:2 You shall take seven pairs of every clean animal with you, the male and its female mate. Of the animals that are not clean, take two (each), of the male and its female mate. 7:3 Also of the birds of the sky, seven and seven,</mark> male and female, <mark>to keep seed alive on the surface of all the earth. 7:4 In seven days, I will cause it to rain on the earth for forty days and forty nights. Every living thing that I have made, I will destroy from the face of the earth."</mark>

<mark>7:5 Noah did everything that Yahweh commanded him.</mark>

7:6 Noah was six hundred years old when the flood of waters swept over the earth. <mark>7:7 Noah went into the ship with his sons, his wife, and his sons' wives, anticipating the waters of the flood.</mark> 7:8 Clean animals, animals that are not clean, birds, and everything that creeps on the ground 7:9 went by pairs to Noah into the ark, male and female, as God had commanded Noah. <mark>7:10 Seven days later, the waters of the flood swept over the earth.</mark> 7:11 In the six hundredth year of Noah's life, in the second month, on the seventeenth day of the month, on the same day all the fountains of the great deep burst forth, and the sky's apertures were opened.

GENESIS 7 – J + RJEP + P

7:1 וַיֹּ֤אמֶר יְהוָה֙ לְנֹ֔חַ בֹּֽא־אַתָּ֥ה וְכָל־בֵּיתְךָ֖ אֶל־הַתֵּבָ֑ה כִּֽי־אֹתְךָ֥ רָאִ֛יתִי צַדִּ֥יק לְפָנַ֖י בַּדּ֥וֹר הַזֶּֽה: 7:2 מִכֹּ֣ל ׀ הַבְּהֵמָ֣ה הַטְּהוֹרָ֗ה תִּֽקַּח־לְךָ֛ שִׁבְעָ֥ה שִׁבְעָ֖ה אִ֣ישׁ וְאִשְׁתּ֑וֹ וּמִן־הַבְּהֵמָ֡ה אֲ֠שֶׁר לֹ֣א טְהֹרָ֥ה הִ֛וא שְׁנַ֖יִם אִ֥ישׁ וְאִשְׁתּֽוֹ: 7:3 גַּ֣ם מֵע֧וֹף הַשָּׁמַ֛יִם שִׁבְעָ֥ה שִׁבְעָ֖ה זָכָ֣ר וּנְקֵבָ֑ה לְחַיּ֥וֹת זֶ֖רַע עַל־פְּנֵ֥י כָל־הָאָֽרֶץ: 7:4 כִּי֩ לְיָמִ֨ים ע֜וֹד שִׁבְעָ֗ה אָֽנֹכִי֙ מַמְטִ֣יר עַל־הָאָ֔רֶץ אַרְבָּעִ֣ים י֔וֹם וְאַרְבָּעִ֖ים לָ֑יְלָה וּמָחִ֗יתִי אֶֽת־כָּל־הַיְקוּם֙ אֲשֶׁ֣ר עָשִׂ֔יתִי מֵעַ֖ל פְּנֵ֥י הָאֲדָמָֽה:

7:5 וַיַּ֖עַשׂ נֹ֑חַ כְּכֹ֥ל אֲשֶׁר־צִוָּ֖הוּ יְהוָֽה:

7:6 וְנֹ֕חַ בֶּן־שֵׁ֥שׁ מֵא֖וֹת שָׁנָ֑ה וְהַמַּבּ֣וּל הָיָ֔ה מַ֖יִם עַל־הָאָֽרֶץ: 7:7 וַיָּ֣בֹא נֹ֗חַ וּ֠בָנָיו וְאִשְׁתּ֧וֹ וּנְשֵֽׁי־בָנָ֛יו אִתּ֖וֹ אֶל־הַתֵּבָ֑ה מִפְּנֵ֖י מֵ֥י הַמַּבּֽוּל: 7:8 מִן־הַבְּהֵמָה֙ הַטְּהוֹרָ֔ה וּמִן־הַ֨בְּהֵמָ֔ה אֲשֶׁ֥ר אֵינֶ֖נָּה טְהֹרָ֑ה וּמִ֨ן־הָע֔וֹף וְכֹ֥ל אֲשֶׁר־רֹמֵ֖שׂ עַל־הָֽאֲדָמָֽה: 7:9 שְׁנַ֨יִם שְׁנַ֜יִם בָּ֧אוּ אֶל־נֹ֛חַ אֶל־הַתֵּבָ֖ה זָכָ֣ר וּנְקֵבָ֑ה כַּֽאֲשֶׁ֛ר צִוָּ֥ה אֱלֹהִ֖ים אֶת־נֹֽחַ: 7:10 וַֽיְהִ֖י לְשִׁבְעַ֣ת הַיָּמִ֑ים וּמֵ֣י הַמַּבּ֔וּל הָי֖וּ עַל־הָאָֽרֶץ: 7:11 בִּשְׁנַ֨ת שֵׁשׁ־מֵא֤וֹת שָׁנָה֙ לְחַיֵּי־נֹ֔חַ בַּחֹ֨דֶשׁ֙ הַשֵּׁנִ֔י בְּשִׁבְעָֽה־עָשָׂ֥ר י֖וֹם לַחֹ֑דֶשׁ בַּיּ֣וֹם הַזֶּ֗ה נִבְקְעוּ֙ כָּֽל־מַעְיְנֹת֙ תְּה֣וֹם רַבָּ֔ה וַאֲרֻבֹּ֥ת הַשָּׁמַ֖יִם נִפְתָּֽחוּ:

GENESIS 9 – J + RJEP + P

9:18 The sons of Noah who went out from the ship were Shem, Ham, and Japheth. And Ham was the father of Canaan. 9:19 These three were the sons of Noah, and from these, the whole earth was populated.

9:20 Noah started out as a farmer, and planted a vineyard. 21 He drank of the wine and got drunk. He lay naked within his tent. 9:22 Ham, the father of Canaan, saw the nakedness of his father, and told his two brothers outside. 9:23 Shem and Japheth took a garment, and laid it upon both their shoulders, walked backwards, and covered the nakedness of their father. Their faces were averted, and they didn't see their father's nakedness. 9:24 Noah awoke from his wine (-induced stupor), and knew what his youngest son had done to him. 9:25 He said, "Canaan is cursed. He will be a servant of servants (serving) his brothers." 9:26 He said, "Blessed be Yahweh, the God of Shem. Let Canaan be his servant. 9:27 May God make Japheth mighty. Let him dwell in the tents of Shem. Let Canaan be his servant."

9:28 Noah lived three hundred fifty years after the flood. 9:29 Noah's entire lifespan was nine hundred fifty years; then he died.

GENESIS 9 – J + RJEP + P

9:18 וַיִּהְיוּ בְנֵי־נֹחַ הַיֹּצְאִים מִן־הַתֵּבָה שֵׁם וְחָם וָיָפֶת וְחָם הוּא אֲבִי כְנָעַן: 9:19 שְׁלֹשָׁה אֵלֶּה בְּנֵי־נֹחַ וּמֵאֵלֶּה נָפְצָה כָל־הָאָרֶץ:

9:20 וַיָּחֶל נֹחַ אִישׁ הָאֲדָמָה וַיִּטַּע כָּרֶם: 9:21 וַיֵּשְׁתְּ מִן־הַיַּיִן וַיִּשְׁכָּר וַיִּתְגַּל בְּתוֹךְ אָהֳלֹה: 9:22 וַיַּרְא חָם אֲבִי כְנַעַן אֵת עֶרְוַת אָבִיו וַיַּגֵּד לִשְׁנֵי־אֶחָיו בַּחוּץ: 9:23 וַיִּקַּח שֵׁם וָיֶפֶת אֶת־הַשִּׂמְלָה וַיָּשִׂימוּ עַל־שְׁכֶם שְׁנֵיהֶם וַיֵּלְכוּ אֲחֹרַנִּית וַיְכַסּוּ אֵת עֶרְוַת אֲבִיהֶם וּפְנֵיהֶם אֲחֹרַנִּית וְעֶרְוַת אֲבִיהֶם לֹא רָאוּ: 9:24 וַיִּיקֶץ נֹחַ מִיֵּינוֹ וַיֵּדַע אֵת אֲשֶׁר־עָשָׂה־לוֹ בְּנוֹ הַקָּטָן: 9:25 וַיֹּאמֶר אָרוּר כְּנָעַן עֶבֶד עֲבָדִים יִהְיֶה לְאֶחָיו: 9:26 וַיֹּאמֶר בָּרוּךְ יְהֹוָה אֱלֹהֵי שֵׁם וִיהִי כְנַעַן עֶבֶד לָמוֹ: 9:27 יַפְתְּ אֱלֹהִים לְיֶפֶת וְיִשְׁכֹּן בְּאָהֳלֵי־שֵׁם וִיהִי כְנַעַן עֶבֶד לָמוֹ: 9:28 וַיְחִי־נֹחַ אַחַר הַמַּבּוּל שְׁלֹשׁ מֵאוֹת שָׁנָה וַחֲמִשִּׁים שָׁנָה: 9:29 וַיִּהְיוּ כָּל־יְמֵי־נֹחַ תְּשַׁע מֵאוֹת שָׁנָה וַחֲמִשִּׁים שָׁנָה וַיָּמֹת: פ

GENESIS 10: J + RJEP + P

10:1 These are the generations of Noah's sons, Shem, Ham, and Japheth. Children were born to them after the flood.

10:2 The sons of Japheth: Gomer, Magog, Madai, Javan, Tubal, Meshech, and Tiras. 10:3 The sons of Gomer: Ashkenaz, Riphath, and Togarmah. 10:4 The sons of Javan: Elishah, Tarshish, Kittim, and Dodanim. 10:5 Of these were the islands of the nations divided in their lands, everyone after his language, after their families, in their nations.

10:6 The sons of Ham: Cush, Mizraim, Phut, and Canaan. 10:7 The sons of Cush: Seba, Havilah, Sabtah, Raamah, and Sabtecah. The sons of Raamah: Sheba and Dedan. 10:8 Cush became the father of Nimrod. He was the first hero on earth. 10:9 He was a mighty hunter before Yahweh. Therefore it is said, "Like Nimrod, a mighty hunter before Yahweh." 10:10 The beginning of his kingdom was Babel, Erech, Accad, and Calneh, in the land of Shinar. 10:11 From that land he went into Assyria, and built Nineveh, Rehoboth Ir, and Calah, 10:12 and Resen between Nineveh and Calah (the great city). 10:13 Mizraim became the father of Ludim, Anamim, Lehabim, Naphtuhim, 10:14 Pathrusim, Casluhim (whom the Philistines descended from), and Caphtorim. 10:15 Canaan became the father of Sidon (his firstborn), Heth, 10:16 the Jebusite, the Amorite, the Girgashite, 10:17 the Hivite, the Arkite, the Sinite, 10:18 the Arvadite, the Zemarite, and the Hamathite. Afterward the families of the Canaanites spread widely. 10:19 The border of the Canaanites was from Sidon, extending to Gerar, to Gaza; and extending toward Sodom, Gomorrah, Admah, and Zeboiim, to Lasha. 10:20 These are the sons of Ham, according to their families, their languages, their lands, and their nations.

GENESIS 10 – J + RJEP + P

10:1 וְאֵ֙לֶּה֙ תּוֹלְדֹ֣ת בְּנֵי־נֹ֔חַ שֵׁ֖ם חָ֣ם וָיָ֑פֶת וַיִּוָּלְד֥וּ לָהֶ֛ם בָּנִ֖ים אַחַ֥ר הַמַּבּֽוּל׃ 10:2 בְּנֵ֣י יֶ֔פֶת גֹּ֣מֶר וּמָג֔וֹג וּמָדַ֖י וְיָוָ֣ן וְתֻבָ֑ל וּמֶ֖שֶׁךְ וְתִירָֽס׃ 10:3 וּבְנֵ֖י גֹּ֑מֶר אַשְׁכֲּנַ֥ז וְרִיפַ֖ת וְתֹגַרְמָֽה׃ 10:4 וּבְנֵ֥י יָוָ֖ן אֱלִישָׁ֣ה וְתַרְשִׁ֑ישׁ כִּתִּ֖ים וְדֹדָנִֽים׃ 10:5 מֵ֠אֵלֶּה נִפְרְד֞וּ אִיֵּ֤י הַגּוֹיִם֙ בְּאַרְצֹתָ֔ם אִ֖ישׁ לִלְשֹׁנ֑וֹ לְמִשְׁפְּחֹתָ֖ם בְּגוֹיֵהֶֽם׃ 10:6 וּבְנֵ֖י חָ֑ם כּ֥וּשׁ וּמִצְרַ֖יִם וּפ֥וּט וּכְנָֽעַן׃ 10:7 וּבְנֵ֣י כ֔וּשׁ סְבָא֙ וַחֲוִילָ֔ה וְסַבְתָּ֥ה וְרַעְמָ֖ה וְסַבְתְּכָ֑א וּבְנֵ֥י רַעְמָ֖ה שְׁבָ֥א וּדְדָֽן׃ <mark>10:8 וְכ֖וּשׁ יָלַ֣ד אֶת־נִמְרֹ֑ד ה֣וּא הֵחֵ֔ל לִֽהְי֥וֹת גִּבֹּ֖ר בָּאָֽרֶץ׃ 10:9 הֽוּא־הָיָ֥ה גִבֹּֽר־צַ֖יִד לִפְנֵ֣י יְהוָ֑ה עַל־כֵּן֙ יֵֽאָמַ֔ר כְּנִמְרֹ֛ד גִּבּ֥וֹר צַ֖יִד לִפְנֵ֥י יְהוָֽה׃ 10:10 וַתְּהִ֨י רֵאשִׁ֤ית מַמְלַכְתּוֹ֙ בָּבֶ֔ל וְאֶ֖רֶךְ וְאַכַּ֣ד וְכַלְנֵ֑ה בְּאֶ֖רֶץ שִׁנְעָֽר׃ 10:11 מִן־הָאָ֥רֶץ הַהִ֖וא יָצָ֣א אַשּׁ֑וּר וַיִּ֙בֶן֙ אֶת־נִ֣ינְוֵ֔ה וְאֶת־רְחֹבֹ֥ת עִ֖יר וְאֶת־כָּֽלַח׃ 10:12 וְֽאֶת־רֶ֔סֶן בֵּ֥ין נִֽינְוֵ֖ה וּבֵ֣ין כָּ֑לַח הִ֖וא הָעִ֥יר הַגְּדֹלָֽה׃ 10:13 וּמִצְרַ֡יִם יָלַ֞ד אֶת־לוּדִ֧ים וְאֶת־עֲנָמִ֛ים וְאֶת־לְהָבִ֖ים וְאֶת־נַפְתֻּחִֽים׃ 10:14 וְֽאֶת־פַּתְרֻסִ֞ים וְאֶת־כַּסְלֻחִ֗ים אֲשֶׁ֨ר יָצְא֥וּ מִשָּׁ֛ם פְּלִשְׁתִּ֖ים וְאֶת־כַּפְתֹּרִֽים׃ ס</mark>

<mark>10:15 וּכְנַ֗עַן יָלַ֛ד אֶת־צִידֹ֥ן בְּכֹר֖וֹ וְאֶת־חֵֽת׃ 10:16 וְאֶת־הַיְבוּסִי֙ וְאֶת־הָ֣אֱמֹרִ֔י וְאֵ֖ת הַגִּרְגָּשִֽׁי׃ 10:17 וְאֶת־הַֽחִוִּ֥י וְאֶת־הַֽעַרְקִ֖י וְאֶת־הַסִּינִֽי׃ 10:18 וְאֶת־הָֽאַרְוָדִ֥י וְאֶת־הַצְּמָרִ֖י וְאֶת־הַֽחֲמָתִ֑י וְאַחַ֣ר נָפֹ֔צוּ מִשְׁפְּח֖וֹת הַֽכְּנַעֲנִֽי׃ 10:19 וַיְהִ֞י גְּב֤וּל הַֽכְּנַעֲנִי֙ מִצִּידֹ֔ן בֹּאֲכָ֥ה גְרָ֖רָה עַד־עַזָּ֑ה בֹּאֲכָ֞ה סְדֹ֧מָה וַעֲמֹרָ֛ה וְאַדְמָ֥ה וּצְבֹיִ֖ם עַד־לָֽשַׁע׃</mark> 10:20 אֵ֣לֶּה בְנֵי־חָ֔ם לְמִשְׁפְּחֹתָ֖ם לִלְשֹֽׁנֹתָ֑ם בְּאַרְצֹתָ֖ם בְּגוֹיֵהֶֽם׃ ס

www.ingramcontent.com/pod-product-compliance
Lightning Source LLC
Chambersburg PA
CBHW041532220426
43662CB00002B/38